D0209583

SUPERPOWER IN PERIL

SUPERPOWER IN PERIL

A BATTLE PLAN TO RENEW AMERICA

DAVID H. McCORMICK

WITH JAMES M. CUNNINGHAM

CENTER STREET

NEW YORK NASHVILLE

Center Street
Hachette Book Group
1290 Avenue of the Americas, New York, NY 10104
centerstreet.com
twitter.com/centerstreet

First edition: March 2023

Center Street is a division of Hachette Book Group, Inc.
The Center Street name and logo are trademarks of Hachette Book Group, Inc.

Library of Congress Cataloging-in-Publication Data has been applied for.

ISBNs: 9781546001959 (hardcover), 9781546001973 (ebook)

Printed in the United States of America

LSC-C

Printing 2, 2023

To my parents, Jim and Maryan, and to Dina and our girls.

CONTENTS

PREFACE

It's tempting to be pessimistic about America these days. Inflation, stagnation, and the lingering effects of the pandemic threaten the American dream. Our values are under assault, and our country is being pulled apart by polarization. The rise of the Chinese Communist Party threatens our security and our way of life. The world is changing rapidly, and our policies, institutions, and leaders are not keeping pace. Our strength and our self-confidence are slipping away.

Yet I remain optimistic. If the true test of a great country is its capacity for self-renewal, the United States of America stands apart. Throughout its history, our country has continually defeated grave threats and overcome domestic divisions when the odds were stacked against us. That's the American story, and we can do it again.

Decline, in other words, is not inevitable, but neither is renewal. What matters is what we do next. That's what this book is about.

The following pages present a vision for how our leaders can break the cycle of stagnation, disillusionment, and decline and begin renewing the greatness of America. I do not attempt to offer a solution to every enduring national problem. Instead, I look to the opportunities to breathe new life into our country and present a plan for victory in the races for global supremacy in talent, technology, and data. These are the critical contests of our time, and I believe the United States can prevail in all three. In doing so, we will unleash the extraordinary potential of the American people and ensure our nation remains the global superpower. However, our success will require more than just big ideas. It will require transformational leadership that shapes America's future by redefining how our government serves our society, renewing the souls of our institutions, and setting forth a unifying vision for our nation.

This book is not about politics or business, nor is it a tell-all autobiography. Rather, it is about the leadership required to save America, as seen through the eyes of someone blessed to have led in our esteemed military, successfully run two companies, and served at the highest levels of government. I began writing this in 2020 while CEO of Bridgewater Associates. I feared our country was headed in the wrong direction and believed I had something to contribute during this national crisis. A year later, for the same reason, I decided to run for the U.S. Senate from my home state of Pennsylvania.

While I lost the race, the experience—and the conversations with the many thousands of people I met along the way—reaffirmed that our path forward is treacherous and uncertain, but it also renewed my confidence in our country. The years ahead will undoubtedly test our resilience and place in the world. But decline is a choice. America, for all its faults, is exceptional. If we rally together and commit ourselves to the mission of renewal, our best days are yet to come.

INTRODUCTION

Duty, Honor, Country: Those three hallowed words reverently dictate what you ought to be, what you can be, what you will be. They are your rallying points: to build courage when courage seems to fail; to regain faith when there seems to be little cause for faith; to create hope when hope becomes forlorn.

—General Douglas MacArthur, at West Point, May 12, 1962

On a rainy Friday in May 2022, I climbed into my pickup truck to drive to Westmoreland County, Pennsylvania, for a campaign event that evening. Eleven days later, Pennsylvanians would go to the polls to pick their Republican nominee for the open U.S. Senate seat. The race was tight, and I was meeting with supporters to build momentum heading into the final stretch.

That same day, Donald Trump also came to Westmoreland County, to hold a rally for my opponent, Mehmet Oz, whom he had endorsed a few weeks earlier. The weather could hardly have been worse for him, and only a few hundred people came out in ankle-deep mud to hear the former president speak at the Westmoreland Fairgrounds.

When my event ended around 9:00 p.m., my colleague and I got back into my Ford F-150 for the hour-long journey back home to Pittsburgh. We turned on the radio and began listening to Trump's rally. Driving through dark, rain-slicked country roads, we heard the familiar refrain of the president bragging about his record and endorsements.

"Every single candidate that I endorsed won their primaries on Tuesday!" "We have a total record of 55 and 0!"

Then I heard my name.

"Dr. Oz is running against the liberal Wall Street Republican named David McCormick."

They say politics is not for the faint of heart, and I was about to be reminded why.

I had met with Donald Trump twice to discuss the campaign. When the news broke that I was considering running, in November of 2021, he called and invited my wife, Dina, and me to Florida.[1] We didn't talk much about the race, except to recognize that, with the incumbent Republican, Pat Toomey, retiring, holding on to his seat would be vital to regaining a Republican majority in the Senate.

The second time was a few weeks before that rainy night in Westmoreland County. At the time, my campaign was surging. We entered the race in January, months after most of the candidates, but in twelve weeks we had sped to the front of the pack. We had all the momentum. Then I heard the former president planned to endorse Mehmet Oz, so I flew to Mar-a-Lago.

When I arrived, I was escorted into President Trump's office. I sat across from him and asked him simply to stay out of the race. "Let us duke it out ourselves," I said. "Let the voters decide on their own."

He listened and then called in his assistant Molly. On a large television against the wall, she pulled up a video of an interview I had participated in in early January 2021, not long after January 6. She played a Bloomberg segment, where, when I was asked about the political divisiveness in America, I said Trump bore some responsibility. In the same segment, the interviewer asked what I thought about President Biden's first days in office and his recently stated goal of unifying the country, and I wished him well. President Trump was unhappy with both comments.

Then the former president looked me in the eyes and warned, "You know you can't win unless you say the election was stolen." I made it clear to him that I couldn't do that. Three days later, Trump endorsed Mehmet Oz.

The endorsement gave Dr. Oz a bump in the polls, but before long, his momentum faded. I remained in the lead. It became clear to all involved that Donald Trump's endorsement wouldn't be enough to close the deal, which would have been an embarrassing loss for the former president in the critical Keystone State. So Trump made his way to Pennsylvania.

When I turned on his rally that Friday night, I didn't expect to hear my name. While President Trump had previously attacked incumbents with whom he had disagreements, he had never attacked other Republicans running for office, particularly a candidate who knew him as well as Dina and I did and who was campaigning on many of his policies. We figured Trump would leave me out of it, but we were wrong.

For the next few minutes, I sat in silence, watching the trees fly by in the dark outside the window and listening as the former president of the United States attacked me at a fairground a mere twenty miles away.

He called me Wall Street, not Main Street. Soft on China, not tough on China. A globalist, not America First. He labeled me weak, not a fighter, and said I'd get to Washington and "fold," like all the establishment Republicans. I'd been called many things in my life—nothing can compare to the rhetorical assaults of a foul-mouthed Army Ranger instructor—but I'd never been called weak or had my patriotism called into question. The man Trump described wasn't me. It certainly wasn't the person my colleagues had known for decades or the man the voters of Pennsylvania had come to know over the preceding months of campaigning.

I couldn't help but smile. The remainder of the election was going to be a hell of a fight.

I was born in Washington, Pennsylvania, a few short miles from that evening's rally in Westmoreland County, and was raised in a small industrial town named Bloomsburg, fifty miles south of Scranton. Bloomsburg was the sort of place where, on the Monday after Thanksgiving, the schools would shut down, and we would head out to the hills for the first day of deer hunting season. While we lived in town, my family owned a small farm, and I grew up working in the summers trimming Christmas trees and bailing hay. On the weekends, I bused tables at the local Magee Hotel on Main Street. I did well enough in school, but I wasn't a great student. I found a home competing on football fields and wrestling mats across northeastern Pennsylvania.

Wrestling was my path to the U.S. Military Academy at West Point. I was the first local kid in decades to attend one of the academies, so when I was accepted, it was a big deal for my hometown.

I arrived at West Point and learned the three words that become what General Douglas MacArthur called the "rallying points" for every cadet: "Duty, Honor, Country." For four years, I studied to be an engineer, trained to be an Army officer, and worked religiously in the weight room and on the wrestling mat. I became cocaptain of the Division I Army wrestling team my senior year and was commissioned a 2nd lieutenant in 1987.

I fought in Desert Storm as part of the 82nd Airborne Division. Graduate school at Princeton came a year later, where I received my PhD in international relations. After completing my doctoral dissertation, I returned home to Pennsylvania, this time to Pittsburgh. And after a couple of years of consulting at McKinsey & Company, I joined and eventually became CEO of a cutting-edge software and services company, FreeMarkets. The company went public with a blockbuster initial public offering (IPO), and we created six hundred jobs in Pittsburgh, contributing to the city's 1990s renaissance. Then I was called back to public service in the George W. Bush administration.

This time I walked the halls of Washington, DC, not the hallowed grounds of West Point. I found myself in the Oval Office with the president of the United States. I flew in Air Force One with President Bush to meetings with heads of state from all over the world. These responsibilities put me at the forefront of the fight to protect U.S. technology from Chinese theft and, as a senior Treasury official, at the center of the response to the global financial crisis.

After leaving government, I went to work at Bridgewater Associates, one of the most successful investment firms in the world, which manages money for large institutional investors ranging from state pension funds for teachers, firefighters, and police officers to corporations and university endowments. After several years at Bridgewater, I became co-CEO, was fired eighteen months later, and eventually became CEO again years later. That's a story for another chapter.

All these experiences came flooding back that Friday night in Westmoreland County. From Main Street to Wall Street to the proving grounds of the 82nd Airborne, I've seen this country from many angles. I've worked in finance, but I've also helped create jobs on Main Street Pennsylvania. I've done business around the world, but I've also played a unique and powerful role in defending America from the predations of the Chinese Communist Party. I've been in government but also in combat in Iraq. It's been an extraordinary blessing to live a life that's only possible in America.

Presumably because of these experiences, President Trump had interviewed me to be Treasury secretary, asked me to be his deputy secretary of defense, and appointed me to his Defense Policy Board. During my Senate run, I supported and campaigned on many of his policies, and my wife had served honorably as his deputy national security adviser. So I'll admit I was surprised to hear the president attack me.

But as I listened, I realized that despite the former president's unfair and inaccurate attacks on me, his words also reflected the tension at the heart of the conservative movement: the forces of traditional, big business pulling against the populist wave. The free trade orthodoxy of old versus the new protectionist impulses. The ongoing debate about America's role in the world, and the uprising of everyday Americans against the elite, Acela corridor bubble. Soon I understood what Trump was also saying: the old Republican Party and the traditional understanding of what it means to be a Republican are dead. He had a point.

We've seen such changes before. In the early twentieth century, my family were Democrats. My grandfather was a Democratic commissioner during the FDR era in Indiana County, Pennsylvania, and my parents, both teachers, were the children of New Deal Democrats.

But the times and the political landscape changed. Though we still hold the same values, those values are now more at home in the Republican Party.

When I was a kid, politics didn't matter much to me. When I went to West Point and joined the Army, I largely followed in the apolitical footsteps of George Marshall, the legendary World War II general and secretary of state. In uniform, my duty was to the country and the commander-in-chief, not to any party.

While attending graduate school, I studied under two brilliant conservative thinkers, during which time the patriotism formed in the Army turned into a deeper appreciation of the exceptional nature of the American founding and of America's role in the world.[2] Later, as a business leader, I came to embrace the wisdom of former president Ronald Reagan's confidence in the free market and entrepreneurship as essential drivers of America's strength. I even led a company called FreeMarkets. These two beliefs—in exceptionalism and free enterprise—carried me into the Bush administration. Like many of my colleagues, I had faith in the power of markets, and I believed there was no substitute for American leadership in the world.

Before long, I began to see the limitations in that orthodoxy. Communities like the one I grew up in suffered as production lines and jobs moved overseas. As someone who had witnessed the horrors of war, after initially supporting the invasions of Afghanistan and Iraq, I started to question what we were doing for such an extended period in both countries, where young men and women sacrificed life and limb for no clear or consistent mission.[3] I further wondered why our national leaders would not do more to stop China's growing abuses of power and the corruption of global institutions that we ostensibly led.

By the time Donald Trump threw his hat into the ring in 2015, the Republican Party needed to change. It had become, in the estimate of two political observers, Salena Zito and Brad Todd, "consumed with the 'big government versus small government' argument,"[4] and given in to the excesses of ideas over prudence, dogma over compassion. The Democratic Party wasn't any better, moving ever leftward. The two sides were locked in ideological warfare, disconnected from the practical needs of voters. A huge swath of America had had enough. They wanted politicians to stop the exodus of manufacturing jobs and to help rebuild communities hollowed out by globalization and technological advances. They wanted someone to stand up to China, to stick it to the elite institutions and so-called elites who had left them behind, and to defend our nation's values. They wanted someone to fight for them. Enter Donald Trump.

President Trump's "nationalist argument," write Zito and Todd, "was economically pragmatic from the start, devoid of the ideological language of the trench warfare that had stalemated presidential politics."[5] Instead he recognized the wave of legitimate anger and disillusionment that cut across traditional party lines, and he rode it to victory in 2016.

Though I had never met Trump, after he was elected, the president interviewed me for his cabinet and eventually asked me to serve as deputy secretary of defense,[6] but I was committed to finishing what I had started at Bridgewater. Nonetheless, I applauded from afar as his administration reset our relationship with China and explicitly put the needs of Americans first in our foreign and economic policies.

The Republican Party had finally wakened from its sleepwalking slumber, roused by the populist movement, which was reflected in and channeled by President Trump. But now what?

No answer to this question was offered at that Westmoreland rally. None has been offered since. President Trump had his moment as the great disruptor, but what matters now—when the present and future of America are in such jeopardy—is what we do next. To save our republic, we need a vision for how we will address the immense problems before us, and we need leaders who can unite our country around that vision.

One of my favorite authors, Ernest Hemingway, wrote that bankruptcy happens "gradually, then suddenly."[7] So it has gone for American strength. When the Cold War ended, America stood alone at the top. It had unchallenged economic, military, political, and cultural force. We were perhaps the most powerful country the world had ever seen. In the generation that followed, our primacy slipped little by little. Our leaders wasted the strategic advantage granted by the fall of the Soviet Union. We disarmed, then got bogged down in foreign wars. Across administrations, America aided and abetted China's rise, and now it has become our gravest economic rival and military threat. At the same time, the dynamism that had powered our economy throughout the twentieth century slowed. Productivity stalled, and entrepreneurship declined. The global financial crisis left millions without a job or savings, and a decade of shortsighted monetary policy enriched the already rich but left the rest behind. Inequality of opportunity grew dramatically.

The Biden administration's abandoning of Afghanistan in August of 2021 was for me a shocking and deeply troubling symbol of that decline. First the White House pulled out most of our troops, seemingly overnight. In their wake, our most strategic position—Bagram Air Force Base—and billions of dollars of military equipment were left open for the taking. Thousands of Americans and tens of thousands of Afghans who had fought alongside us, as well as their families, were left exposed to the depredations of the radical, evil Taliban.

I will never forget sitting in my home with my girls watching in horror the television news coverage of the thirteen service members killed at the gates of Kabul Airport. I will never forget the tragic spectacle of Afghan civilians so desperate to flee the fate that awaited them that they clung to the wheels of hulking cargo planes, some falling to their deaths, others found hours later mangled in wheel wells. How could Dina and I explain to our six daughters that this was not the America we know?

Dina, who had served in senior roles in the White House under both President Bush and President Trump, stayed up night after night trying to get Afghan women and American citizens out of the country. She was joined by veterans and heroes all around the country, all trying desperately to ease, in some way, the pain and shame brought upon us. Only there was no balm. America was humiliated before the world.

Six months later, Russia invaded Ukraine. Russian forces landed in the south and surged north from Crimea. Tanks rolled down from Belarus and in from the east. Airplanes and missiles bombarded and murdered innocent civilians.

Except it wasn't just Afghanistan or Ukraine. In recent years, the southern border has become a freeway for drugs and human trafficking. Inflation hit forty-year highs. Food and gas prices skyrocketed. Cities saw record levels of violent crime, carjackings, and robberies. COVID took over one million American lives. Our schools continued to struggle, and violent mobs tore down statues of our nation's founders. We suffered through the reverberations of the indefensible and shameful violence on the steps of our Capitol on January 6, 2021. Our country confronted an unprecedented assault on her values, history, and liberties.

It began to feel to many as if America was coming apart and the national fabric fraying. The future I had dreamed of for my children appeared darker than I could have imagined.

As I watched the horror unfold in Afghanistan, I couldn't help but think back to the 1970s. Then, as now, we saw disasters in the Middle East, inflation, empty grocery shelves, gas so scarce people could fill only half a tank, and what President Jimmy Carter called a "crisis of confidence" in the soul of the nation. Many anticipated America's best days were behind her. We hear the same chorus again today, from politicians, talking heads, and even business leaders, who are predicting our demise.[8]

Yet the profound challenges before us today, which loom so large in my mind, begin to shrink in the shadow of our nation's remarkable story. Throughout our history, America has confronted grave threats at home and abroad and defeated them all.

There is nothing inevitable about American decline. What matters is what we do next.

As a renowned scholar once wrote, "The ultimate test of a great power is its ability to renew its power."[9] By that standard, America stands alone. This nation has an unparalleled ability to overcome its own circumstances, thanks in no small part to the restless, courageous, and indefatigable spirit that dwells within the American heart.

Our very founding achieved perhaps the greatest political revolution in human history. It reimagined how people could organize themselves for liberty and prosperity. Never before had a nation committed to a creed like ours. Never before had government been constructed explicitly of, for, and by the people. With that same spirit, our forefathers continually, often too slowly, amended and expanded the founders' vision. It drove the pioneers west, the astronauts to the heavens, and our nation to glory.

America was born of and sustained by the audacity of its people, and that spirit makes us exceptional.

Over the course of my career, I have had the great fortune of traveling all around this country and meeting Americans from all walks of life. I have seen immigrants congregate in classrooms with the descendants of Allegheny coal miners. I served in government alongside the children of émigrés and blue bloods from New England alike. I had the honor of serving in the Army with those from all backgrounds—each with their own incredible story.

There's a reason people come to America from all over the world: our shores promise liberty and opportunity, and all we ask in return is patriotism. They do not cross oceans and deserts for the promise of this or that government program or safety net. They come in search of the freedom to live their lives as they see fit. They come for the American dream and the promise of a better life. They come because here they will be treated and respected as individuals. Here they can practice their faith freely. Here they can make a home, join a community, open a business, and send their children to school to become a scientist, surgeon, or whatever they want to be. They come because they can become Americans and be privileged with the wondrous blessings that entails.

To some, America is a dream. To others, an inspiration. It's freedom. It's art. It means the great wide open of the West or the soaring Rocky Mountains. Or maybe it's the welcoming hamlets of the Gulf Coast or the blue-collar ethos of Pittsburgh. But for all, it means freedom and possibility. There are some who despise us for these very reasons, but for most, our country remains a beacon of hope and opportunity.

There's a tendency these days to see American exceptionalism as a dirty word. Some argue it is an empty slogan, and we are no different from any other country in celebrating ourselves. As then-President Barack Obama put it in 2009, America is exceptional "just as I suspect that the Brits believe in British exceptionalism and the Greeks believe in Greek exceptionalism."[10] Others reject the notion altogether. In classrooms, dorm rooms, and newsrooms, America is often seen as irredeemable and born in sin. Republicans and Democrats see those on the other side of the aisle as the enemy. American exceptionalism has even been labeled a dangerous myth: a lie we tell ourselves to justify imperialism.[11] The common theme is that our history isn't glorious but full of sin and failure.

To those who question our goodness, I say show me a better country. Show me a freer country. Show me a more artistic, innovative, diverse, or welcoming country. Show me a country that has done more for the world in its short history. Show me a country that gives more opportunity and liberty to more people. Show me the country as willing to admit when it is wrong and then change to make it right.

Now, show me the country formed for the singular purpose of securing human liberty and opportunity. The truth is, in absolute terms, relative to other countries, and across history, no nation can compare to America in the advancement of freedom, democracy, prosperity, progress, and equality.

I do not object to those who believe the dark chapters of our past have not been fully illuminated. I do object to those who would have our children conclude that America is not a force for good in the world or that our present is infected by the sins of the past. That isn't history but revision.

Though we have too often fallen short of our own ideals, we have continually worked to redress the injustice and form, as the founders said, a more perfect union. That's who we are. Those hell-bent on revising our history are a distraction. The past is past. The future is ours to define. And that's what this book is about—defining the future of this great nation.

About a month into my Senate campaign, on a cold February morning, I attended a "meet and greet" breakfast in a local diner in Lehighton, an industrial town in Carbon County, in northeastern Pennsylvania. As the questions wound down, an elderly woman stood up. Her husband was seated at her side, and before a hushed room, she thanked me for my military service, then told me about her son, Michael.

A local standout, Michael had volunteered for the military after September 11 and fought in heated combat in Afghanistan. Upon returning home, he quietly suffered and, after years of struggle, took his own life in 2013. He left a wife and young daughter behind.[12]

As she told Michael's story, she began to cry, and so did I. When she finished, she handed me a gold star coin representing her patriot son. She asked me to carry it with me and to promise that as senator I would fight for all the Michaels across Pennsylvania and across America. All the veterans who came home to peace but for whom inner peace proved elusive. All the people left behind, who lost jobs to globalization, who lost loved ones in or were left damaged by war, who lost someone due to COVID, who devoted their lives to this country they loved so dearly.

In that moment, I knew, no matter what happened, I had made the right choice to run for the Senate. This country gave me everything I have, and I believed I had something more to give it in return.

I lost the primary campaign to Mehmet Oz—more on that later—but this book is a continuation of that journey. It is my effort to answer the defining question facing our national leaders: What comes next?

A starting proposition is that while America is imperfect, it is both exceptional and worth defending. Let me offer two more: First, every generation has a duty to this country, and ours is to renew it. Second, American renewal is not possible without a revival of the American spirit.

America is a work in progress—an experiment in human liberty and self-governance. As such, we continually struggle with big, often recurring problems. Democratic elections are contested and hard to run, particularly as our country grows and modern technology and social media revolutionize how we communicate. Government officials are incapable of living within our national means, so debt and deficits balloon. In times of relative peace, we neglect to maintain our military might, then struggle to restore it when needed. Our society—big, diverse, and spread out—never exists in perfect harmony. The list goes on. Each, as we've seen, can stymie our nation's leaders, but each is enduring. Every generation must contend with them. They must, in other words, do the hard work of preserving our republic.

But there come times when Americans are called upon to *renew* it. When everything seems to be crashing down and the future looks dark—in these moments of great trial, America has always found hope and opportunities to grow stronger, to expand the frontiers of our power, and to begin a new era of American leadership.

The pages that follow present a plan for national renewal, built around the unique opportunities of our moment. They begin by taking stock of where we stand—the state of our union. They then put our present moment in the context of history and of Ronald Reagan's Morning in America. As we will see, we have been here before, and the sources of American strength remain the same. The question is: What does it take to renew them?

My answer to that question is that we need our leaders to put forth policies to secure victory in the three defining contests for global leadership in our time: talent, technology, and data. First, I present a plan to invest in *talent* by advancing school choice and education reform, promoting workforce development, and crafting a strategic immigration policy. Second is a bold reimagining of how our nation pursues *technological supremacy*. And third is a strategy for *data* that addresses the challenge of Big Tech and secures American leadership in the digital age.

Finally, the book explores the kind of leadership necessary to accomplish renewal. I first address the ultimate external risk to American renewal—the Chinese Communist Party—and what our leaders must do to overcome this existential threat. I then discuss the chief obstacle to our renewal—the decay in our national institutions—and how America's leaders should reform them, and I conclude by defining the kind of transformational leadership needed to drive our country forward.

Our national "to-do" list is too long for any book, and I don't attempt to address every issue here. This book is not about our dismal fiscal situation and exploding debt. It doesn't fix our broken tax policies or enumerate the broader set of pro-growth economic policies needed to stimulate the economy. It does not offer a holistic plan to rebuild the military nor to tame inflation. And it is not about electoral reform, gun control, or the other contentious social issues.

Instead, it is about what's distinct in our time and what should stand at the vanguard of our country's renewal agenda.

My argument is straightforward: America is stuck in a downward spiral of stagnation, disillusionment, and decline. To reverse course, America needs leaders who not only successfully develop and implement plans to achieve global superiority in talent, technology, and data but also take the steps necessary to make renewal possible, by confronting China, reforming our institutions, and guiding our nation forward.

Because I am a conservative, this book is anchored to conservative principles, chiefly the understanding that America's success has come from ensuring individuals have the opportunity to strive, innovate, and flourish, secure in the knowledge of their liberty from tyranny and oppression. Because I am a Republican, I believe the ideas in these pages should become building blocks of the party's future agenda. Free-market conservatives and national security advocates alike must get on the same page. Now, more than ever, our economic interest and security concerns go hand in hand. Our national policies must reflect that truth.

But this book isn't about Republicans or Democrats. It's about what our leaders must do to heal the country. To create common ground in the fight against the great challenges of our day. To renew America.

Our success will ultimately depend on the quality of that leadership.

In his recent book, former Secretary of State and National Security Adviser Henry Kissinger elegantly captures the criticality of leadership in times of transition: "Leadership is most essential during periods of transition, when values and institutions are losing their relevance, and the outlines of a worthy future are in controversy."[13] Is there any doubt we are in such a moment, one made all the more challenging by the fact our country is so deeply divided?

Our leaders must meet this moment with a transformational vision for our country—one that spans government, business, technology, and the military and unites the majority of Americans around a shared national purpose. I have lived squarely at the intersection of these arenas my entire professional life, moving between the elements of our society and seeing how they can work together. And though this book is rich with policy prescriptions, if there's one thing I've learned along the way, it's that government is not the answer to all our problems. The best thing our political leaders can do is unlock all that's great about this nation and its citizens. This book offers a plan to do just that.

We sit atop an untapped reservoir of potential energy: the courage and restlessness of the American spirit. If we can cultivate and unleash that spirit—and endow it with the gratitude of patriotism—America will remain exceptional.

Every December for the last twenty years I have tried to take my family to the Army-Navy football game. It's one of my favorite days of the year. My wife and I and our six daughters descend on Philadelphia, where the game is usually held. My and Dina's parents, my brother and his wife, and our friends meet us there for dinner the night before. Early the next morning, despite occasional complaints from my daughters about cold or rainy weather, we go for a family run. We make our way through the city streets to the Philadelphia Museum of Art, where we climb the "Rocky Steps" and look out over the city, down the Benjamin Franklin Parkway.

I first saw that view as a kid. One of my dad's friends had tickets to the Army-Navy game and invited us to go with him. It was incredible. The stadium was packed. People came from all over Philadelphia and all over the country. Former players and their families and veterans from as far back as World War II and Korea made the trip. There were Philadelphia dockworkers, New York lawyers, and everything in between.

My brother and I both played football growing up, but we had never seen anything like this atmosphere. The roar of the crowd, the pageantry, the grandeur of the game. Seventy thousand people packed together to watch two teams play without pro contracts or national championships on the line but in what may be the greatest rivalry in American sports.[14] And as the saying goes, the Army-Navy game is beautiful because whether you're cheering for Army or Navy—America always wins.

When I went to West Point in 1983—not to play football, as I'd initially hoped, but as a member of the varsity wrestling team—I came to understand that the two teams didn't need any trophy to motivate them. They were playing for honor, glory, and the lifelong memory of defeating their greatest rivals, who also happen to be their brothers-in-arms.

The game is mandatory for all cadets. Most years, we would hop on buses the night before and drive down from West Point to Philadelphia. In the bitter December cold, we would descend upon the parking lot of Veterans Stadium the next morning, often with head-pounding hangovers, to prepare for the pre-game "march on."

If you haven't been to the game, the march on is the first of many game-day traditions. The entire Corps of Cadets and the Brigade of Midshipmen, up from Annapolis, parade onto the field and take their places in the stands. I vividly remember lining up with my cadet company and marching out of the tunnel. I remember standing ramrod straight as the National anthem played, something I do to this day. I remember the crowd, as big and wonderful as ever, coming alive as Army skydivers jumped into the stadium and Navy jets flew overhead. Then the whistle blew, and all bets were off.

This is the biggest game of the year for both teams—if you lose most of your games but win this one, it's a successful season. Few, if any, of the players will go on to play professionally. For most, when the game ends, the normal pace of academy life will continue: predawn wake-up, inspections, physical fitness, classes, and training. The linemen will immediately start to cut weight to make Army or Navy regulations. For the seniors on both sidelines, it's the last hurrah before putting on their military uniforms. When future games are played, they might be running counterterrorist operations in the Horn of Africa, standing guard at Europe's Eastern Front, or navigating through the Straits of Malacca. Soon enough they'll serve shoulder to shoulder with the guys on the other sideline. But for four quarters, they fight like hell for bragging rights and the thrill of beating their sworn rival.

When the game ends, the crowd stays in place, and the stadium grows eerily quiet. Players from both teams take their helmets off as the alma mater of the losing team and then the alma mater of the winning team are played. The Corps of Cadets in their gray dress coats and the Brigade of Midshipmen in blue and brass stand at attention as they sing. The crowd watches in reverence. Even the TV announcers go silent.

More than thirty-five years after I first sang West Point's alma mater with the long gray line of cadets, the closing ceremony never fails to bring a tear to my eye. In that moment, the young men on the field, the cadets and midshipmen in the stands, everyone in attendance and everyone watching from home joins with all who have watched and played these games over decades past. All the passion and rivalry of four hard-fought quarters of football melt away. In their place ring what Abraham Lincoln called the "mystic chords of memory, stretching from every battle-field, and patriot grave, to every living heart and hearthstone, all over this broad land."[15]

With the writing of this book already well underway, I attended the Army-Navy game in December of 2021. As I stood at attention listening to the final chords of "Alma Mater" fade away, everything I love about America came into focus. I was overwhelmed with a profound sense of gratitude for all those who have sacrificed for the country and a deeply held confidence in our ability to once more "swell the chorus of the Union" and renew our country.[16]

The pages that follow detail the American dream I've been blessed to live, the state of our union, and the steps we must take to restore this great nation.

PART I

Decline, Renewal, and What Comes Next

CHAPTER 1

Decline Is Not Inevitable

For America today, decline is not a condition. Decline is a choice.

—Charles Krauthammer, in his Wriston Lecture at the Manhattan Institute, 2009

The order came in the middle of the night, broadcast over my Humvee radio: get back to Fort Bragg. We were given a set of coordinates and told to go there and wait for a transport plane. We didn't know why, but we knew it was urgent. We packed up our gear, secured the communications equipment, and moved quickly to the pickup site. When we landed back in North Carolina, it was clear something big was happening. Transport aircraft lined the runways at nearby Pope Air Force Base, and vehicles and pallets full of ammunition and supplies stood waiting to be loaded. Military police directed traffic. The place was abuzz with frenetic activity and the immense logistical burden of a rapid full-scale mobilization.

A few days earlier and a thousand miles away, my unit—C Company, 307th Engineers, 82nd Airborne Division—had parachuted into the woods of Arkansas at the Joint Readiness Training Center, one of the Army's most realistic and demanding training grounds. The around-the-clock exercise was meant to simulate actual combat in a jungle environment. We faced off against a well-trained opposing force designed to mimic a Soviet-equipped insurgency. The men on both sides were armed with laser-fitted weapons, and we wore sensors that would signal if the enemy had hit us. The rounds we fired were blanks, but the explosives were real. The Arkansas woods in August are no place for the fainthearted. Mosquitoes and chiggers are everywhere, and the heat is oppressive. With the stifling surroundings, the relentless pace of operations, and the realism of the training, this was serious business. The members of my unit had worked hard to prepare and were fired up for the challenge.

I arrived at the storied 82nd two years before as a new lieutenant straight out of Ranger School, which had followed the officer basic course and Airborne School. My time in that elite paratrooper unit was everything I had hoped for. In my first assignment as a platoon leader, my unit included a Southern Baptist from Alabama, a Black man from Newark, a farm boy from Kansas, a well-to-do college dropout from Boston, and, thankfully, a platoon sergeant from Puerto Rico, who took this green lieutenant under his wing. In the fast-paced and mission-driven environment of the 82nd, misunderstandings and prejudices faded away, soon replaced by loyalty, teamwork, and patriotism.

I was honored to be the leader of this courageous, committed group of young Americans, who had volunteered twice—once for the Army and a second time to be a paratrooper—and I worked hard to be worthy of their trust and to lead them well. Sadly, my time at the 82nd was slated to come to a close. Not long before we jumped into Arkansas, I had been posted to a one-year assignment to help build an airfield in Turkey and was preparing to leave Fort Bragg after this final training rotation.

What happened next was a turning point in my life, and in the course of history.

It was August 1990, and 100,000 Iraqi soldiers had just invaded Kuwait, a small, oil-rich nation wedged between Iraq, Saudi Arabia, and the Persian Gulf, on which Saddam Hussein had set his sights long ago. He wanted Kuwait to reduce its oil production to drive up prices and help Iraq recover from its grueling war with Iran, which had just ended two years prior. He also wanted Kuwait itself, which he saw as a rightful part of Iraq. Unable to strongarm Kuwait, Saddam instead took it by force, thinking it would be a low-cost operation. The assault began on August 2, and Kuwait quickly fell. And now the 82nd Airborne was headed to Saudi Arabia to block further aggression south.

My duties were clear. As executive officer, I was responsible for getting the 130 paratroopers in C Company ready to deploy. Every soldier needed ammunition, food, and gear. Every vehicle needed to be cleaned and inspected. And we had one day to do it. Overnight, we boarded C-141s and flew to Ramstein Air Force Base in Germany. The planes refueled, and we continued on to Dammam, Saudi Arabia.

Almost overnight the nation was mobilizing for war, and all of America watched anxiously for minute-by-minute updates on CNN.

Once we arrived in Saudi Arabia, we did what soldiers have always done: we waited. The company initially set up in Dammam, near some of the largest oil fields. We conducted live fire exercises, practiced clearing minefields, and constructed all types of fortifications. We received regular intelligence briefings, and our ranks swelled with specialists and supporting forces, most ominously Army surgeons.

Initially, we were deployed as a screening force on the Kuwaiti border to deter Iraqi forces from crossing toward the Saudi oil fields.

We would not have been able to do much against the Iraqi tanks, but that wasn't our job. Our job was to make clear that if they invaded Saudi Arabia, they would invite retaliation from the full might of the U.S. military.

In the chaos and secrecy of the mission, we didn't get a chance to call home before we deployed, nor were we able to be in touch with our families except by mail for the many months that followed. I sent my parents letters as often as I could. My mother still has them in a box at home. After we moved to the border, it became even harder to keep in touch. The Army brass had all sorts of restrictions for operational security reasons, so mail made it to our unit only episodically. But one day, shortly before Christmas, a huge box showed up at our camp. We opened it and found a Christmas tree that my dad had picked out from the family farm. By some miracle, it had made it past all the censors and restrictions. For a few days, we had proper Christmas cheer in the middle of the Saudi desert—an unexpected blessing that made even the most hard-bitten soldiers smile. After Christmas, we moved back to an airfield near Riyadh, to help protect against any attack on the city, which held the Kingdom's military headquarters.

By this time, one of the largest build-ups of military power in modern history was well underway. Every hour, troops, tanks, and helicopters flew in from the United States. We partnered with allied nations to stand up to Iraq's aggression and assembled on the Trans-Arabian pipeline road—dubbed the Tapline Road—along the Iraqi border. Amid this consolidation of forces, I had the responsibility of preparing for a broad range of contingencies. I took a day trip into Riyadh and returned with bulldozers hauled by 18-wheelers, power tools, and assorted equipment that might be needed once we crossed the border. We didn't know what the mission would be, so we prepared for just about everything a combat engineer could expect.

An American-led coalition, orchestrated by President George H. W. Bush, had given Saddam Hussein an ultimatum: leave Kuwait by January 15, 1991. He didn't, and on January 16, the world witnessed what the greatest fighting force ever created could do.

The invasion went in two phases. First, an air war where the combined might of American and allied militaries rained thousands of tons of ordnance on the Iraqi army. Weeks later the coalition smashed through Iraq's barricades and military in a two-pronged ground attack. To the right, American-led forces surged into Iraq near the Kuwait border. Meanwhile, another contingent launched a left hook across the Iraqi desert. My unit joined that assault. At the last minute, we had been attached to a French tank division charged with protecting the left flank.

We crossed the border into Iraq early on the morning of February 25, our Humvees cutting through the desert with close air support in the distance. When the sun came up, carnage met my eyes. I remember vividly the skeletons of enemy tanks, trucks, and artillery that had been hit by precision-guided missiles. The bombing campaign, so precise and watched on TVs around the world, was unprecedented in human history. Pushing farther in, we encountered some resistance from retreating Iraqi Republican Guard forces, but the majority shed their uniforms and blended into the populace or surrendered by the thousands.

My unit was assigned the missions of clearing minefields and destroying Iraqi munitions and military equipment. A platoon from the 27th Engineer Battalion, also from Fort Bragg, was attached to my company. Soon after crossing into Iraq, it was assigned the mission of clearing munitions from airfields, after coalition bombing had rendered them inoperable. Sadly, when clearing cluster munitions, the bombs went off, killing seven, including their platoon leader, 1st

Lieutenant Terry Plunk, whom I'd gotten to know well. It was a tragic and very personal reminder of the costs of war.[1]

Not long after my company and others from the 82nd were tasked with destroying the Khamisiyah weapons depot, an enormous and remote desert facility housing over 18,000 tons in munitions. Our goal was to ensure the Iraqis would not regain control of all that firepower when U.S. troops withdrew. The depot held entire city blocks of missiles and ammunition, mostly stored underground in hundreds of protected bunkers. It took time, but we disabled and destroyed everything we found.[2]

My company successfully executed this pressure-cooked mission, and as a result, several key leaders, myself included, were awarded the Bronze Star for meritorious service in "support of actions against hostile forces" in Iraq. I was proud of our unit and its performance, but our efforts paled in comparison to the remarkable bravery and sacrifice that so many U.S. service members have exhibited over the past two decades of combat in Iraq and Afghanistan.

By the end of February, Iraq had retreated from Kuwait, its forces in disarray. Having achieved its war aim, the United States, on behalf of the coalition, moved to a cease-fire with Iraq, and on April 11 signed an armistice agreement.

About a year before, I had visited East Berlin during a week of leave. I walked to where the Berlin Wall had once stood and picked up a piece from a fresh pile of rubble, an artifact of the Cold War to celebrate the Soviet Union's ongoing dissolution. Then, one year later, as my unit crossed the border from Saudi Arabia into Iraq, with Apache helicopters and A-10 Warthogs flying in the distance, I was present at the creation of the unipolar moment, one that would define America's role in the world up to today.

In that small corner of the Middle East, America passed its first test as the world's singular superpower. With its decisive victory over Saddam Hussein's forces, it affirmed its primacy. Our military was unrivaled, and our moral authority extended around the world, as seen in the relentless march of liberal democracy and free market orthodoxy across the globe.

The groundwork for that moment had been laid over the preceding decade, with Ronald Reagan's Morning in America. Old challenges of energy price instability and inflation had been contained, and the information revolution was opening new frontiers. The military was reequipped with new, high-tech weaponry—and lots of it—making it the unstoppable force that would decimate the Iraqi army. The green shoots of the technology boom of the 1990s began to show, and the deft, adaptable statesmanship of Reagan, George Shultz, Jim Baker, George H. W. Bush, and many others set the Soviet Union on a path to peaceful dissolution.

By virtue of their leadership, "the core feature of global politics was U.S. dominance," as Charles Krauthammer put it in 1990. As we would soon prove in the Iraqi desert, America was indisputably "the unchallenged superpower."[3]

Thirty years later, the unipolar moment has passed. I still have that piece of the Berlin Wall, but it now seems like a memento of a bygone era. America can no longer claim to be "unchallenged," and the principal sources of national power have changed dramatically. Renewal requires us to recognize these changes and to adapt. But first we must take stock of our condition. Where do we stand? By assessing the state of American strength—our relative economic, military, and diplomatic power—and of our exceptional values, we can begin to see the path forward.

Is America in Decline?

The first U.S.–China summit of the Biden administration in 2021 started as most do. Secretary of State Antony Blinken and National Security Adviser Jake Sullivan welcomed their counterparts and laid out their view of the state of the relationship. Then came the Chinese response. The Chinese Communist Party's foreign affairs chief, Yang Jiechi, looked across the table and began reciting China's achievements—how far it had come and how strong it was and stronger still it would soon be. He then turned his sights to America. America must accept decline, Yang declared. Stop promoting democratic values. Stop thinking of itself as the global leader. The dialogue grew heated. After a response from Secretary Blinken, Minister Yang shot back: "The United States does not have the qualification to say that it wants to speak to China from a position of strength."[4] If it weren't already clear, this message crystallized China's view: the sun is setting on America.

Is it? It's not easy to measure a country's "power," its strength and ability to shape the outcome of world events. The best approach is to compare its pillars of power—its economic heft, military might, and diplomatic tool kits—to those of its competitors and to see how that comparison has changed over time. Measuring these pillars, and the competence with which they are used, can give us a sense of America's relative power and the direction in which we are currently headed.

In China, the United States faces its first true economic rival since the 1940s. China's growth from when I first traveled there thirty years ago is nothing short of remarkable, and it may soon surpass ours in overall size.[5] Not even the Soviet Union at its height could aspire to that. However, China has many problems, and we have many advantages. America's share of the global economy has held steady for decades, and U.S. capital markets remain at the center of the global financial system. Americans are far wealthier than Chinese citizens, and our demographic outlook is brighter. As one scholar put it, China is slated to grow old before it grows rich.[6]

China also struggles with its own economic challenges, including significant slowdowns in growth and productivity, national debt totaling over 250 percent of the country's GDP, over $100 billion in overseas loans going bad, a real estate crisis and insolvency, nearly 20 percent unemployment among young people, and the structural challenges of trying to enforce Xi Jinping's goal of "common prosperity."[7] Moreover, the U.S. dollar's reserve status gives us unparalleled abilities to influence global transactions and borrow extensively.

Sadly, we have abused that privilege. Our national debt greatly exceeds our GDP and is growing quickly.[8] More than a decade of low interest rates have made our payments on that debt manageable, but as rates return to their historic levels, more and more taxpayer money will be required to pay our creditors—thereby causing the deficit, which hit nearly three trillion dollars in 2021, to continue to grow. That spending is mortgaging our nation's future and contributing to inflation hitting its highest rate in forty years. All this leads to my greatest concern: the long-term slowdown in economic growth and opportunity. We're stuck in a productivity rut, and the rate at which Americans are starting businesses is declining.[9] Americans do not share equal chances to pursue their aspirations, and that opportunity gap threatens the dynamism that has long characterized our country.

An analysis of our military power tells a similar story. We may have the most powerful military globally, but regionally, where wars are fought, we are outmanned, outgunned, and out of position. Since the

Cold War, the U.S. military has shed personnel and matériel. Meanwhile, China's military budget increased almost a thousand times over, and when adjusted for purchasing power, off-books budgets, and the fusion of civil and military technology, China now rivals the United States in military spending.[10] They built the largest Navy in the world, measured by number of ships, and in 2020 alone built as many major naval vessels as the United States has deployed in the entire Western Pacific.

We are also losing our military technological edge. China has modernized with the intent to defeat U.S. forces, developing an unmatched missile arsenal, advanced aircraft, and combat ships and investing in high-end cyber and anti-satellite capabilities and lethal drones. Russia likewise built a large fighting force and then decided to unleash it on innocent Ukrainians. Smaller militaries and even non-state actors also now have access to devastating drones, cyber capabilities, and other advanced military tools.

Meanwhile, two decades of war, continual underfunding, bureaucratic impediments, and cultural drift all inhibited much-needed innovation in the U.S. military, and the armed forces have readiness and personnel crises on their hands. The services struggle to give their people the training and working equipment needed to perform their mission. Each is falling short of its recruiting goals, and radical, progressive politics are making their way into the leadership and education of our war fighters, distracting from the common purpose and missions that should define service.[11]

A former Pentagon war planner summarized the situation succinctly in 2019: in war games, "when we fight China or Russia . . . We lose a lot of people, we lose a lot of equipment. We usually fail to achieve our objective."[12] That is, we have lost military primacy.[13]

Our allies still, for the most part, stand by us, and though we have plenty of work to do in forging new partnerships, America has made tremendous progress with the strategic grouping of the United States, Japan, Australia, and India, known as the Quadrilateral Security Dialogue, or simply the "Quad"; a groundbreaking realignment in the Middle East with the Abraham Accords; and a new defense pact with the United Kingdom and Australia. Russia's unjust and unprovoked invasion of Ukraine also galvanized our allies, who have finally begun to take seriously their NATO commitments and the dangers looming in the shadows of our world.

American leadership remains in high demand around the world. Yet Washington has been much too slow to adapt to emerging technologies that will define power in the digital age. China has clear plans to shape how technologies are developed and used around the world, plans that give the state access to user information and reject notions of privacy and liberty. The United States has pushed back selectively, as in the effort to block Huawei's 5G systems from U.S. and allied markets. Otherwise, Washington has failed to muster an alternative vision for a free and innovative digital world.

China has also usurped much of our leadership of the major organs of global governance. The sins of the World Health Organization (WHO) at the outbreak of COVID-19 revealed the rot. Those tasked with protecting global health covered up bad news out of China and allowed political pressures to get in the way of their mission. Similarly, the World Bank continues to effectively subsidize China by categorizing it as a developing country, which makes it—one of the richest countries in the world—eligible for favorable loans. We have not held these institutions accountable for undermining U.S. interests, and now authoritarianism is on the march.[14]

All told, in surveying the pillars of American power, a common theme appears: America is strong but sclerotic. The United States is still the wealthiest country but risks becoming a stagnant one.

Likewise, we maintain the strongest military, but it is losing its technological edge and lacks the men and matériel it needs to do what the nation asks of it. Finally, though the beacon of freedom still shines, U.S. diplomatic influence in both big global institutions and foreign capitals is fading. The humiliating withdrawal from Afghanistan and our failure to deter Vladimir Putin's aggression signaled to many that America was in retreat. Moreover, China has sought to dominate the next generation of diplomacy: forging new relationships and shaping the rules of the road for emerging technologies.

It need not be this way. These outcomes are the result of choices, and it is past time to make different choices that renew America. To renew our nation, however, we must do more than strengthen our economy, military, and geopolitical power. America is a great country not because it is the most powerful but because it is exceptional. And it is exceptional because it protects liberty, promises opportunity, and inspires patriotism, all of which we must cherish.

America the Exceptional

The tapestry of America is woven in many threads. Songs, myths, and heroes captivate us. History, soil, and war unite us. The Constitution binds us. But it is a creed that defines us. The creed holds that all people are endowed with the rights to life, liberty, and the pursuit of happiness, and if you work hard and follow the rules, you can make your life what you want it to be—you can live the American dream.

This creed is the grand proposition of the American experiment. The Founding Fathers believed that a country could be constructed to protect it, and for generations, Americans have fulfilled their obligations. They have confronted the injustices of slavery, oppression, and bigotry and overcome the Depression, pandemics, and malaise. They turned our land red with blood defending it, so that we may all have the blessing of freedom and opportunity.

The American creed, in other words, sets forth the virtues of liberty and opportunity, and the desire to preserve it instills a third: patriotism. Together these virtues make America exceptional. When we uphold them and bring them into harmony in our souls, America flourishes. We unleash the boundless energy of millions of individuals, tempered by patriotic and civic duty. When we don't, all else suffers. Our economic, military, and diplomatic might rest on a foundation of sand.

On each account, we stand out when compared to other countries, and though we have often violated them, we are distinguished by our willingness to discuss our failings openly and by how far we have come to rectify them over time. However, the foundation is faltering. The American experiment is falling short in key dimensions.

When the Founding Fathers finally gathered in Philadelphia in 1787, they did so, as the preamble the Constitution declares, to "secure the Blessings of Liberty to ourselves and our Posterity."[15] American government, they emphasized, exists to secure the innate rights of the people, most especially liberty. This, in the words of one historian, was "the exceptional idea" of the American founding, and it is embedded in our political system.[16] From local school board elections to races for state office, Senate seats, or the presidency, Americans get to vote for their representatives more than any other peoples.

Liberty is also embedded in the American character. We are an unruly bunch. We hold tightly to our freedom, exercise it freely, and commemorate it in our treasured national symbols, from Lady Liberty to the Liberty Bell. In that, we are different from even our closest democratic compatriots. When a Pew poll asked Americans and Europeans what they valued in their governments, nearly six in ten

Americans cited the preservation of individual liberty. By contrast, a similar portion of British, French, German, and Spanish respondents believed government existed to ensure no one was in need.[17] Americans are distinguished by their embrace and prioritization of liberty.

For too long, many Americans were denied their liberty, but we have continually sought to correct course and accumulate progress. It has been a bumpy road. Hundreds of thousands of Americans fought and died to abolish the evil of slavery, but then Jim Crow laws and the Ku Klux Klan instituted a new form of racial repression. Civil rights activists marched for freedom, but evil men bombed the 16th Street Baptist Church in Birmingham, Alabama. In time, equality secured victory in law. Likewise, America expanded the right to vote to women and others originally denied it. All the while, we upheld a free press, freedom to practice religion, the right to bear arms, and protections from illegal government intrusion into our lives.

Though we have made tremendous progress in the protection of liberty, serious challenges remain. Racial bigotry still robs some individuals of their God-given rights, and some seem ready to embrace socialism or other political ideologies that reject economic liberty and free enterprise. We've also just lived through a pandemic in which politicians and an unelected public health bureaucracy saw it within their powers to shut down businesses and schools, mandate vaccines and masks, and force people to abide by their rules, however arbitrary or divorced from evidence they may have been.

Americans are defined by what they do and what they aspire to, not by any class or ethnicity. For that reason, we mythologize those who achieve the unthinkable: the frontiersmen, the artist, the innovator, the astronaut. We praise those who build their own lives, families, and communities, and we honor the rights of the individual above all else. In that sense, America truly stands apart. We believe much more than Europeans, for example, in the primacy of the individual.[18] We likewise are far more religious than other Western societies, and we encourage religious expression of all kinds.

Sadly, there is a tendency today to reject our individualism, our diversity, and the pluralism that allows us to coexist and thrive together. Woke ideologues on the far left would divide our country into groups based on race, ethnicity, sex, or any other convenient identifier. They would reject perspectives they disagree with and close down the kind of productive disagreement that allows our pluralistic society to come together. At the same time, extremists on the right argue "real Americans" are of a certain race and ethnicity, and they look down on our diversity, seeing it as an infection, not a beautiful and productive feature of who we are. Both sides see others as members of a group, not as unique individuals. Neither understands America. They divide it and polarize it.

America's embrace of liberty cannot be disconnected from the promise of opportunity. Where I'm from in northeastern Pennsylvania has long been the destination for many immigrants, especially from across Europe. As memorialized in *The Molly Maguires*, a classic film starring the iconic James Bond, Sean Connery, they came to America as cheap labor to work in the coal mines and later manned the assembly lines in small manufacturing firms across the state. My father was the president of the local college, Bloomsburg State—now called Bloomsburg University—and the children of these laborers and immigrants filled the school.

During my dad's time as president, my brother, Doug, and I would sometimes attend the college's graduation ceremony. I will always remember seeing the rows of proud faces in attendance. These parents had traveled far and worked hard so that their children could go to college and enjoy a brighter future. As their children marched across the stage to receive their diplomas, all that sacrifice came to fruition, and in that moment, they lived their version of the American dream.

My wife, Dina, is living her American dream too. She was born in Egypt to Coptic Christian parents. Her father served as an officer in Anwar Sadat's army, yet her family was discriminated against for their beliefs. When she was five, they emigrated to Texas. Her parents worked multiple jobs to put food on the table. They learned the language and began the process of becoming Americans. Dina worked her way as a waitress through college at the University of Texas and deferred admission to law school to go to Washington and intern for Senator Kay Bailey Hutchison. After a few years on Capitol Hill, she found herself in the White House as the assistant to the president for presidential personnel, at the age of twenty-nine the youngest person to ever hold the position. She has since gone on to reach the pinnacle of success in business, serving on the management committee at Goldman Sachs, and in senior government roles. Only in America.

In his journeys through a young America in the 1830s, Alexis de Tocqueville marveled at what he called the "equality of conditions" and "immense liberty" of its citizens. He saw a country where anyone, regardless of their station, could pursue their definition of happiness. That's the promise of America: each of us, whatever our unique dream, will have the opportunity to pursue it.

That promise made America the economic superpower it is today. As two conservative writers put it, "a commerce-loving, striving, and endlessly inventive people hustled its way to become the greatest economic power the world."[19] We have maintained an unrivaled track record of growth and dynamism through wars, economic downturns, and strife, and as a result, America is the wealthiest major country and the most economically free.[20] The expanding wealth gap gets lots of attention, but even the bottom quintile of Americans by income are better off than those in almost any other country.

As America grew freer, opportunity expanded. The abolition of slavery in Northern states gave Black Americans access to the American dream. Expanding rights for women, including finally allowing them to go to work in large numbers, freed them to exercise their potential, and we have also welcomed immigrants.

Yet, for too many Americans today, that intergenerational promise of opportunity has been broken. Lincoln once said, "I hold the value of life is to improve one's condition."[21] What a distinctly American principle, but one I fear we are losing.

Early in my campaign, I sat down with a middle-aged woman in Cambria County. Our conversation turned to the drug epidemic sweeping the Commonwealth of Pennsylvania, and she told me she had recently lost a family member to an overdose. Everyone in her community, she said, was affected. From then on, I started asking the same question to every group I met with: "By a show of hands, who here has been personally impacted by fentanyl?" I never entered a room where a large percentage of those gathered did not raise their hand. Over one hundred thousand Americans are killed each year by opioids, primarily fentanyl, including over five thousand in Pennsylvania in 2021. Many come from communities buffeted by globalization and ravaged by COVID-19. All are robbed of the opportunity for a better life.

But fentanyl is just one tragedy among many. Intergenerational mobility has declined, and today's young adults often do not have the same prospects their parents did. According to one study, 92 percent of children born in 1940 earned more than their parents, but only 50 percent of those born in 1984 do.[22] Despite the miraculous reduction to child poverty in my lifetime, those born into the lower socioeconomic class today are less likely to make it to the middle class than their parents. Worse yet, the loss of mobility hits those in minority and rural communities the hardest. Increasingly, someone's status at birth determines their lot in life.

An economist recently observed that "capitalism was designed for outsiders," but the American economy has become increasingly closed to them.[23] Washington has erected obstacles to entrepreneurship. Universities resemble expensive credentialing facilities, not gateways to knowledge. We've built barriers to opportunity. In a nation dedicated to the promise of growth and opportunity for every American, expectations matter. We compare ourselves to each other, to our ancestors, and to our aspirations.[24] We ask ourselves: Am I getting promoted? Will I be better off than my parents? Will I be able to give my kids a better childhood than I had? There can be little doubt that for many Americans, the answers increasingly are "no."[25] This growing gap will hold us back if we fail to address it.

If liberty and opportunity power the inventive and restless side of America, patriotic duty holds it intact. Lincoln defined it at Gettysburg: to ensure that "government of the people, by the people, for the people, shall not perish from the earth." That duty binds us to a shared American project. We are called to be grateful for and to uphold our founding principles, to care for one another, and to take an active role in preserving the American experiment. These are the responsibilities of citizenship, and they hold the national fabric together. When we lose them, the tapestry frays.

We see evidence of this happening all around us. America has become a deeply polarized place, in large part because the loudest voices among us are making it so. Activists want to teach our kids radical ideas, like the ridiculous notion that America was founded to protect the institution of slavery. We are even fighting over what it means to be an American, encouraged by social media platforms, which promote echo chambers and incentivize groupthink, and by traditional media, which cherry-picks facts to feed their preferred narratives. There's a cost to all this. Many young people think America is worse than other nations. Many say it's not worth defending.[26] They reject our patriotic duty to preserve the American experiment.

Perhaps I shouldn't be surprised. Surrounded by partisanship and unmoored from strong institutions, Americans now trust one another less than they once did.[27] They don't agree on the core tenets of citizenship. But if such divisions persist, our country will be pulled apart. We will continue to become, in the words of David Brooks, an atomized society "caught in a distrust doom loop."[28]

This is the condition of our country. What do we do about it?

The State of Our Union

Skeptics on both sides of the aisle say it's time to give up the burdens of a superpower and become a normal nation. We aren't cut out for leadership anymore, they claim. We don't have the capacity, and it's a distraction from the problems that matter. So we shouldn't waste our time trying to rebuild our military or firm up our role in the world.[29] The critics are wrong. They miss the inextricable relationship among what America does at home, what it does abroad, and how it remains exceptional.

America is not like other nations, nor should it be. America is exceptional. For our sake and the world's sake, we ought to endeavor to keep it that way.

American strength makes it possible for us to practice and preserve our exceptionalism. As Alexander Hamilton explained at the

Constitutional Convention in Philadelphia in 1787: "No government could give us tranquility and happiness at home which did not possess sufficient stability and strength to make us respectable abroad."[30] That is, by being strong and wielding that strength in service of American interests, our nation creates the space for each of us to exercise our liberty and to chase our American dream in peace.

This was the central insight behind American leadership following World War II. President Harry Truman and the wise men at his side looked back at the preceding decades of depredations, depression, and disease at horrifying scale and at the Iron Curtain descending across Europe, and they recognized that they would see more of the same unless America helped build a better world. So they set about creating a stronger America and a more stable world.

Truman and his successors took great pains to build up the pillars of American strength. They spent a far greater portion of the national treasure on the military. They invested in U.S. scientific and technological leadership. And, most of all, they unleashed the potential of the American worker, who then turned us into the richest country the world had ever seen. At the same time, they enlisted allies to share the burden of stability and security and established big international institutions to formalize our leadership.

This wasn't pie-in-the-sky idealism or global charity but an enlightened understanding that America and its citizens are most secure and most well-off when others share our interests and join us in defending them. There were missteps along the way, and our nation did, at times, use its power recklessly. Still, the results are undeniable: seventy-five years of unprecedented peace and prosperity both at home and abroad and the greatest expansion of freedom and opportunity in world history.

Global politics is a messy business. Over millennia, empires sought wealth and dominion. They saw the accumulation and use of power as zero-sum: either you have it or others will use it against you. As two Athenian envoys reportedly said, "The strong do what they can, and the weak suffer what they must."[31] The Chinese Communist Party shares that view. It wields its power cruelly, subjecting its own citizens to totalitarian control and threatening nations that dare stand against it. It aspires to supplant America and enforce its will around the world. If it succeeds, we will suffer. It doesn't share our values—our respect for liberty and human dignity—or our principles of property rights and individual autonomy. It doesn't respect trade rules or commerce. It wants to create client states, not fair partnerships.

Who else will stand up to Communist China? Who else can or will uphold the peace, prosperity, and liberty we have enjoyed for generations? The Chinese Communist Party has explicit plans to lead the world.[32] Who will stop them?

Only American leadership, exercised properly, will protect the interests of Americans.

But we must lead from a position of strength, because like all authoritarians before them, that's the only language Beijing understands. Right now we're not strong enough, and we're growing relatively weaker. To confront China and preserve our prosperity, freedom, and independence, we must rebuild the pillars of our national power. We will need a thriving economy that generates opportunity, good jobs, and growth. We will require the most advanced, powerful military and the inclination to stand up for American interests around the world. We will, in other words, have to renew our nation.

But where to begin? At the source of our problems. We must look past the symptoms of decline to its root causes. And there we find a self-reinforcing cycle of stagnation and decline.

America promises progress. It depends on it. What is the American dream if not the promise that each generation will outperform the previous? Why do we have liberty if not to move freely, to better ourselves, and to make something for our families? What is our patriotic duty if not the continual pursuit of a stronger, better republic? If our nation stalls, it loses her loveliness—and sadly, that's what's happening.

History shows that great powers do not so much decline as stagnate. In their ascent to the top, they exhaust the easy paths to wealth and turn from growth to haggling over the harvest. The dominant cultures and institutions come to favor the status quo in order to preserve their position and their piece of the pie. In turn, one well-regarded scholar observed, they "slow down society's capacity to adopt new technologies and to reallocate resources in response to changing conditions."[33] They rust up the engines of national power, creating inertia against national renewal.

By any measure, the United States is headed down that path. Slow productivity growth and declining entrepreneurship stink of stagnation.[34] Globalization has left too many workers behind and undermined our industrial competitiveness—our ability to produce goods at a fair price and to raise the real incomes of our citizens at the same time. The U.S. military is being "out-innovated" by adversaries and rapidly losing its ability to deter China, especially when it comes to Taiwan, and America's diplomacy and global leadership are on life support.

Stagnation has gripped our core institutions as well. You can see it in the unrelenting growth of government rules, bureaucracy, and the administrative state. You can see it in the slow creep of politics into fundamentally apolitical institutions. And you can see it in the cultural fever gripping our society in which, to quote the writer Bari Weiss, "the equality of opportunity is replaced with equality of outcome as a measure of fairness."[35] Institutions trapped in this maelstrom drift from their proper roles in our society, become platforms for social posturing, and compromise basic standards of excellence and merit. They become barriers to, not organs for, progress, dynamism, and moral formation.

We are caught, in other words, in a cycle of stagnation and therefore of decline. That cycle is the root cause of much of our fiscal problems and domestic strife today.

Our country has left those among us most in need behind. The free-trade regime, though good for overall economic growth, took a toll on American workers, and we did not do enough to help them adapt. Men, particularly those without college degrees, have steadily left the labor force for decades, and roughly one in six men with only a GED is out of work.[36] More and more citizens depend on government support, and many more children grow up without a stable, two-parent family than in previous generations.[37] Many Americans live in what one journalist called "Alienated America."[38] Their communities have deteriorated. Jobs are scarce, drugs plentiful, and loneliness pervasive. These numbers are even more discouraging for racial minorities, particularly Black families.[39] All of this—the expanding opportunity gap, the imposition of government mandates, the radical cultural pressures that silence dissent, and the divisions and disunity—are a product of our stagnation. How can we ask each other to commit to the American experiment when that experiment is not living up to its promise?

America remains exceptional, but the national fabric has begun to fray. The inclination toward illiberalism, the loss of opportunity, the rejection of individualism and diversity of thought, and the distrust pull it apart. You and I can feel it. I heard it at every stop on the campaign trail. Pennsylvanians have an unmistakable sense that America is on the verge of losing its greatness, and they're not alone. One poll found that 58 percent of Americans think the next generation will be worse off.[40] Another found 88 percent thought we were headed in the wrong direction.[41] The sense of decline is pervasive. In the fall of 2020, a septuagenarian Trump supporter told the *New York Times* that "he never felt this way about our country." A Biden supporter echoed him: "We're just teetering, and it's scary as all get-out."[42]

America has descended from the pinnacle of the unipolar moment, but it bears repeating: we are not bound to fall any more than we are destined to remain the strongest nation. There's nothing inevitable about national decline—no inexorable power pulling us down or unstoppable adversaries destined to overtake us. There is no doubt America is an exceptional nation. We now have an opportunity to prove it by what we do next.

CHAPTER 2

We've Been Here Before

It is time for us to realize that we are too great a nation to limit ourselves to small dreams. We are not, as some would have us believe, doomed to an inevitable decline... So, with all the creative energy at our command, let us begin an era of national renewal. Let us renew our determination, our courage, and our strength. And let us renew our faith and our hope.

—Ronald Reagan, in his first inaugural address, January 20, 1981

On July 15, 1979, Jimmy Carter declared that America suffered from a "crisis of confidence" that "strikes at the very heart and soul and spirit of our national will." The crisis, he warned, threatened "to destroy the social and the political fabric of America."

I was just fourteen at the time and worked in the summers trimming Christmas trees. To be selected as part of the crew, I had to arrive at the local jail by six thirty a.m., where the man who owned the tree farms would pick up the volunteers in his pickup truck—men and teenagers like me—and drop us off in one of the untrimmed fields to work our way through rows of trees. We worked under tight supervision beneath the scorching sun and got paid by a wad of cash at the end of each day. I loved it. But even then, as I watched the unemployed men trimming trees by my side, I sensed Carter was right. Growing up in rural Pennsylvania, most people expected to go to work at the local textile mill, or other small manufacturers in the region, but many of those had begun to shut down. Pennsylvanians were losing jobs. The future they had planned for and the American dream they had hoped for appeared to be slipping away.

By the end of the 1970s, malaise had settled over the country. However, in the years that followed, this sentiment would quickly disappear and be replaced by recovery and optimism. Not that I was focused much on geopolitics during those hot summer days trimming trees, but if you had told me then that the Soviet Union would soon dissolve, the Cold War would end peacefully, and America would stand alone in the world as a superpower, I'm not sure I would have believed you. Yet the election of Ronald Reagan sparked a revival at home and abroad that laid the foundation for decades of unprecedented American prosperity and strength.

I arrived at West Point in the middle of that remarkable period of national renewal. No one from my immediate family or even close family friends had served in the military, and I'd had high hopes of competing as a Division I athlete at a good college with a less monastic social life. But I was not a particularly strong student, and my admission was aided by the fact that West Point recruited me to play football and wrestle. While my parents would have supported whatever decision I made, my dad insisted I at least apply to West Point to see if it was a possibility.

To my surprise, I was accepted, and the possibility of attending West Point began to take on a life of its own. No one from my hometown had attended any of the service academies since Vietnam, and my acceptance was announced in the local paper. My teachers and coaches were encouraging. Everyone I spoke to assumed that I would accept the appointment. I did and this turned out to be one of the best decisions of my life.

On a balmy day in early July 1983, my parents dropped me off at West Point's Michie Stadium. A short briefing to parents and their soon-to-be cadets ended abruptly with "Parents exit to the right and 'new cadets' exit to the left." My military career had begun. By the end of the day, after hours of vaccinations, uniform fittings, a buzz cut, and parade practice, the West Point "Class of 1987" marched across the parade field with the reviewing stands chock-full of teary-eyed parents looking down upon their transformed—and, in some cases, teary-eyed—new cadets.

The rising seniors, or first classmen, "firsties," ran the show. They bombarded us with information and barked orders as they herded us around West Point's historic grounds. There's no gentle orientation day at West Point or the sixty-day "beast barracks" that follows. They intentionally shock the system with a time-tested process that takes this cohort of wide-eyed teenagers and begins to break them down, to be remolded as leaders and officers. It was all perfectly orchestrated, a test for the older cadets who are responsible as well as the new "plebes" in their charge. I'd realize only years later, when it was our turn to welcome the new class, just how much work went into preparations for this century-old tradition.

At times I thought the upperclassmen were speaking in tongues, throwing acronyms and terms at us. Soon we would also be able to speak this new language, but not yet. For now, we listened, learned, and bonded with our classmates—all in hope of surviving plebe year. We were limited to three responses: "yes, sir," "no, sir," or "no excuse, sir."

For those preparing to put on the uniform, the growing confidence in the U.S. military and America were palpable. The military had struggled to regain the public's confidence and to adapt to the end of the draft after the Vietnam War. That stain had begun to wash away before I arrived at West Point. By the time I left, it was gone. Lee Greenwood's "God Bless the USA" released in 1984 captured the national mood.

This capacity to reverse our fortunes and overcome the challenges we face has been a persistent thread throughout American history. Americans confronted the original sin of slavery and fought a war to preserve our union, and we have stood against Fascism, Communism, and external threats to our way of life.

In the wake of the Great Depression and World War II, the United States emerged victorious in a world torn apart by war. Europe had been devastated by years of brutal fighting. The United Kingdom's time in the sun was rapidly ending, and Japan, once a dominant Pacific power, was powerless. It was a moment of great potential—for good and ill. The grip of Communism was tightening as Maoist forces conquered China, and the Iron Curtain descended across Eastern Europe. However, the war also brought forth great advances in technology and human flourishing. Nations rapidly advanced air flight, radars, medical care, precursors to computers, and of course, nuclear power.

At this precarious moment, the United States laid the groundwork for the American century. It acted swiftly to secure its leadership through institutions like NATO and the United Nations and through creative statecraft, like the Marshall Plan to shore up Europe. The United States also went to work on the home front. Through the GI Bill, our federal government made a profound commitment to helping Americans returning from war pursue their dreams. Motivated by

Vannevar Bush and the success of wartime innovation, we invested in scientific discovery to spur further advances.

In the decades that followed, that foundation carried the nation to unprecedented heights, but not without American renewal along the way. When the Soviet Union launched the Sputnik satellite into space in October 1957, Americans saw their technological edge slipping. Then Soviet cosmonaut Yuri Gagarin beat the Americans into space in April 1961. America answered with the National Aeronautics and Space Administration, the National Defense Education Act, and an embrace of freewheeling innovation, backed by cash and hands-off oversight. John Glenn orbited the earth just weeks after Yuri Gagarin, and on July 20, 1969, Neil Armstrong took one small step out of the lunar landing module, onto the surface of the moon.

The durability of the American experiment is undeniable. Even in my lifetime, we have gone through another remarkable period of renewal: Ronald Reagan's Morning in America. Our country proved, yet again, what Americans are capable of when we put our minds to the task of strengthening our country. That turnaround holds a special place in my mind because I was there. I lived this renewal and saw the good it did for America.

More important for us today, we find ourselves in a similar sort of malaise now as we did in the years leading up to Morning in America. By looking back at that story of renewal, we can see what it will take to turn things around again—and we are reminded of all that we as Americans inherit and are charged to uphold.

By reflecting on the past, we can also see some of the risks we face in the present. One of the great benefits of our representative democracy, with all its shortcomings, is our tireless pursuit of a brighter future for all Americans. Sadly, we have too often fallen short of that goal. Morning in America was no exception: it set us on the path to becoming the world's lone superpower, but also unleashed forces that would upend the livelihoods of millions of Americans and leave far too many behind. Renewal, as we'll see, takes perception, vision, and the hard work of execution. It requires great statesmen to lead it. But it does not occur overnight, nor is the work ever completed. Renewal requires relentless focus and constant evolution—and leaders who value both.

A Crisis of Confidence—Then and Now

Mark Twain is said to have observed that history does not repeat itself, but it often rhymes. When I look back at the 1970s, the verse rings true. Though the comparison isn't perfect, it looks a lot like today.

In my hometown, the Magee Carpet Company was the largest employer. It was central to the community and had been since the turn of the century. James Magee II was the son of an Irish American carpet maker in Philadelphia. His father had founded James Magee and Company shortly after the Civil War. He grew up around the factory's twenty-five looms. Though his father ran the place, he still worked his way up from a floor-sweep to superintendent. Before long, Magee realized he did not have a future there, so he set out to start his own business, an ingrain carpet shop in Philadelphia, and later relocated to Bloomsburg after civic leaders enticed him to move his operation and set up a factory with thirty-five looms.

Within a few years, the market shifted—ingrain carpets were going out of style, and the Magee Carpet Company pivoted and started making tapestries. The business took off, and within two decades, Magee had erected one of the largest carpet mills in the country and employed hundreds of workers in Bloomsburg. Magee's son, Harry Magee, grew up in our town. Harry went to school at Dickinson College, just a few hours south, and by the time World War II broke out, he had ascended to become president of his father's company. Harry and his father became patrons of Bloomsburg by starting the local radio station, bringing a small airport to town, helping fund and govern the local hospital and banks, and serving on the town council and board of education. Under his leadership, the Magee Carpet Company rivaled international competitors and earned the nickname "The Mill of Two Thousand Dinner Pails."

Then on June 20, 1972, disaster struck. Hurricane Agnes was the first of the 1972 season. It formed in the Yucatan Peninsula and slowly worked its way up to Florida, eventually pummeling the Eastern Seaboard of the United States and wreaking havoc on Pennsylvania. A foot of rain fell in the Susquehanna Valley, stranding thousands, flooding homes and businesses, costing dozens of lives, and severely damaging the Magee carpet mill. A few months later Harry Magee died. The company had to be reorganized. Business slowed. Layoffs followed. It was clear to me even as a kid growing up in the 1970s that the biggest employer in town was struggling and, in many respects, the town would never recover.

The Magee Carpet Company was not alone. Across Pennsylvania and across America, deindustrialization had begun. For one hundred years, the towns and valleys of the Commonwealth of Pennsylvania had been the industrial heart of America. Anthracite coal mines in Pottsville, Hazleton, Wilkes-Barre, and across northeastern Pennsylvania provided the critical energy source to power American industry. In places like Homestead, Bethlehem, Johnstown, and Aliquippa, Pennsylvanians forged the steel and rolled the metal that made American cities. Pittsburgh, at the confluence of the Allegheny,

Ohio, and Monongahela rivers, became the industrial capital of America.

Then the mills, steelworks, and mines began to close. Factories laid off workers by the thousands, and rail lines went quiet. In 1950, the United States accounted for half the world's steel production. By 1980, that portion dropped to nearly 10 percent.[1]

Some jobs went overseas. Some were automated. As the clock struck midnight on 1982, much of the region reported over 20 percent unemployment. The day after Christmas, thirteen hundred steel workers in Johnstown lost their jobs. Many more would find themselves out of work around the region in the years to come.[2] Deindustrialization left more than quiet mills and empty mines in its wake; it changed how Americans worked, led to shuttered businesses, and hollowed out communities, erasing the futures that many had long envisioned for themselves.

We confront a similar process today. We have entered the so-called Fourth Industrial Revolution, marked by rapid advances in robotics, automation, digital sensors, advanced manufacturing, and the rise of artificial intelligence. Technological progress is already redefining how we produce goods, but the changes go well beyond just production. Amazon lists thousands of books on the "future of work," all of which raise a fair question: What will Americans do for a living in ten years?

It's fair to assume that the average American will change jobs more than their parents did. Young men and women entering the workforce today likely have no idea what their career will look like. This is not necessarily bad, but it comes with more risk. The technological progress driving these changes could be among the critical keys to rebooting American productivity and wage growth, but not without a cost. Just as deindustrialization helped lead to both the boom of the 1990s and the hollowing out of Middle America, so too will today's changes both help and harm Americans—but only if our leaders move quickly and decisively to seize the advantage.

This brings us to the second parallel between now and then: a growing gap in leadership. Throughout the 1970s, when confronted with a rapidly changing world, government struggled to deliver economic growth, domestic stability, and international security. Richard Nixon, for example, responded to the economic turmoil of the time by attempting to control the growth in wages and prices that presaged inflation. His strategy backfired, and inflation surged.[3] Jimmy Carter's administration spent a lot of time reorganizing government but seemed less interested in solving the country's biggest challenges.[4] He projected weakness, and our enemies noticed. Trust in government plummeted. In 1968, three in five Americans said they trusted government to do the right thing. By the end of the 1970s, only one in five did.[5]

A crisis of confidence in our leadership looms again today. When a recent Gallup poll asked Americans what institutions they trusted, only 7 percent said Congress. Media organizations did slightly better, and the presidency enjoyed the confidence of just 23 percent of the respondents. Across the board, trust is falling.[6] As in the 1970s, the loss of trust reflects government's shortcomings. Over the past few decades, we have spent trillions on the war on poverty, yet poverty rates have hardly budged. Our schools have shown little improvement and too often underserve their children. The handling of the COVID-19 pandemic revealed the politicization and unseriousness of much of our governing infrastructure, robbed a generation of students of vital years of schooling, and deepened the severe mental health crisis. Meanwhile, thousands of Americans gave life and limb in Afghanistan and Iraq, to little avail. Then, as now, in the absence of principled and visionary leadership, and therefore of sound policy, our country is suffering through economic uncertainty, political disorder, and decline.

In the 1970s, inflation and unemployment were so acute that Americans turned to a "misery index" to capture the situation. The misery index summed the rates of unemployment and annual inflation. It sat in double digits for much of the 1970s and, in a testament to how far we slipped, surpassed 20 percent during the Carter years.[7] The stock market did not appreciate from the start to the end of the 1970s. Productivity growth slowed by a half, meaning wages stagnated as well.[8] In Columbia County, where I grew up, unemployment hit double digits in the mid-1970s.[9] "Stagflation," as it came to be called, undermined any confidence in the future of the U.S. economy. *Time* magazine even ran a cover in 1975 asking, "Can Capitalism Survive?" The 1973 oil crisis exacerbated matters when the Organization of Petroleum Exporting Countries (OPEC) cartel embargoed shipments to the United States as retribution for supporting Israel in the Yom Kippur War. Gas lines went dry as the price of crude oil grew by over 900 percent between 1972 and 1981. Americans not only had to wait in line for hours for a tank of gas, but worse yet, couldn't keep their heat on or light up their Christmas trees.

Here we are again. Throughout the 2010s, Obama administration policy favored those who owned property, invested in the stock market, and generally had assets, at the expense of those who did not. The pandemic then further expanded the opportunity gap, hitting those already worst off the hardest. Coming out of the pandemic, easy monetary policy and the excesses of the Biden administration's fiscal plan contributed to the highest inflation since the days of the Misery Index, while also engorging the national debt. The disparate impact widens the inequality gap, and our shared economic future looks increasingly ominous. In the land of opportunity, that's a terrible thing.

The 1970s also beheld extreme political disorder—assassinations, violent protests, and domestic terrorism—and decay. The Federal Bureau of Investigation reported twenty-five hundred bombings on American soil during an eighteen-month period in the early 1970s. Popular films like *Taxi Driver*, *Death Wish*, and *Dirty Harry* imagined lone-wolf vigilantes taking to the streets to clean up the violence and restore order to civic life. The rot permeated national politics. The Watergate scandal led to Nixon's resignation. His two successors—Gerald Ford and Jimmy Carter—failed to win reelection. Both left office with few successes to their name. The core foundation of civil society seemed to be breaking down.

We again see far too many examples today of growing political violence and unrest. On June 14, 2017, James Hodgkinson opened fire on Republican congressmen practicing for the upcoming congressional Baseball Game. Five men were wounded, including Congressman Steve Scalise. Hodgkinson had gone in search of Republicans, radicalized by political hatred. His heinous act was one of many instances of political violence in recent memory. In the summer of 2020, violent looters took advantage of protests for racial justice to inflict billions of dollars of property damage—much of it on unsuspecting small business owners. That same year, there was a dramatic increase in homicides, and some cities saw historic highs in murder rates. Then, on January 6, 2021, we witnessed unprecedented violence at the Capitol. While most of those outside our Capitol that day were protesting peacefully, those who instigated violence and desecrated the halls of one of the most sacred symbols of our democracy should face the due process of our justice system. Whether on the streets of Minneapolis or the steps of the Capitol, such violence is unacceptable and un-American.

In the 1970s, American leadership in the world seemed at risk—just as it does now. The sense of decline took hold quickly. On July

16, 1969, Neil Armstrong transcended the bonds of earth, but the next year, Henry Kissinger privately fretted that the United States "has passed its historic highpoint like so many earlier civilizations."[10] Over the decade that followed, it became clear that America did not have the power or authority it once claimed on the world stage.

I still remember from my childhood the black-and-white television images of the last helicopter departing Saigon, a searing illustration of failure in Vietnam. The international architecture we had established also began to crumble. In 1973, the Bretton Woods system, which had governed international monetary policy and economics since World War II and pegged international currencies to the U.S. dollar, dissolved. America's share of the global economy had shrunk dramatically since the early 1960s, and the Soviet Union seemed to be, if anything, growing stronger.

Then as now, a sense of decline took hold. In the mid-1970s, a group of scholars, led by Samuel Huntington, presented a report on "The Crisis of Democracy," which warned, "the United States is more likely to face serious military or diplomatic reversal during the coming years than at any previous time in its history."[11] Today, nearly half of Americans surveyed believe our country's influence in the world is declining, compared to just nineteen percent, who believe it to be growing.[12] As I described in the previous chapter, our chief competitors similarly foresee American decline as well and have closed the gap with us economically, militarily, and strategically. America's standing is again at risk.

In sum, deindustrialization and technological change coupled with deficient leadership triggered economic uncertainty and sclerosis, political decay, and the weakening of America's position in the world. The situation was dire—every bit as dire as the one we face today—and it seemed to get worse as the 1970s limped to a close.

In 1979, the American-backed regime in Iran fell to Islamic revolutionaries, and the Soviet Union marched into Afghanistan. America's future seemed, to many people, very much in question.

Yet within a few short years, it was "Morning in America." How did that remarkable turnaround happen? Answering that question helps to bring our own future into focus.

Morning in America

While many factors contributed to the reversal that followed, President Reagan and his team took three practical steps that made it possible. First, they recognized the major challenges before the country and the opportunities implicit in each. Second, they crafted a visionary agenda to restore American power. Third, they turned that vision into reality through sound policy and political will. Perception, vision, and execution: these are what my friend and former professor Aaron Friedberg called the "three general prerequisites for an integrated, national response to relative decline."[13] While there is no simple explanation for how America went from malaise to the unipolar moment in just over a decade, there is also no doubt that Reagan's leadership during this period and the story of Morning in America that resulted was consistent with Friedberg's assessment.

The Roots of Renewal

Carter took a beating for his "malaise speech," but his diagnosis wasn't wrong. He saw the fraying of American society. He recognized that we faced real-world challenges of stagflation, loss of opportunity, and a seemingly resurgent Soviet Union. He likewise saw the depth of the spiritual crisis in the country. The national consciousness was in crisis. Reagan saw the same thing.

Contrary to the view of him as a political elitist obsessed with cutting taxes for the rich, Reagan was, as one political observer puts it, "the working-class Republican."[14] The son of uneducated, hard-working parents—neither of whom graduated from high school—Reagan grew up a New Deal Democrat. He appreciated the value of a government that cared for Americans in places like his hometown of Tampico, Illinois, and for those left behind. Over time, he refined his political philosophy, but he never lost sight of where he came from or of the people he grew up around.

Their struggles animated his administration. His first inauguration speech, on January 20, 1981, opened with their plight: inflation threatening to "shatter the lives of millions of people," "human misery and personal indignity" caused by shuttered factories and unemployment, taxes denying workers "a fair return for their labor," and regulatory obstacles stifling ingenuity. Then he pivoted to the future. The men and women struggling under the weight of these burdens remained, in his words, heroes:

> You can see heroes every day going in and out of factory gates. Others, a handful in number, produce enough food to feed all of us and then the world beyond. You meet heroes across a counter—and they are on both sides of that counter. There are entrepreneurs with faith in themselves and faith in an idea who create new jobs, new wealth and opportunity. They are individuals and families whose taxes support the Government and whose voluntary gifts support church, charity, culture, art, and education. Their patriotism is quiet but deep. Their values sustain our national life.[15]

In his mind, those Americans, so often forgotten by Washington, were the center of gravity of American life. He believed American renewal began with them, and government's job was to support them and help them overcome the worst that life could throw at them and otherwise to get out of the way. That belief and his deeply felt compassion for the needs and dreams of the average American fueled his confidence in America's future.

By the time Reagan became president, America was poised for a technological explosion that changed the course of history. The microprocessor had unleashed a wave of computer innovations. Apple and Microsoft were gaining steam, and in 1981, IBM released its first commercially available personal computer, running on Microsoft's MS-DOS operating system. *Entrepreneur* magazine launched in 1977, hailing the ascent of the American innovator and businessman in the public eye.

This was the dawn of the information age, and Reagan rightly believed America was ready to take advantage of it, both in the market and in the military. And he correctly surmised that our chief competitors in Moscow could not adapt. In a commencement address at his alma mater, Eureka College, in 1982, Reagan declared that "the Soviet empire is faltering because rigid, centralized control has destroyed incentives for innovation, efficiency and individual achievement."[16] Reagan drew a clear line in the sand between America's commitment to liberty and opportunity and the Soviet command-and-control model. The latter, he believed, could not long survive. Not everyone agreed with him, but he understood that the Soviet Union was an aged, weakened beast.

"The American resurgence," according to one historian, "would not have been possible without the tectonic shifts that commenced in the 1970s." However, it was not enough to perceive our conditions. He continues, "By recognizing the trends in play and deploying American power to accentuate them, and by acting decisively at points of great fluidity in world affairs." Reagan and his team put America on the path to the unipolar moment.[17]

Visionary Leadership

Reagan excelled at what George H. W. Bush called the "vision thing."[18] He spoke plainly but forcefully, and he brought into office three big ideas for how to renew America: revitalize the American dream, rebuild the military, and take on Communism. Guided by that vision, the government went to work rebuilding the pillars of American power.

The economy was first. Jim Baker, then Reagan's chief of staff, identified three priorities for the administration's first hundred days: "economic recovery, economic recovery, and economic recovery."[19] Chiefly, the Federal Reserve needed to get inflation under control. It was debilitating. People's savings lost their value, and their wages didn't fare much better. Productivity stalled. The economy did too. Americans could not save or find jobs, much less innovate or reach their full potential.

For America to recover, those burdens had to be lifted. Wealth, as Reagan put it in 1983, "is born in the hearts and minds of entrepreneurs all across Main Street America," so Washington must tend to Main Street.[20] Prices needed to stabilize, and government had to clear the way for entrepreneurship. To fulfill that mission, he promised tax cuts and continued deregulation. His administration also boosted federal support for research and development by 25 percent from 1983 to 1986, and Reagan extolled the transformative power of innovation, saying "Technology is not the enemy of job creation, but its parent—the very source of our economic dynamism and creativity."[21]

Alongside the economy, the U.S. military needed a rebuild. The Vietnam War and the years that followed took a toll on the armed forces. The transition from a draft to an all-volunteer force created substantial turmoil, and the services struggled to stay ready and armed for a fight. By the late 1970s, consensus held that the Soviet Union's conventional military power exceeded that of NATO's.[22] Jimmy Carter's secretary of defense, Harold Brown, set out to reverse that consensus. Under Brown's guidance and that of his research and development czar and future secretary of defense, Bill Perry, the Pentagon developed the F-117 fighter-bomber and B-2 bomber, the first two stealth aircraft. It began to field precision-guided missiles that could strike with greater accuracy than any existing weapon and revolutionized military communications and satellites. Most important, Brown made sure the efforts were budgeted and paid for, and the technology revolution in the military was well underway.

The Reagan administration inherited Carter's military transformation and doubled down. To go into the world effectively, America needed a powerful military at its back, so Reagan and his defense secretary Casper Weinberger stepped up defense investment, oversaw tremendous advances in stealth and other military technologies, and launched the Strategic Defense Initiative. They showed the Soviet Union it could not keep up with us and in the process created the most formidable military the world had ever seen. This was the force I joined when I arrived at West Point.

Reagan's vision began at home, with the revitalization of American economic and military power, but extended abroad. His strategy for taking on the Soviet Union was simple: "we win, they lose."[23] He gave clear markers of what he wanted to do. America would challenge Communism in all corners and bring its economic might to bear against the Soviets. Radio Free Europe and Voice of America blasted Western news behind the Iron Curtain, and Reagan formed tighter relationships with similarly visionary leaders in London, Berlin, and even the Vatican. At the same time, Reagan understood that conditions changed. From a position of strength, he could reach across the Iron Curtain to Moscow. George Shultz began quiet negotiations with his Soviet counterparts. They built trust and began to work at bigger problems—all part of the clear mission of victory in the Cold War.

Reagan gave the country direction. He laid out a vision of renewal and strength, grounded in his faith in everyday Americans and in a conceptual understanding that American strength, prosperity, and leadership are inseparable. To have one, we must have the others. The lessons are simple: We need visionary leadership, and we need to remember that what we do at home echoes abroad.

The Hard Work of Renewal

Ronald Reagan came into office promising renewal. He offered his vision, and few could question his devotion to it. Yet rhetoric and vision amount to nothing if we do not commit ourselves to actual reform. Renewal requires courage and the willingness to take short-term hits for the long-term benefit of the country. It requires us to work together as Americans, not partisans, to advance our common goals. It requires backbone and investment, but also the ability to adapt to ever-changing circumstances.

One example of such leadership was the fight against runaway inflation, which had bedeviled the United States for a decade and even reached double digits. Carter, struggling to get it under control, had appointed Paul Volcker as chairman of the Federal Reserve. The decision turned out to be a momentous one. Volcker understood that to control inflation the Federal Reserve would have to limit the money supply—the amount of money in circulation in the economy—and allow interest rates to rise. But doing so would inevitably hurt the economy. Interest rates soared in 1980 and 1981, with the federal funds rate, which is the one rate the Federal Reserve can set, hitting 20 percent. America entered a recession. Unemployment peaked into double digits.

The economic damage took a political toll. Republicans lost twenty-six seats in the 1982 midterm elections, yet Paul Volcker stuck to his strategy. The economist John Taylor, my predecessor once removed as Treasury undersecretary, has recounted that when pressured to stop his onerous means, Volcker replied that, "he couldn't stop fighting inflation until he ended it."[24] Reagan backed him up, even as critics pilloried them both. In the end, the strategy worked. Inflation subsided, and America's economic foundations stabilized. Uncertainty and volatility no longer held back growth and investment, but the administration still had to work to preserve the gains. During Reagan's second term, Baker, then secretary of the Treasury, negotiated an array of international agreements on exchange rates, trade, and financial coordination, effectively adapting the Treasury's strategy to strengthen America's economic position even further.

Reining in inflation cleared the way for Americans to unleash their restive spirit. They were aided by the opening of the economy. The Carter and Ford administrations, along with Congress, had already begun to deregulate key industries, breaking barriers to American innovation and dynamism. The Reagan administration accelerated this work. This would become a theme. In their biography of Jim Baker, two reporters write that while Reagan was devoted to his conservative agenda, he was "not so wedded to the details that it stopped him from reaching across the aisle to achieve many of his priorities with bipartisan support."[25]

Reagan placed his faith explicitly in the power of free markets and individual liberty to power economic growth and won Democratic support for that objective. The 1981 tax reforms, which slashed top tax income rates from 70 percent to 50 percent, earned eighty-nine votes in the Senate. The 1986 reform bill further chopped income taxes down to 28 percent for the top bracket and corporate taxes to 34 percent, passing both chambers with substantial bipartisan majorities. The administration likewise took select actions against cronyism and monopolies, closed tax loopholes that big businesses could exploit and, through expansive deregulation and labor reforms, helped light the embers of innovation and entrepreneurship.

The accumulated impact of Reagan's bipartisan economic reforms was profound. In the 1980s, newer, more innovative firms rose to challenge old stalwarts. The economy took off, growing by over 7 percent in 1984. The unemployment rate, which sat at around 7.5 percent when he took office, dropped to 5.2 and stayed low, aside from a brief spike in the early 1990s, until the global financial crisis.

Reagan showed that same principled commitment to rebuilding the military. Defense spending grew by 40 percent in the first five years of the Reagan administration. It wasn't enough to develop new technologies; the administration fielded them in incredible numbers. America's military power became unrivaled. In both the economic and military arenas, Reagan proved himself a stalwart leader. George Shultz would later praise that aspect of his friend and former boss, writing that he had "a spontaneous, natural ability to articulate the nation's most deeply rooted values and aspirations, and a readiness to stand by his vision regardless of pressure, scorn, or setback."[26]

He carried that same fortitude into the diplomatic arena as well. Reagan viewed nuclear weapons as an abomination, but he and his advisers understood that the Soviets would never reduce their stockpiles simply because nuclear weapons were so dangerous. America needed a show of strength to bring them to the negotiating table. In 1979, the Soviets had started deploying SS-20 intermediate-range nuclear missiles into Western Russia, putting NATO at risk. In response, Carter had announced plans to position American nuclear weapons, named Pershing II missiles, and cruise missiles around Western Europe. Europeans protested. The Vatican opposed it. Reagan stuck with the plan and negotiated an agreement in allied capitals. The missiles started moving into Germany in 1983. Over one hundred missile launchers stood in Germany by 1986.

The Soviets saw American strength displayed and recognized the seriousness of the American position. Before long, Reagan was able to bring the Soviets to the negotiating table and laid the foundation for groundbreaking arms control deals. It took guts to stand up to our allies, many of them close friends, and to ignore the doomsayers. Together, Reagan and his team, and all the men and women who worked with them, took on the Soviet Union. A few years after they left Washington, the Cold War ended, and the Soviet Union peacefully disintegrated, orchestrated by the steady hand and leadership of Bush and his advisers.

American Revival

The Reagan playbook for renewal was guided by certain timeless principles. Chief among them were the belief that America's strength comes from its people, the faith in America's potential, an understanding that America's economic might and military strength are the vital foundation for international leadership, and the recognition that American leadership abroad makes our nation stronger at home. From there, his administration crafted a broad, dynamic policy agenda. There's no denying the effectiveness of that agenda, but Reagan's success came not just from practical policy but also from a revival of the American spirit. As Senator Ted Kennedy once observed, Reagan "stood for a set of ideas...and he wrote most of them not only into public law, but into the national consciousness."[27]

First, Reagan believed in America. His boundless optimism for what America could accomplish was infectious—and well documented. It was also necessary to restore the nation's confidence in itself. Upon accepting the Republican nomination in 1980, Reagan rejected those that would "say that the United States has had its day in the sun; that our nation has passed its zenith."[28] He bet on America's ability to revive itself and "managed through sheer force of personality to infuse the nation with his belief in a better tomorrow."[29] This was not a lazy optimism. Things would not simply work themselves out, but, with strategic direction and better policies, America could outpace the Soviet Union and launch a new birth of freedom.

Second, Reagan's optimism was matched by his ambition for America. Already an accomplished actor, Reagan had launched his political future during the 1964 election, when he spoke in support of the Republican nominee Barry Goldwater. "You and I have a rendezvous with destiny," he declared. America, "the last best hope of man on earth," had a duty to stand against Communism.[30] The speech became famous and took on a life of its own, but his conviction about America's role in the world did not change. It reappeared in his simple "we win, they lose" formulation of strategy against the Soviet Union. It explains his unfailing commitment to building the most powerful, innovative military imaginable and to moonshot projects like the Strategic Defense Initiative.

His domestic aims achieved the same grand heights. He called for a "rebirth of the American tradition of leadership at every level of government and in private life as well."[31] America was exceptional, Reagan reminded us, so "we have every right to dream heroic dreams."[32] After a decade of scandal and malaise, Americans embraced that confidence and the ambition he had for our country. It reminded us of what we could achieve.

Third, Reagan's optimism and ambition for America sprang out of his faith in liberty and the power of citizens: "If we look to the answer as to why for so many years we achieved so much, prospered as no other people on Earth, it was because here in this land we unleashed the energy and individual genius of man to a greater extent than has ever been done before."[33] That belief animated much of his policy agenda. In his famous 1982 Westminster address to the members of the British Parliament, Reagan declared that the "march of freedom and democracy will leave Marxism-Leninism on the ash-heap of history as it has left other tyrannies which stifle the freedom and muzzle the self-expression of the people."[34] The notes varied speech to speech, but the theme held constant: If given space and opportunity, Americans could change the world. And Americans believed it because it was true. Critics often paint this notion as support for an aberrant individualism that rejects social obligation or national duty.[35] Surely some have taken it too far, but the antidote, as Reagan understood, comes not from Washington but from within our citizens. It is gratitude for our national inheritance and a commitment to preserving it.

Reagan had a striking sense of where we stood in the course of American history and a well of gratitude for our exceptional inheritance as Americans. In his first inaugural address, in January 1981, Reagan looked out across the National Mall from the west steps of the Capitol. He then lifted his gaze across the river to Arlington National Cemetery, where thousands of American patriots lie in rest. Each gravestone, as Reagan said, "is a monument to the kind of hero" that you find in every neighborhood of this great country. We are the beneficiaries of their service and courage, he intoned, and the inheritors of a profound legacy of strength, courage, and resiliency. He revisited that theme in his final days as president. His farewell address called for Americans to inhabit an "informed patriotism." Study the nation's history, he urged. Know where we come from—the triumph of the Constitution, the stony road and the lash, and the bloody battlefields—and be grateful that after two hundred years, America "still stands strong and true on the granite ridge, and her glow has held steady no matter what storm."[36]

Why spend so much time looking at the distant past? That was a different time, a different century. It's true: we cannot simply roll out the Reagan platform or attempt to re-create a time long gone. But we can learn a thing or two from this history, like the importance of vision for national renewal or the timeless truth that it's the American people, not the government, who make our great nation tick. Most of all, this history should fill us with hope for our time. However, even as morning broke in America, our renewal was far from perfect, and its benefits and costs unevenly shared. Steel mills continued to close across my home state of Pennsylvania. High costs, low productivity, and foreign competition emptied out the industrial heartland of the state. Big Steel left and never came back. Communities across America suffered.

I grew up in one of those communities. One of my best friend's dad was the sheriff, and I played football and wrestled with the sons of millworkers, farmers, and laborers, as well as a few doctors and college professors.

While some of us seemed better off than others, it wasn't something my friends and I ever thought about or talked about—everyone was equal. But with time, I began to realize how much some of my friends' parents were struggling. Unemployment rates in our county hit double digits in the mid-1970s and stayed high for years.[37] I began to see fathers out of work. As my team traveled to neighboring towns for football games, we'd often see boards on storefront windows and chains on factory gates.

When the mills, factories, and mines closed, life became less certain and more difficult for many across America. Today, that same young man or woman who once had stability would be less likely to start a family or find a stable job. We have seen American families weakened, with more and more children born to unmarried parents. But that same interval saw tremendous advances in healthcare, public safety, and all manner of conveniences, from air-conditioning to dishwashers to the all-powerful smartphone.

The era of free trade and globalization that kicked off in the 1980s powered economic growth for a generation, but the benefits of that growth were not shared widely enough. The men and women left out of work by automation or factories moving overseas still needed jobs, and too many could not find them—nor did they get the support they needed to adapt to a new environment. Those without a college degree and especially Black families saw their wealth fade.[38] A subset of America bore the costs, and unconstrained globalization became untenable.

American renewal, in other words, has brought both triumph and tragedy. Our nation has repeatedly overcome terrible circumstances but often failed some citizens in the process. Morning in America was no exception. As we turn to our own renewal, let us recall the example of America's ascent after World War II, its journey into the next frontier of space, and the restoration of American might under Ronald Reagan. But let us also pause and remember the stain of racism midcentury, the civil unrest of the 1960s, and all those left behind as America surged toward and beyond the unipolar moment.

We should share Reagan and Lincoln's faith in America as we embark on our own renewal. But in doing so, we can—and must—do better. The remainder of this book attempts to show how.

CHAPTER 3

The American Way of Renewal

When the world looks to America, they look to us because we are the most successful political and economic experiment in human history.

—Condoleezza Rice, at the Republican National Convention, August 29, 2012

Pittsburgh holds a special place in my heart. I was born a few miles outside the city, as were three of my daughters. And I experienced one of the most formidable decades of my professional life immersed in the technology renaissance of the Steel City.

Pittsburgh stands at the confluence of three rivers: the Monongahela, the Allegheny, and the Ohio. The Allegheny flows clear and blue, down from the New York–Pennsylvania border to the north. At Point State Park, it meets the Monongahela, and together they form the Ohio, which flows on to the Mississippi. For decades, the Monongahela was the central artery of the nation's steel industry. Steelworks and mills lined its valley, which runs from the West Virginia mountains up through southwestern Pennsylvania, turning Pittsburgh into the steel capital of the world.

At the start of the twentieth century, Pittsburgh produced half of the country's iron and steel, twice as much as was produced in all of England at the time.[1] When World War II began, Pittsburgh turned its industrial might to arming America. Local companies like H. J. Heinz, Dravo, Westinghouse, and Pittsburgh Plate Glass built weapons, parts, and matériel. The city contributed ninety-five million tons of steel to the war effort, and the Commonwealth of Pennsylvania matched the Axis powers in steel production by war's end.[2] In the years that followed, the region turned out at least a quarter of the nation's steel.[3] Men working in downtown offices used to bring an extra shirt to work to change at lunch, as the soot in the air would soil their white collars by lunchtime.

Thirty years later, when Ronald Reagan took office, the city was struggling. It lost three-quarters of its manufacturing capacity in the 1970s.[4] In the 1980s, southwestern Pennsylvania lost at least 150,000 manufacturing jobs, and, by one estimate, Pittsburgh's population shrank by 176,000 people.[5] The Pittsburgh area had consistent double-digit unemployment, even hitting 18 percent in 1983.[6] U.S. Steel's famous Homestead Steel Works shuttered in 1986, and the Monongahela Valley fell silent.[7] The entire region was knocked on its back. It experienced what some have called a second Great Depression.[8] Yet somehow, even then, the silhouette of recovery began to take shape.

I returned to Pittsburgh in 1996 after leaving the Army and completing my PhD. For almost a decade, I would go on long weekend runs through the city. Cutting across the Carnegie Mellon campus and through Schenley Park, I watched that part of the city's journey from rust to renewal. I would look down on the muddy Monongahela and the skeleton of steel mills that once lined its banks. I would turn up past the University of Pittsburgh into the Hill District, which inspired the old cop show, *Hill Street Blues*. This was a struggling neighborhood of predominately Black communities living in poverty, with an inadequate education system and minimal opportunity. Then, back on to Carnegie Mellon's campus, I would pass world-class research facilities and innovation incubators. Pittsburgh was in the middle of an extraordinary but incomplete renaissance.

Pittsburgh's exceptional colleges and universities, particularly Carnegie Mellon University and the University of Pittsburgh, were at the center of the city's revival. In 1984, Carnegie Mellon established its Software Engineering Institute, one of just ten federally funded research centers backed by the Pentagon. The next year, Gulf Oil turned over its research campus fully to the University of Pittsburgh, establishing what is today known as the Applied Research Center. U-PARC, as the campus is called, quickly attracted big-name corporations, like General Motors, and smaller businesses alike.

In time, the two schools continued to draw government and business partnerships. Carnegie Mellon's famed robotics institute, founded in 1979, began offering the nation's first doctorate in robotics and became a magnet for engineers around the country and the world and in 1996 created its own commercial arm, the National Robotics Engineering Center. The university—where I served as a trustee and adjunct professor—ranks among the best engineering schools in the country, led the U.S. Army's AI Task Force, and has partnered with such American titans as Apple, Google, and General Electric. Meanwhile, the University of Pittsburgh Medical Center became a world leader in cutting-edge research into transplants and medical devices. The area around the two schools—the Oakland district—blossomed.

Innovation districts receive a lot of attention these days, but few developed and grew as organically or beautifully as Pittsburgh's did. The two world-class educational facilities drew in government funding. In a reinforcing cycle, brilliant, entrepreneurial people flocked to the area, the start-up scene took off, and government and private capital followed. In 1994, the two universities, local business councils, and the city joined forces to form the Pittsburgh Technology Center. Built along the north bank of the Monongahela River, the center turned the old J&L Coke Works into a hub of public-private investment and research.

Among the technology firms driving the city forward was FreeMarkets, a hot start-up with its name in neon on the city's skyline. Founded by two dynamic McKinsey alumni and entrepreneurs, Glen Meakem and Sam Kinney, FreeMarkets was a rocket ship and the talk of Pittsburgh with a multi-billion-dollar initial public offering (IPO) in 1999. The blue-chip Silicon Valley venture capital firm of the day, Kleiner Perkins, invested in the company, and a rotating list of its iconic partners from John Doerr to Vinod Khosla to Ray Lane sat on our board. FreeMarkets created hundreds of jobs around the city, and money and talent were flowing into the technology sector around us. It resulted in a remarkable period of American innovation.

Glen Meakem recruited me to join FreeMarkets in 1999, and after a short time in McKinsey's Pittsburgh office and several years spent learning the business, I took on the role of CEO in 2002. Our business created software and services that allowed transparent online bidding for parts and supplies for everyone from automotive manufacturers in Detroit to the U.S. Navy and the Commonwealth of Pennsylvania. In most of these markets, buyers would rely on a small group of suppliers and one-off manual negotiations of prices and contractual terms to acquire everything from castings and forgings to electrical circuits to paper goods and other supplies. The inefficiencies were enormous. This outdated process drove up prices and in fact weakened the strength, quality, and competitiveness of the U.S. manufacturing base. FreeMarkets disrupted that model by creating online tenders and transparent price discovery and introducing a whole new set of players into the supply chain through online connections. The efficiencies derived from our work and the emergence of technology and competition triggered enormous disruption but also helped lay the groundwork for much of the innovation we've seen in manufacturing industries since.

By any measure, FreeMarkets was an extraordinary success, one I was proud to be a part of. However, creative destruction along with the bursting of the tech bubble eventually found its way to our sector as well. FreeMarkets had great relationships with its clients, but we didn't move fast enough to become one of the true "software as a service" companies that would eventually dominate the landscape. As CEO, I hadn't built a team around me capable of evolving our business model quickly enough, and therefore we concluded that the best path for keeping up with the fast-moving, competitive business environment was to sell FreeMarkets to Ariba, another business-to-business service provider, as part of a rapid industry consolidation. It was a difficult decision that ultimately turned out to be a wise one—the combined company, which I joined for a time as president, was a big success for Pittsburgh, FreeMarkets' employees, and its shareholders.[9] But it also taught me an invaluable lesson. It was my responsibility, as leader, to set the vision for the company, get the right team in place, and move fast enough to stay in the lead. There are no off days or time for resting on your laurels. Adapt or die, as the saying goes.

At the same time, our sale delivered a reminder of the harsh realities of our technological age. The pace of change is so fast, so unrelenting, that even innovative companies like FreeMarkets get caught in the riptide of technological evolution—which means their employees do too.

As part of the negotiations for Ariba to buy FreeMarkets, I explicitly ensured that Pittsburgh would remain a central hub for the company and that the large majority of our six hundred employees based there would be offered jobs in the combined company. But a small number of jobs were ultimately eliminated. As a leader, not being able to secure jobs for each and every FreeMarkets employee still weighs on me.

I remember attending a Kleiner Perkins CEO conference in the late 1990s, at the height of the technology bubble. I was introduced to two up-and-coming innovators out of Silicon Valley, also backed by Kleiner Perkins: Sergey Brin and Larry Page. They had a new company with a funny name and only $100 million in revenue—much less than ours. But then the bubble burst. While we sold FreeMarkets, for Larry, Sergey, and their company, Google, the future was just beginning. And so it was for Pittsburgh.

Pittsburgh has become, as the saying goes, the land of "eds, meds, and tech."[10] Its world-class universities in 2016 spent two and a half times the national average on research and development.[11] In the past twenty years, technology companies have flocked to Pittsburgh, sparked by FreeMarkets' success. Facebook, Amazon, Microsoft, Google, and Apple all opened offices in the area. Uber and Ford headquartered autonomous vehicle research labs there, and local stalwarts like PNC and Kraft remain vibrant. All the elements of America's innovation ecosystem—talented people, academic research institutions, private capital, and federal R&D funding—meet in Pittsburgh, and few images better capture the city's new identity than the transformation of a 355,000 square foot turn-of-the-century Ford assembly plant into a cutting-edge center for cancer research in 2022.[12]

On my weekend runs through Pittsburgh, I saw the building blocks of renewal: talent fostered by schools like Carnegie Mellon and the University of Pittsburgh, capital investment from the public and private sector alike, the open exchange of knowledge and data across sectors, and the capacity to turn good ideas into something real and tangible. Just as the confluence of rivers made Pittsburgh an industrial capital for decades, so too did the confluence of these factors make it a hub of economic dynamism and technological advancement. I also saw the universities and incubators, government-backed research facilities, and businesses: the institutions that sustained the city's renewal and fostered cultures of experimentation, risk-taking, and constant evolution, without which the innovation ecosystem around Pittsburgh would wither.

One city's experience cannot easily be replicated across the country—and Pittsburgh still has its fair share of problems—but its experience still illuminates a path forward for America. Like our country today, Pittsburgh once stood at a crossroads. It could have continued down the path of stagnation and decline, but it chose a different path. America must do the same.

The Timeless and the Novel

Both Pittsburgh's revitalization and Morning in America reveal to us the timeless aspects of renewal. They began with a rebirth of economic dynamism and growth, powered principally by people operating in an environment of free-flowing capital and ideas. Both cases were sustained by strong institutions. In Pittsburgh, it was the universities, businesses, and the like. In the 1980s, the United States benefited from a well-run Federal Reserve, a smaller government, innovative companies, and visionary leadership from Reagan.

Of course, national renewal differs in important ways from that of a city like Pittsburgh. A nation must defend itself, engage with the world, and balance a far more complex and ungovernable set of interests and challenges. Reagan and his advisers accomplished all three. They rebuilt the military, building on Jimmy Carter's earlier efforts, and they reasserted American leadership to begin the dissolution of the Soviet Union and the proliferation of democracy. They embraced the founding notions of limited government and individual responsibility and agency. Their example reaffirms the most important principle: national renewal occurs when we rebuild the pillars of our power and strengthen our foundation of exceptionalism.

The more interesting question, though, is how do we do that? What made Morning in America possible in its era and Pittsburgh's renaissance in its? What will make renewal possible in our time?

Recall the first prerequisite of national renewal: perceive the challenges before us, but also the opportunities implicit in each. Every episode of American renewal has occurred because wise men and women followed that rule. They saw the dangers of decline and stagnation, and they found new ways to reverse course. Put another way, they adapted and innovated.

This story has played out across our nation's history. America is an unquiet giant, spurred on by the restlessness of her citizenry. We succeed when we make the space for talented individuals to strive, innovate, and flourish, to collaborate and access capital, and to live secure in the knowledge of their liberty. In so doing, we build a reserve of national energy. When crises hit, as they inevitably will, we unleash those energy reserves in outpourings of national power. This was the story of our "Arsenal of Democracy" in World War II and the formation of the postwar order that followed, of the landing of *Apollo 11* on the moon in 1969, and of the creation of the semiconductor industry and the emergence of Silicon Valley in the decade that followed.

From its beginning, America has been a cauldron of potential energy. The genius arrayed in Philadelphia in 1787 cannot be denied.

Americans explored west to what George Washington called the "second Land of Promise,"[13] then built a maze of rail lines connecting coast to coast. Alexander Graham Bell invented the telephone, and Thomas Edison designed the incandescent light bulb. The electricity they tinkered with began to light homes and power factories. Entrepreneurial men and women from foreign lands flocked to America, and some of those, like Andrew Carnegie, became industry titans. The steel they produced built cities. The coal and oil they extracted powered cars, factories, and people's homes. In time, American innovation reached new frontiers. Americans explored space and built microchips. The computer, the cell phone, and the suite of digital technologies we take for granted today emerged from the American laboratory.

All that innovation turned the United States into an economic powerhouse. It was the principal driver of economic growth for the past century, boosting productivity and accounting for 80 percent of the growth in GDP per capita in the second half of the twentieth century.[14] In more recent times, the information revolution, which began in the dark days of the 1970s and took off after Morning in America, transformed the workplace and the economy. I was in the middle of that revolution in Pittsburgh and saw how the flurry of technological adoption overhauled entire industries. That kind of creative destruction has a cost, but it had a tremendously positive effect on American businesses and, more important, American workers. They became dramatically more productive, and firms hired more of them. All in all, Americans earned more for their hard work.[15]

Innovation likewise turned America into a military juggernaut and eventually a superpower after World War II. In the prewar years, the U.S. military had developed innovative techniques for using aircraft carriers and airplanes, but it lacked much capacity when war erupted. Then the nation shifted to a war production footing. Factories became military production lines, and U.S. industry built the Arsenal of Democracy. As the war progressed, Dravo and the American Bridge Company shipyards on the Ohio River produced hundreds of LSTs, the landing ships that ferried tanks ashore at Sicily, Normandy, and across the Pacific, and Bethlehem Steel in Pennsylvania produced over one thousand ships. That's over one ship *per day*.

Meanwhile, U.S. scientists and engineers revolutionized military technology. They invented the radar and built computers to help guide aircraft and munitions and aid in cryptography. Extraordinary advances in medicine saved the lives of countless American GIs. And the Manhattan Project, which President Truman called the "greatest achievement of organized science in history,"[16] created the atomic bomb that ended the war. These were hardly the first instances of American military innovation, but the accumulated advances in American science, technology, and industry helped us win World War II. In the ensuing years, we continued to set the pace of innovation. Ronald Reagan helped ensure the Soviet Union's collapse by rebuilding the most technologically advanced military in the world, and we have benefited from that might ever since.

Every instance of national innovation and advancement looks different, but each follows the same basic pattern. Like Pittsburgh turning from rust to robotics, our country has continually adapted to an ever-changing world.

What We Do Next

What, then, are the challenges and opportunities before us now?

America's principal economic challenge is the loss of productive dynamism. Essentially the value of a worker's output, productivity is one clear indicator of how well off a country is. When growing, people produce more, get paid more, and can purchase more and better products and services. The economy and quality of life improve.

Innovation is critical to productivity growth, and it is necessary to reenergize it again.[17] But we must also attend to the ecosystem that fosters innovation across society and distributes the benefits. This is productive dynamism, and, as the economist Oren Cass observed, it "requires both disruption and the productive re-allocation of those disrupted."[18]

Consider a factory that automates its production lines. Too often the story ends there with some workers out of a job. In a thriving society, the story continues. Most workers will get trained to work alongside the machines, becoming more productive. Those who do lose their jobs will find opportunities to move to new ones or new industries where they can be more productive and in turn get paid more. They and their communities would become more prosperous.

That kind of dynamism is the hallmark of a thriving society, but we have constructed barriers against it. America's institutions and economic system have come to favor insiders over outsiders.[19] They have created extensive obstacles to innovation, from occupational licensing laws that require an aspiring hairdresser to take a thousand hours of classes to the credentialism that biases four-year college degrees over skills and hard work.

Indeed, we too often cling to anachronistic institutions unfit for an era of rapid change and the digital economy. Congress, media, and businesses all have grown stale or decayed, and the administrative state has responded as always with new, complicated rules that harm competition and deepen the cycle of distrust and stagnation.

It's not just the economy. The U.S. military is losing its technological edge and its capacity to do what the nation asks of it. American leadership is faltering, neither shaping the next generation of technology and trade nor proving nimble enough to adapt to a complex world. Behind these challenges lies a tattered national fabric pulled apart by distrust. Our government, duty-bound to preserve our union, is so captured by partisanship and bureaucracy that it cannot solve the big problems before us. Our institutions are decaying, and our leaders have yet to meet the moment.

Those are the challenges. Here are our opportunities.

After returning from the Gulf War, I made the difficult decision to leave the Army and pursue a graduate degree in international affairs. This wasn't my original plan. I'd studied mechanical engineering and chosen to become a combat engineer with the expectation of a likely military career. But an experience shortly after I graduated from West Point inspired me to change course.

In my final year there, my knee was injured during a wrestling match. Committed to finishing out the season, I put off the surgery until spring, which meant it was still healing when I limped across the stage at graduation. The injury prevented me from beginning my Army career right away, so I stayed on at West Point as an assistant coach for the wrestling team. In the evenings, I would drive down to New York City and take graduate courses at Columbia University. One of them was taught by Roger Hilsman. He had lived an extraordinary American life. A West Point graduate himself, he had served in the Office of Strategic Studies—the precursor to the CIA—in the Pacific behind Japanese lines during World War II, before going on to become a scholar, diplomat, and senior adviser to presidents. He taught diplomatic history as someone who had lived it.[20]

He was an inspiration. I wanted to be like him, to be in the arena, to live and participate in American history. The Gulf War gave me a taste of that experience, and I wanted more. So in the fall of 1991, I sent off applications to a dozen schools, then left the Army. With a year to kill and a year's worth of combat pay in my pocket, I bought an "around the world" airline ticket from TWA. The ticket, which drained about a third of my Gulf War savings, let me take as many flights as I wanted, as long as they took me in the same direction, circumnavigating the globe.

I trekked overland through the Middle East, including Turkey, Syria, and Jordan, then spent three weeks in the Holy Land. It was my first time in Jerusalem, and I had the opportunity to visit and pray at the Western Wall, one of the great holy sites in the world. From there, I scuba dived off the beautiful reefs of the Sinai Peninsula in Sharm El-Sheikh and saw Coptic churches for the first time—a memory that would come flooding back when I met my wife and her devoutly Coptic family.

After three months in the Middle East, my travels continued farther east. I spent almost a month exploring the incredible rain forests of Borneo before making my way north to Malaysia, Thailand, Taiwan, and eventually China, where I saw a nation on the cusp of modernity. Eight months and about twenty flights later, my adventure ended at Schofield Barracks, Hawaii, where my brother was stationed.

Doug had attended West Point as well, and, like I had before, served as cocaptain of the wrestling team. On other dimensions, he was far more accomplished. Unlike me, he was at the top of his class academically and was also the first captain at West Point—the highest-ranking officer among the cadets, an honor reserved for the strongest leaders. Unsurprisingly, he has since gone on to a successful business career. But at the time, he was a new lieutenant posted in Hawaii, so I took my chance to see him. It was there I learned that I had been accepted into graduate school at Princeton.

The journey opened my eyes to the world. The end of the Cold War had shaken everything up. Germany had reunified. Japan was

America's chief competitor. China was a waking giant, and the Middle East was reeling.

Fifteen years later, I found myself traveling the world again, this time as a senior official in the George W. Bush administration. In 2005, I was confirmed by the Senate as the undersecretary for export administration at the Commerce Department, in charge of managing export controls, the rules governing what products and information were deemed too sensitive to be traded abroad. Export controls protect American technologies, technical data, and information relevant to our national security from getting into the hands of our adversaries. They are a vital line of defense for our country's military technological edge and innovation leadership, and they were becoming even more central to U.S. foreign policy when I came to Washington.

Early in his presidency, President Bush warned that "science and technology have never been more essential to the defense of the nation and the health of our economy."[21] It was a prescient observation. Microsoft, Apple, and other technological powerhouses had begun to dominate global markets, an early glimpse of the digital domination we see today. Military leadership likewise spoke constantly of the need to innovate. Meanwhile, China was rapidly becoming a major economic power and a primary importer of U.S. technology, and it was my job to manage the dynamics of that aspect of the relationship.

I quickly began advocating tighter controls on what technologies China could acquire from U.S. manufacturers. I worried they would use our know-how to strengthen their military, and I warned that their rampant theft of American intellectual property made them an untrustworthy partner.[22] My Chinese counterparts took notice. One of my first visits to the White House Situation Room in 2005 resulted from China's President Hu relaying directly to President George W. Bush his frustrations about overly restrictive technology controls, which I had put in place. In response, Stephen Hadley, the president's national security adviser, convened a meeting of key cabinet officials, where I was the primary briefer, and we agreed the restrictive technology controls on exports to China were appropriate. Within six months, I was offered a role as deputy national security adviser for international economic affairs, where my remit focused on issues at the intersection of national security and economic policy. Eighteen months later, I became the undersecretary of the Treasury for international affairs, and remained in that post during the global financial crisis and until President Bush left office.

For nearly four years, I sat through hundreds of meetings with the most senior ministers and officials from around the world, including heads of state. I participated in debates on issues ranging from the proliferation of nuclear technology to the transfer of dual-use technologies and intellectual property, to restrictions on inbound investment to the protection of key data and the underlying infrastructure of financial markets as the global economy staggered through 2008. With each meeting, it became increasingly clear that technology, economics, national security, and geopolitics, though always related, were fast becoming nearly inseparable.

Now almost two decades later, their convergence is complete. The interdependence of national economies allows countries to weaponize commercial ties for political purposes. Transformational technologies—such as 5G telecommunications networks and the suite of AI-enabled tools—have emerged as drivers of commercial success for their developers and national power for the countries that lead in fielding them at scale. And the digital age, with billions of people connected via the internet and terabytes of data transmitting from device to device every second, has advanced human prosperity while continually introducing new security vulnerabilities. The ability to innovate and adapt now underwrites a nation's military, economy, and geopolitical power to an extent never seen before.

All these transformational forces have led us to an inflection point and created three opportunities for renewal.

First, we sit atop an untapped reservoir of national power: the ingenuity and spirit of the American people. Given access to opportunity, Americans will drive our country forward, yet we have too long neglected this timeless principle. Second, we are in the midst of a global technological revolution. New advances in everything from artificial intelligence to biotechnology to microprocessors have the potential to spur economic growth and strengthen our national security if we lead the way. Third, in the digital age, control over data confers national power. Just like we shaped the post–World War II era, we can make a digital world that protects the privacy and rights of individuals and ensures the free, prosperous flow of data.

The national renewal agenda should focus on these three areas of opportunity—talent, technology, and data. A commitment to investing in our nation's talent could generate new opportunities up and down the income ladder, restoring the American dream. It would also trigger greater entrepreneurship and job creation. Meanwhile, technological and data leadership could spur innovation, which would in turn boost productivity and economic dynamism.[23] Together, they would reverse the cycle of stagnation that holds our country back and form the foundation of the great American renewal.

The Building Blocks of the National Renewal Agenda

Global leadership in talent, technology, and data holds the key to renewal but is not guaranteed. We are in a race for each. We have neglected our standing in these races, but with smart policy choices and focused leadership, we can lead all three.

Cultivate Our Nation's Talent

A central premise of this book is that the American people are our country's greatest source of strength. Whether we call it human capital, talent, or just people, it's the ingenuity and hard work of individuals that drive progress.

Throughout my career, I have been reminded over and over again that the teams with the best mix of people usually win. This was true in high school football, in the Army, and in business. It's doubly true for nations. A country's people and their talents are its most precious resource.

This is especially true for America. At its best, our country gives its citizens the opportunity and the freedom to strive and the freedom to strive for what they want. Americans in turn go after their dreams, providing a limitless supply of energy for national growth and renewal. This cycle explains why the country has accomplished the most extraordinary feats over its short history.

Americans and their families, in other words, sit at the center of national life, and America's strength emanates outward and upward from them. When they have access to good schools, training, and jobs, our country does well. When they lose access, our country suffers.

Just look at recent years. From 2016 to 2020, America experienced a wave of economic growth, job creation, and prosperity. The unemployment rate dropped from 4.7 to 3.5 percent. Seven million new jobs were created, drawing people back into the workforce. Traditionally underserved populations benefited most, and women and people of color saw massive surges in employment.[24] Wages grew, especially for blue-collar workers, and 6.6 million people were lifted out of poverty.[25] The Trump administration accelerated progress by expanding workforce training opportunities and advocating school choice and innovation in schooling.

This was the American economy working as it should. Economic growth created jobs, which led to a tight labor market. Workers were in high demand, so wages rose. Americans up and down the income brackets saw their fortunes improve. The American dream looked more real than it had in a generation.

Then the pandemic hit. Businesses shut down. Schools went remote. Unemployment spiked, and women left the workforce in droves.[26] In addition to the terrible human tragedy, the impact on workers and businesses was undeniable. It also was uneven. Small business owners and working-class Americans suffered most of all. Those who could work from home did fine—many even did well—but waiters, bartenders, haircutters and beauticians, factory workers, and countless others saw their lives turned upside down. On top of that, we still don't know the extent of the damage done by expelling a generation of kids from the classroom, some for over a year.

The COVID crisis stripped many of access to education and opportunity. But for the few years preceding it, we saw clues for how to expand the American dream. That, after all, should be the primary goal of U.S. domestic policy and the guiding light of our talent strategy: to give all Americans, in the words of Abraham Lincoln, "an even unfettered start, and a fair chance, in the race of life."[27]

Not everyone can take advantage of the opportunity afforded by the American dream, and we share a duty to care for them. We have a mental health crisis in our country, and those afflicted by it need our support. We likewise must tend to those struggling with health problems, addiction, or other debilitating challenges. And when someone loses their job or is down on their luck, we ought to help them get through and bounce back stronger than before. It is vital that we provide the resources necessary to fulfill these societal responsibilities. Such is the bare minimum of a wealthy, compassionate society. However, my focus here is on the next step—the question of how to expand the American dream and unlock the potential in our country.

America is brimming with potential. Are we doing everything we can to unleash it? Are we giving Americans access to the opportunities they rightfully deserve? The answers are a resounding "no." Students and workers do not get the support they need. You don't have to look far for signs of failing schools, mismanaged campus affairs, or struggling workers.

At the same time, our nation also faces a skilled labor shortage. During my campaign, leaders of small and large businesses across Pennsylvania told me they were struggling to find the needed labor, from welders to roughnecks to laboratory technicians. Americans need good jobs, and companies need skilled workers. We can close that gap, and, when there are still jobs to be done, we should look to the best and brightest around the world to do them.

The great American renewal, in other words, begins with people. It has three parts. First, we must improve the quality of our schools by expanding school choice, committing to free expression, and valuing civics and the formation of good citizens. Second, we must create new workforce training programs and accord job training and community colleges the same respect—and financial support—our country directs toward a four-year college education. Finally, we should compound American talent through a strategic immigration policy that secures our borders, preserves our sovereignty, and protects our security, while at the same time attracting the world's best talent in service of American innovation, prosperity, and strength.

These proposals, some of which have been discussed for years, are the critical starting point for renewal. Each on its own is important but insufficient. Together, they can ensure America remains the land of opportunity and a beacon of promise.

Win the Race for Technological Leadership

Over the past decade, the world has made extraordinary technological breakthroughs. The combination of more powerful computers, cloud services, and available stored data makes it easier for everyone from a small start-up to a multinational titan to take advantage of artificial intelligence. New capabilities, like the suite of data analytics enabled by machine learning or smart factories wired together to track performance, anticipate when maintenance is needed, and optimize output, promise to revolutionize how companies do business. We're continually finding new ways to detect, treat, and even prevent diseases. Clean and renewable energy is cheaper than ever before. We are able to manufacture and produce products in novel ways, from pharmaceuticals to buildings and cars.

We can't go back in time to an old American economy any more than Pennsylvania could revive the industrial skeletons of the Monongahela Valley. Instead, like Pittsburgh, we must create new opportunities for Americans through innovation—but we cannot simply lift cities like Pittsburgh. We must spread opportunity far and wide.

We will have to do the same for the military, creating new capabilities and new ways of operating to preserve our military strength. The traditional model of government-led innovation is increasingly insufficient. Cutting-edge technologies tend to blur the line between military and civilian uses and will likely come out of commercial industry, rather than a national laboratory. This is a reality the defense ecosystem—the Department of Defense, research labs, the defense industry, and Congress—has been slow to embrace.

Technological leadership, in other words, is critical to America's economic success and national security, and therefore to national renewal. The United States needs a new innovation strategy to preserve our edge.

Despite lots of talk about innovation and high-tech competition, our country still has a largely aimless approach. Funding innovation is risky, regardless of the funding's origin, public or private. The trail of failed government ventures, from solar panel manufacturer Solyndra to a hodgepodge of aborted weapons programs, speaks to the risks. Perhaps as a result, public R&D funding recently hit a sixty-year low relative to our national wealth. The private sector now leads the way, but businesses must confront what the management guru Clayton Christensen called the "innovator's dilemma," the capacity to divest from what makes them successful today in order to invest in what will make them successful in the future.[28]

At the other extreme is the Chinese Communist Party's approach, which amounts to a high-tech industrial policy. The CCP draws no meaningful distinction between military and civilian technology, invests accordingly, and has made meaningful progress. Its Made in China 2025 plan made clear that, in sectors it deems important, such as information technology, robotics, and power storage, Chinese firms will enjoy substantial state support and that non-Chinese firms will compete on uneven ground.[29] Beijing has also taken creative steps, such as creating venture funds where the state accepts most of the risk in order to incentivize private investment in artificial intelligence. If Beijing wants capital to flow to a technology, it will.

We need a new, uniquely American approach, distinct from the status quo of neglect we have today and the CCP's top-down, statist industrial policy. This new approach will have to adhere to the wisdom of capitalism but also address the market failures, anti-competitive landscape, and vital national interests at play in the race for technological leadership. In addition to making significant increases in basic R&D, Washington should use modest levels of government capital to incentivize greater private sector investment in technologies of strategic importance and harness market forces to create competition around these critical sectors. It will also have to spur investment through tax credits and by clearing away regulations and rules that hinder innovation and stifle the innate inventiveness of the American public.[30] We must be bold and creative while at the same time careful to avoid drifting into industrial policy. More on that—and the specifics of a market-driven technology strategy—in the coming chapters.

Lead the Digital Age

The third and final pillar of the renewal agenda is data. Not long after World War II, the godfather of the wartime innovation effort, Vannevar Bush, observed that "a record if it is to be useful to science, must be continuously extended, it must be stored, and above all it must be consulted."[31] All the research done during the war had generated an extraordinary wealth of human knowledge. It would have been a tragedy to lose it. Bush recognized that this was just the beginning and anticipated a coming information revolution that would enable researchers to share knowledge in novel ways. Even as the complexity of science and technology increased, humanity could bridge across specialties and make use of the ever-expanding wealth of knowledge available to them. Data storage, access, and learning would catalyze human progress.

Bush was right. The information revolution resulted in the greatest expansion in information and knowledge the world has ever seen. And in the past decade or so, data has proliferated. From 2013 to 2020 alone, the amount of data stored in the world increased by a factor of 10, up to 44 zetabytes—that's 44 followed by 21 zeros.[32] Every day, computers, smartphones, and all other manner of machines generate reams of new information cataloging how they are being used, whether they are running well, where they went, and on and on. Much of it flows from country to country. Measured by bandwidth, cross-border data flows grew roughly 112 times over from 2008 to 2020.[33] All of this data can contain sensitive information about people or intellectual property that companies, and citizens, want guarded. It is not something to handle lightly. It is, however, central to trade, security, and innovation—and therefore to national power.

Advances in computing power, cloud storage, and machine learning triggered the explosion of data as a source of power. The algorithms at the heart of artificial intelligence, for example, benefit particularly from vast quantities of high-quality data, which they use to learn and gain efficacy. Data can also trigger and enable world-changing innovations, like the COVID-19 vaccines. On January 10, 2020, months after cases appeared in the city of Wuhan, Chinese scientists posted the genetic sequence of the novel coronavirus online. Armed with this essential data, scientists at the U.S. company Moderna would create the blueprint for what became the company's COVID-19 vaccine in just two days. This might seem too fast to be safe, but Moderna had already researched the concept of a vaccine based on messenger RNA. The capability was in place. All it needed to create something valuable was new data.[34]

Unlike oil, which you deplete when you use it, data is a near-limitless resource. It can power innovation again and again without being depleted. The important thing, then, is to have access to large quantities of high-quality, uncorrupted data.

Data confers power—economic, national security, and governmental. For that reason, China has created a techno-totalitarian regime designed to control data, strip individuals of their privacy, and to dominate the digital era. Europe has offered an alternative vision, built, as usual for the EU, around heavy-handed regulations. The United States has been out of the game without a clear data strategy. That must change.

America's data strategy must have two lines of attack, one domestic and one global. At home, the imperative is to address the abuses of data by foreign adversaries and by Big Tech. To do so, we'll need to pass national privacy laws, step up protections against Chinese intrusions, and reduce Big Tech's monopoly over information and speech. With our own house in order, we can take on the burdens of leadership abroad. We must put forward an American vision for the digital age that encourages the open sharing of data, protects the privacy of our citizens, and ensures America continues to set the rules of the road long into the future.

The Path to Renewal

Talent, technology, and data promise to stimulate economic growth, generate new opportunities for Americans to pursue their dreams, sharpen our military edge, secure the nation, and preserve our leadership abroad.

Or rather, they *can* power our renewal. Technological progress will proceed whether we like it or not. The digital revolution will as well.

The Chinese Communist Party has grand plans to seize the initiative and lead the way. The question is whether America will take the steps necessary to remain at the vanguard.

Shortly before Christmas in 2020, Roger Zakheim, the director of the Ronald Reagan Institute, and Eric Chewning, a former senior Pentagon official, came to me with a proposition. The Reagan Institute planned to assemble a group of business and government leaders to assess the state of American manufacturing and its implications for America's national security, and Roger wanted me to lead it. My cochair on the effort was the indomitable Marillyn Hewson. The former chief executive officer and chairman of Lockheed Martin, one of the nation's largest defense contractors, Marillyn brought decades of experience in strategic production. She had served on President Trump's commission to support the American workforce and knew instinctively the challenges that manufacturers and small-scale suppliers faced. Marillyn was the ideal partner.

We assembled a bipartisan group of lawmakers, industrialists, technologists, and financiers to investigate the costs of and solutions to our nation's manufacturing crisis. For the better part of a year, we met regularly with the men and women in the industrial arena: executives of technological powerhouses like Intel, semiconductor designers and fabricators, defense start-ups, and government officials. It quickly became clear that the loss of America's industrial competitiveness endangers our national security and our future prosperity to an extent few appreciate.[35]

President Reagan defined competitiveness as "the degree to which a nation can, under free and fair market conditions, produce goods and services that meet the test of international markets while simultaneously maintaining or expanding the real incomes of its citizens."[36]

On both accounts, the United States has fallen behind. Across industries, wages have not grown for decades, and America's decline as a producer of high-end goods speaks to its slipping position in global markets.[37] Perhaps most glaring of all is semiconductors.

Often known as chips because of the silicon wafers they're cut from, semiconductors are the critical component of everything from televisions to cars to fighter jets. Yet, despite their essential role in our economy and national security, we're falling behind. As one chips leader put it to me, America's semiconductor industry is amid a "long-term death spiral." Two Asian firms own three quarters of the semiconductor manufacturing market: Taiwan Semiconductor Manufacturing Company (TSMC) and Samsung.[38] While American-based firms may excel at the design of leading-edge chips, the smallest and most advanced, TSMC and Samsung dominate their production.[39] Worse yet, we rely on fabs—short for fabrication plants—in Taiwan, one hundred miles offshore of our chief geopolitical competitor, China, for arguably the single most important item in our economy.

China is catching up. From 1990 to 2020, it built thirty-two large-scale fabs while the United States built none.[40] U.S. fabs make up just 12 percent of global production, down from 37 percent thirty years ago, and most of those are less advanced analog chips, the kind needed for simpler electronics and cars. Moreover, China is home to far more new chip industry start-ups and entrepreneurship than the United States is, and it is outpacing us when it comes to investment in semiconductor ventures, fabs, and even R&D.[41] Under current trends, over 80 percent of all chip production will be centered in Asia by the end of the decade.

When I spoke to representatives from some of the biggest chip designers and producers in the United States and abroad, they all pointed to the same fundamental obstacles to U.S. competitiveness in the chips industry: talent, capital, and international competition. Each new semiconductor fab requires thousands of trained engineers and technicians. Already, given plans for new TSMC, Samsung, and Intel plants here, the workforce will have to grow by as many as ninety thousand people by 2025 to keep up.[42] In addition, it costs at minimum $10 billion to build a new semiconductor fabrication plant. Twice that in operating costs every five years. And the United States has to compete with countries like China and Taiwan, which offer subsidies, land grants, infrastructure support, tax incentives, trade protections, and many more inducements to attract capital by reducing the costs of each of their fabs by over 25 percent.[43]

And that's just one industry. We run a trade deficit of over $300 billion per year in advanced technologies. Advanced batteries, for example, are critical for everything from next-generation military capabilities to consumer products like electric vehicles to the future of our electric grid, and China dominates the supply chain from end to end.[44] We also depend on China for pharmaceutical ingredients, and most phones used in America are assembled in southeast China. A single American firm once controlled nearly 60 percent of the global telecom equipment market. That dominance is gone completely.[45]

A Pentagon assessment commissioned by the Trump administration found disturbing weaknesses in the nation's defense industrial base as well.[46] Semiconductors are one weak point. So are the rare earth materials needed for advanced batteries, specialty chemicals for munitions, and scores of other small components. The United States military even has weapons that are built with elements available only in China. Moreover, the defense industrial base lacks the facilities necessary to produce ammunition, weapons, or ships rapidly. Were America threatened, these weaknesses could prove disastrous to our security.

This state of affairs, in other words, endangers our national security and economic prosperity. As we've already seen during the pandemic, relying on a few concentrated chip fabricators an ocean away puts American consumers in the hands of fate. Imagine if a war had broken out or a natural disaster had struck a crucial port. Not only would prices have climbed even higher and shelves have been emptier, but our very ability to defend ourselves would have also been at risk. This isn't the stuff of science fiction. These are real risks, and we have to do something about them, or Americans will find themselves living on the razor's edge of fate, geopolitics, and the whims of the Chinese Communist Party.

The American Way

Let's return to semiconductors. One-off, hotly contested subsidies and narrow tax breaks for chip fabricators will not solve the problems in America's semiconductor supply chain.[47] Instead, Washington will have to work closely with state and local leaders and with industry to develop a larger, skilled workforce, boost the returns of capital investment in chip factories, research, and related activities, and reduce the costs of doing business. At the same time, we will need to promote innovations that increase the productivity of U.S. fabs, keep U.S. design as the leading edge, and make U.S. firms more competitive abroad. Higher paying, more attractive jobs will follow. And we will need American leadership abroad to make the entire supply chain more resilient, to level the playing field in trade, and to ensure the United States can stay at the forefront of digital innovations.

But try though we may, we will never produce all the chips we need at home, nor will we assemble, package, or test them all at home. That's not a bad thing. Global supply chains mean cheaper microprocessors, which means cheaper TVs, cars, appliances, planes, and even weapons systems. We just need those supply chains, ranging from the rare minerals used in chips to the assembly of microprocessors, to become more geographically diversified—away from China—and more resilient.

The details vary hugely, but the same basic template applies across critical sectors. We need patience, vision, and a national approach that builds American competitiveness from the bottom up, not the top down as some in Washington would like. And we'll need the same virtues in the international arena as well.

We have to out-compete China, not become China. The Chinese model puts the Communist Party state at the center of all national and economic life. Ours puts the individual and their families, communities, and businesses at the center. The Chinese model grants people and companies license to innovate and build. Ours guarantees them the right. The Chinese model desires control over society at all costs, even over the most powerful businesses and captains of industry in the country. Ours seeks to unleash our society. Some commentators like to dream about America becoming like Communist China, but to do so would be to sacrifice everything that makes our nation exceptional. We must not adopt a top-down industrial policy in Beijing's image.

However, our leaders also can't stand by while other countries distort markets, hand out subsidies to their favored industries, and steal our intellectual property, putting Americans and U.S. companies at an enormous disadvantage. Instead, Washington must help our nation escape the cycle of stagnation and decline that has killed communities and jobs and made us dependent upon the world, especially China. But it must do so while staying true to our principles that protect liberty and promise opportunity.

The American way is most dynamic when it enables the natural entrepreneurship and abilities of the American people. That means

Washington must position itself correctly as a *catalyzer* for innovation, industry, and dynamism, not the principal source of it. To borrow from my friend Kevin Warsh and his Hoover Institution colleague John Cogan, the American model, when sound, "liberates the individual, encourages the promulgation of new ideas, and ensures the proper functioning of institutions." It preserves free and competitive markets, which "give individuals the opportunity to apply their talents, ideas, and skills" in the pursuit of their dreams, and it rewards us with a "country marked by abundance, governed by values of hard work and decency and secure from foreign adversaries."[48]

Everything proposed in the coming chapters is intended to advance the American way. The talent strategy will give Americans an opportunity for a better education and a better job and help them find good, rewarding work throughout their career. The technology strategy will spur the development of new companies, new technologies, and, therefore, new jobs in areas of strategic significance. The data strategy would protect citizens' privacy and rights while also making sure our country is on the forefront of the new economy. Together, they would unlock the intrinsic adaptability, innovative spirit, and dynamism of private companies and people, then let them run. But there's a missing piece: leadership.

A Rebirth of Leadership

The next three chapters describe the talent, technology, and data strategies our leaders must put in place to achieve renewal. They do so by drawing on personal stories from my childhood growing up in Pennsylvania as the son of two teachers, from my time leading FreeMarkets in Pittsburgh, and from my tours through government and

Bridgewater. I also draw on anecdotes from the campaign trail to show why these issues are so important to the well-being of all Americans.

Fair warning: in some instances, my proposals are heavy on the specifics of workforce development programs, public-private partnerships, global data governance regimes, and all manner of topics you'll find debated in offices around Washington. I'm specific because these problems are complex, and they require thoughtful pragmatic solutions to get things done. I'm also specific because if we are not careful, government itself can become even more of the problem. It has a unique capacity to create the conditions for or erect obstacles to America's renewal.

Public policy, however, is little more than a set of plans and rules for how to accomplish a goal. The questions become: Who sets the goal? Who sets the rules and the plans? And who puts the plan into action? The three building blocks, described above, are only half of what's required for renewal. The other half of the equation is leadership.

We need leadership in government to take on the greatest external threat to renewal, China, and to drive the policies of renewal. We need leadership to reverse the chief obstacle to renewal, the decay in our institutions, and to reorient them toward their proper missions. And we need leadership across society to set the vision for renewal and guide our country forward. Those three elements of leadership comprise the final section of this book.

We begin with leadership in government and in the long-term struggle against Communist China. The existential competitor of our time, the CCP presides over the second largest economy, a dynamic growing technology sector, a rapidly expanding and high-tech military, and the world's largest navy. With Xi Jinping at the helm, China is led by a man who desires not just to dominate its neighborhood but also the world stage—and who sees technological and industrial power as the key to achieve all that. This is a threat unlike any before, and one for which our leadership in government seems woefully unprepared.

During my time in Washington, I saw the weaknesses up close: the gaps in policymaking and execution when it comes to economic warfare or technological competition, the siloed decision-making processes that led to the Treasury, Commerce, and Defense Departments working against each other, and the short-term thinking that preferences big, splashy legislation or speeches over effective, focused solutions. Those gaps will kill us in the competition with China, and piecemeal changes won't suffice in the face of an existential contest. We need bold, visionary leadership in Washington to take on the Chinese Communist Party and push forward an agenda of national renewal.

The challenges, though, go well beyond the ins and outs of policymaking. America has become sclerotic. That may be too soft. The status quo is unacceptable, and our institutions are to blame. Too many schools fail our children. Our universities have become closed-minded and elitist. Many businesses have lost their soul. On the one hand, they posture politically and succumb to an increasingly woke agenda. On the other, they devote themselves slavishly to financial metrics of success, without thinking of their purpose.

Worst of all, our national government seems increasingly incapable of getting things done. Twenty years of fighting in Afghanistan ended in a haphazard, incompetent withdrawal that endangered thousands of Americans and thousands more Afghans who had fought and sacrificed alongside us. Our military, meanwhile, is too small, its equipment too old, its people overworked, and its culture decayed. Geopolitical competition at an existential scale is back, but it has taken us years to realize it.

The root cause of these failings is a rot at the soul of our nation's institutions. Government at all levels, businesses, schools, civic organizations, the media—all these institutions have an honest purpose and a given role to play in our society. However, they have in many instances drifted from their true mission. They have been captured by elites or bureaucracies, twisted by politicization, lost their integrity, or some combination of the three. As a result, the public distrusts them, and many want to tear the whole system down.

I understand the impulse, but we shouldn't burn it all down and start from scratch. Let's rebuild them from within instead, through profound and radical shifts to their cultures, the kinds of people they value, and their processes for decision-making. But to do that, we'll need leaders across institutions to refocus on this evolution and the fulfillment of their proper missions.

Finally, we come to the fever in our national culture. One poll found 79 percent of Americans thought the country was "falling apart."[49] Another found a majority of Americans are no longer proud of their country.[50] Political polarization pulls our nation apart, and those entrusted with its future have squandered the public's faith. In the face of this pessimism, loss of patriotism, and division, the great American renewal doesn't stand a chance.

The only hope is a rebirth of visionary, virtuous, and transformational leadership across our society. Visionary because our leaders must, like Reagan, set the course to renewal. Virtuous because they must guide the nation down that path with courage, humility, and selflessness. And transformational because the challenges before us demand more than incrementalism. Our leaders must boldly move our country forward into unchartered waters while preserving the principles that make America exceptional.

Ultimately this is a question of what kind of country we want to be. The American way looks messy, even chaotic. It is. It does not have the ordered discipline of a government-guided economy like China's. But look closely and you'll find beauty in the chaos of free people pursuing their dreams.

President Reagan's words to the schoolchildren of America after the explosion of the *Challenger* spacecraft capture the sentiment well: "The future doesn't belong to the fainthearted; it belongs to the brave."[51] A restless courage runs deep in the soul of America. It manifests in our constant pursuit of a more perfect union, and it drives us to believe that tomorrow can—indeed it must—be better than today. It was our founding. It has been our life preserver in the most difficult, unforgiving of times. And it will be the key to our renewal.

A path forward for America is clear. Our leaders must implement the three building blocks of the renewal agenda to protect and unleash that courageous spirit, stand up to China, reform our institutions, and lead with the vision, courage, humility, and selflessness that is worthy of a great nation. If we as a country can manage that, if we keep striving, keep learning and growing, and keep fighting for a better future, we will renew our republic.

PART II

The Renewal Agenda

CHAPTER 4

Talent: The Foundation of Our Future

Our future as a nation rests in the quality of the teaching and learning in our schools today.

—Maryan G. McCormick, lifelong teacher, learner, and my mother, from our family history project, 2018[1]

When I returned home in May of 2009 to deliver the commencement address at Bloomsburg University of Pennsylvania, the graduates, most first-generation college goers, were headed into a battered world. The United States was still reeling from the global financial crisis. Jobless rates climbed steadily each month, and many of these students had job offers rescinded or struggled even to find a post-college career in the first place. They had spent two decades going to school in preparation for this moment, yet when the time came to enter the workforce, they were graduating amid a recession and uncertainty.

A college graduation is meant to be celebration, and this was. However, there was no use in pretending that their hard work was over or ignoring the reality staring them in the face. I wanted them to understand what I had learned decades earlier when arriving at West Point amid the uncertainty of Cold War tensions with the Soviet Union. "Our country is in the midst of a crisis," I warned them. We needed graduates like them to help get us out of it. Like so many generations before them, these students would lead us down the difficult path that lay ahead—and it was up to them which direction we went.

The speech was a homecoming for me. From the dais, I could see the building named after my dad, James H. McCormick, when he was president there twenty-five years earlier.

We had moved to Bloomsburg in 1973, after my dad was named the school's president. I was eight years old when we moved. My dad's predecessor had been fired after only two years. As a sign of the times, student demonstrators put an exclamation point on his departure when they threw a cinder block through the plate-glass window of the sitting room in the president's residence.

Dad knew early in his life that he wanted to be a teacher. In high school, he would spend his study hall sessions working in the office of the supervising principal, Bill McCreery, a lifelong family friend. My dad knew then that he wanted to follow in "Uncle Bill's" footsteps. He went on to the former Indiana State College in Indiana, Pennsylvania, where he graduated a year early, and then he began to teach.

My dad taught history, economics, and democracy in Punxsutawney High School and went to the University of Pittsburgh at night to get a master's degree in education. When my mom graduated from Wilson College in Chambersburg, Pennsylvania, they married and moved closer to Pittsburgh so my dad could continue his graduate studies. He soon became the assistant superintendent for the schools in Washington, Pennsylvania, where I was born in 1965. My mother became a schoolteacher as well, teaching fourth- through sixth-grade classes in the neighboring district.

The next year, they moved again, this time to Shippensburg State College, now called Shippensburg University of Pennsylvania. My dad quickly climbed the ranks from assistant professor to professor to vice president and then to acting dean of academic affairs and of teacher education. My mother, meanwhile, began her own graduate program. Her commitment to my dad, my brother, and me prevented her from completing it. Years later, she would try again, only to be delayed by my deployment to the Gulf War. My mother bet my dad a pair of earrings she would finish her degree. She did. She received her doctoral degree from Lehigh University in 1994, and she still wears those earrings proudly to this day.

Finally, in 1973, my dad, at the ripe age of thirty-four, was named president of the Bloomsburg State College. The position came with a residence called Buckalew Place, which we had been told was a stopping point on the Underground Railroad. It sat on a hill overlooking campus, and two or three times a week, my brother, my mom, my dad, and I would walk from our house down through campus to the student dining hall. My parents would greet the students that walked by and stop and chat with the groundskeepers, maintenance workers, and professors we met along the way. When we'd get to the cafeteria, we would get in line with the students waiting to have their IDs checked to get their meals, then sit at the tables with them.

My brother and I loved those trips to the dining area mainly because of the unlimited supply of soft-serve ice cream, but my dad found joy in this opportunity to talk directly to the college community. It didn't matter if they were freshmen, seniors, professors, or cafeteria workers—my dad talked to them all in the same way. He could always find common ground.

Taking an interest in and listening to people was how he learned what was going on and how he could improve their experiences. If my dad heard or saw that a lawn wasn't mowed or a fountain wasn't working, he would immediately go to a phone and call not the maintenance workers but the vice president in charge of facilities and give him hell. As far as my dad was concerned, the grounds had to be beautiful because the students *deserved* for them to be beautiful. They *deserved* good food and good teachers. My dad never wavered on that. To him, the goal was always to create the best environment for students to learn, grow, and prepare to go out into the world.

My mother had the same spirit. While she was an irreplaceable partner in his efforts to lead the college, she also devoted herself to expanding access to education for students with disabilities. She spent her time building curricula and worked with school districts across central Pennsylvania.

Both my parents saw the education and development of the next generation as the most important thing we must do as a country and devoted their lives to seeing this realized. Like countless teachers over the years, they have faithfully played their parts, and their life's work always reminds me that the nation's future is formed in the classroom and on the playing fields of schools across America. I had them in mind when I stood before the Bloomsburg University class of 2009 and urged the graduates to take their education and "to make a difference, to build a life, a community, and a country that best reflects America's values."

My parents are on my mind now as I write this chapter. Our

country faces a far greater challenge today than it did when I stood before the graduating class of 2009, but it has only become more important that new generations grab the torch. More than ever before, the skills and dedication of our citizens are the key to America's future.

The centerpiece of the renewal agenda, therefore, is talent. It is about improving the quality of education and making radical improvements to our K–12 educational system, which has steadily declined compared to other advanced nations around the world. It is about restoring the soul and proper societal role of colleges and universities as a place for open-minded debate, amicable disagreement, and pushing the frontiers of understanding. It is about increasing opportunities for Americans to learn new skills and find meaningful work. And it is about remaining the beacon for top talent from around the world.

Doing this will require us to reimagine how we educate, train, and attract people and to foster a sense of civic duty in each new generation. It will ask us as a nation to reconnect ourselves to my dad's aspirations at Bloomsburg University: to create the best environment possible to educate students, grow America's human capital, and develop the future leaders that will energize the country's renewal.

Nothing Matters More than Education

Our talent strategy begins in the classroom. Access to a good education is the gateway to the American dream. It gives students a base of knowledge and the ability to learn, which opens endless doors. A good education also makes students into better citizens. Through civics and American history, they learn our nation's story and what good citizenship entails. Finally, a good education empowers Americans. It not only teaches them skills but also gives them the ability to exchange ideas and wrestle with hard problems. But you only get one shot at a K–12 education, and sadly our education system has work to do on all accounts.

The numbers are staggering. Only 25 percent of graduating seniors could keep up with a college-level math class, and 37 percent were ready for college-level reading.[2] The average high school graduate today is no better educated than she would have been twenty-five years ago, and neither poor nor rich students are doing better.[3]

As a result, American students are falling behind the rest of the world.[4] Students do not graduate from high school with a solid foundation in math, science, and computer science, and they do worse, especially in math, than their counterparts in much of Europe.[5]

School closures during the pandemic deepened the hole. Across the board, students fell behind in their educations. One study estimated it will take three to five years to undo the damage to elementary school children, and that assumes those students will get extra help along the way. Unsurprisingly, the pandemic lockdowns hurt students from poorer neighborhoods the most, widening the achievement gap between rich and poor. And we still don't know the full extent of the learning and maturation that was lost.[6]

The chief problem is a public school system with a bad habit of putting the interests of school systems and teachers' unions above the needs of students.[7] Throughout the pandemic, the national teachers' unions fought to keep schools closed despite mounting evidence of the damage being done to students. These unions have also long obstructed much-needed reforms to improve, however incrementally, the quality of the education given to students. On top of that, the more than $700 billion our country spends on education each year is increasingly going to administrators and overhead, not classroom instruction. Spending per student, even adjusted for inflation, has increased 280 percent since 1960.[8] Yet, since 2000 alone, the number of teachers increased just 7.7 percent—roughly equal to the increase in student enrollment—while administrative staff grew by 75 percent and principals by over 33 percent.[9]

Our money, in other words, favors the preservation of a monopolistic education system and serves the whims of teachers' unions at the expense of the education of our children. You can see the misplaced priorities at work in the unions' opposition to reopening schools during the pandemic but also in the desire to teach a one-sided view of American history as a story of oppression and evil, which ignores the good in our national story, and in radical curricula that are molded by critical race theory or that teach sexually explicit content to elementary school kids.[10]

The situation continues to get uglier on college campuses, where speech and intellectual diversity are stifled. When I was a kid, my dad would invite outside speakers to come to the college, and each would come to our house for dinner. I can recall my parents hosting everyone from the award-winning author Alex Haley—just as his most famous work, *Roots*, was aired on television—to Senator Sam Ervin, of North Carolina, who had chaired the Watergate Committee. Many, including Ervin, were controversial, but my mother and father believed the value of an education is found in wrestling with hard questions and the free exchange of ideas.

That virtue has been lost. Outside speakers and the professors hosting them have been assaulted on campuses. Two-thirds of college students consider it acceptable to shout down or block campus speakers they didn't like.[11] And the lack of intellectual diversity among faculty turns campuses into echo chambers.[12] As a political scientist has written, what happens on our college campuses "reflects and magnifies the broader tensions that define the cultural conflict that pervades the larger society."[13] We have, he warns, "forgotten how to disagree," and colleges make it worse.[14]

In effect, America's education system has lost sight of its purpose. It does not consistently provide students with the skills or the ability to learn that they need to succeed in the modern economy or with the creativity they need to power American innovation. Elementary to high schools place the considerations of unions and established structures over the needs of students. Colleges stifle speech and dissent and favor a cultural elite. Our nation is not inculcating the virtues of citizenship into the next generation.[15]

A Plan to Fix Our Schools

I am not an education expert, but I know three things to be true. First, the status quo must change. Second, there is no shortage of ideas for how to improve schooling, only a shortage of action. And third, education in America is, in the words of one education expert, "first and foremost about the kind of people we want to be."[16]

The ideas that follow will not address every issue. Instead, they are intended to break the mold. To put children and their families first. To refocus our schools on raising informed citizens. To teach students how to think, not what to think. And, most of all, to ensure as much equality of opportunity as is possible.

Let's begin at the start of the talent pipeline: early childhood education. Good preschool and pre-kindergarten programs set children on a path to success and to greater educational achievement.[17] But the key word is "good." Not all programs provide the same value, and there's no cookie-cutter solution for improving early education. The answer, instead, lies in supporting a diversity of options for educational childcare and in helping parents take the approach they find best. This can be achieved through block grants to states and voucher-type programs. But the guiding principles should be to empower parents and to encourage innovation. In fact, those principles hold true all the way up the education pipeline.

With thirteen thousand school districts spread across fifty states and the District of Columbia, the American approach to education creates plenty of opportunities for innovation. Let's start by empowering families. Every family should have a choice in where their children go to school and a say in what their children learn. It is the responsibility of local, state, and federal governments to ensure they have the opportunities and funds needed to exercise that right.

The public school model, which dates to the 1800s, places students into schools based on where they live. Their parents have some diluted say in how the school operates, through school board elections and public hearings, but little input on curriculum—and even that requires time that many families don't have to spare. In some places, it works well. Most parents like their local schools.[18] But this model is "monopolistic."[19] Like any other monopoly, it lacks accountability and stifles competition. At its worst, it disenfranchises parents and imprisons kids in bad schools.

School choice offers an alternative. It gives students the most opportunities to get a good education.[20] In 1999, nearly half of the fourth graders in Florida could barely read, and the high school graduation rate sat around 50 percent. Twenty years later, Florida students excelled in testing. In that time, Florida had created what then-governor Jeb Bush called "the largest private school choice programs in the country."[21] Parents took advantage, and their kids—many of them minorities or from struggling families—now have much higher rates of college attendance and graduation than those who did not.[22] Similar stories have played out around the country. Pennsylvania's tax credit scholarship program has opened doors to disadvantaged students, and charter schools in Washington, DC, have helped drive a dramatic improvement in the city's schools.[23]

States should follow suit and fund children, not school systems. No child should be trapped in a failing school, in a school that violates their families' core beliefs, or in a dangerous school environment because of their zip code. States should support the expansion of charter school networks and ensure families have access to taxpayer money to help them find the best school for their children. Voucher programs, for example, have proven to improve the quality of education and help disadvantaged students, but there is not a single solution for every school district.[24]

The pandemic created momentum in this direction. Parents saw how school closures hurt their kids. They also saw the quality and content of their children's education and found it wanting. That pressure led twenty-two states in total to create, expand, or improve their school choice offerings—the best year ever.[25] Charter school enrollment spiked around the country. And my friend Glenn Youngkin was elected governor of Virginia largely because he stood up for the parents and students left behind by a failed education system.

This momentum is a welcome sign, but we should still be prudent. To quote a bipartisan statement from two Washington-based think tanks, we still need to "foster rigorous accountability for new and existing approaches."[26] States should help parents identify what the right school is for their kids.[27] They should also make each school's curriculum public to parents. But the ultimate form of accountability is the ability of parents to leave a school that isn't working for their son or daughter. In the current framework of our K–12 system, the opposite happens: a bad school just gets more money.

We also must resist the campaign to dumb down education in the name of "equity," which holds that equality of outcome, not opportunity, is what matters. In recent years, Oregon has suspended proficiency standards in reading, math, and writing for high school graduates, and school districts have abolished honors math programs.[28] Similar efforts are underway across the country. These campaigns are designed not to help students learn, succeed, and overcome the racial achievement gap, but to limit them. They rob children of opportunity and deny the essential truth that each is unique and blessed with their own talents and potential. Rather than act as if the educational achievement gap is insurmountable, we must, in the words of Ian Rowe, a longtime charter school leader in the Bronx, "empower young people to believe that they possess the power—and, yes, agency—to surmount it."[29]

These proposals are entirely *pro teacher.* I'm a child of educators who devoted their lives to serving students, often to those most in need of help. Society should show deep respect and admiration for the critical work teachers do. They have hard, often thankless, jobs, but currently, they are forced to work in a bureaucratic model that makes their jobs even harder. Choice lets funding follow the student to the best schools, often to schools with clever business models or with fewer rigid and arcane rules, meaning teachers get to do what they care most about—educate. These schools recognize the importance of good teaching and pay accordingly. Educators deserve more. But greater opportunity comes with responsibility too. We should hold educators accountable, just as we must hold school systems accountable.

We also need to address the poor quality of STEM (science, technology, engineering, and math) programs at the K–12 level. If given the opportunity, talented young men and women can develop a love of math, sciences, and engineering. School choice programs and magnet schools help, but schools also need more teachers who are knowledgeable about and can teach math, science, and computer subjects, whether or not they have an education degree or other credential. Beyond that, federal and state governments should invest in the tools that young people need to learn technical skills: good data and computing power, quality facilities and teachers, and high-speed broadband. An opportunity to be inspired can spur more innovation than we can imagine. You never know which student will create the next best idea, but without equipping students with the tools, the pursuit of that idea will never be realized.

Finally, we must develop not just good students, but good citizens. As Henry Kissinger warns, "No society can remain great if it loses faith in itself."[30] The preservation of the American experiment requires citizens who understand the American system and are grateful for that inheritance. Therefore, it is imperative that students learn our country's history honestly, including the injustices and missteps, but also how exceptional America is and how far it has come. That's not always a popular position among professors, the majority of whom have an undeniable bias.[31] The classroom is not the place for indoctrination.

Citizenship also requires us to disagree well. In 2016, Robert Zimmer, the president of the University of Chicago, wrote that one word summarizes the proper college education: "questioning." Students need an environment of open exchange, debate, and thought. That is the hallmark of a valuable college education. Sadly, the culture of cancellation on college campuses undermines it. If anything, it teaches students that shouting down those with whom they disagree is not only okay but also effective. There is a time for civil disobedience in the face of true injustice, but the widespread urge to stifle speech just because you disagree with it is deeply at odds with the duty of citizenship.

The best antidote is leadership among college administrators. The university must remain, in Zimmer's words, "a crucible for confronting ideas and thereby learning to make informed judgments in complex environments."[32] His university codified that principle in the "Chicago statement," an affirmation that freedom of expression and debate would always be welcome on campus.[33]

Other schools should follow suit. They should adopt governing principles defending curiosity, debate, and the notion that the answer to bad ideas is not silence, but more speech. They should seek to build a more intellectually diverse faculty. And they should welcome groups that bring a diversity of opinions to campus, like the Alexander Hamilton Society, a national organization dedicated to educating young men and women about the role of American leadership in the world and inspiring them to pursue a career of service to our national security, which I have supported since its early days.

Much of what is proposed here is already underway. More than half the states have some school choice, and organizations like the American Federation for Children have been fighting hard to get that number higher. I'm also not the first to call for a greater focus on math, science, and engineering programs or a healthier college campus. What's missing is the sense of urgency, the scale, and the recognition of how these steps go hand in hand with fixing a broken system. If we do this right, we'll empower the next generation. We'll create the opportunity and speed necessary for American renewal.

An equally pressing problem is the shortage of skilled workers and the dearth of programs to create them across our economy. In Somerset, Pennsylvania, as an example, not too far from the Maryland border, there's a family-owned machine shop called Leiss Tool & Die.

Founded in 1972 by Peter Leiss, it employs about one hundred and fifty people machining and fabricating metal components for multinational manufacturers like GE and local customers alike. Pete and his son Dan showed me around the shop in April of 2022. In one section, computer-aided mills and lathes were cutting metal. In another, a few longtime welders showed me the tricks of the trade. Business was booming, Pete told me, but they needed more welders. He could grow his business significantly if he could hire dozens more skilled workers, but he can't find them.

Peter isn't alone. I heard the same story over and over again on the campaign trail in places like Guy Chemical down the road from Somerset and at General Carbide, a tooling manufacturer in Greensburg. All across Pennsylvania, business leaders tell me they're struggling to fill jobs. They need more mechanics, technicians, and other tradesmen, and they simply can't find them.

Two years ago, the COVID-19 pandemic triggered what some are calling the "Great Resignation." Nearly eight million skilled workers left the workforce. Some retired. Some went part-time. Some just stopped working. As I write this, four million skilled-labor jobs remain unfilled—eleven million jobs total. That gap is holding our country back.[34] One industry survey found a "technical skills gap" to be the single most likely cause of derailed manufacturing plans in the next two to four years.[35] Another reported that 87 percent of executives surveyed complained that they had trouble hiring employees with the necessary skills. As a result, by the summer of 2021, there were 942,000 unfilled manufacturing jobs around the country.[36]

The situation won't improve on its own. America's manufacturing industry is on pace for 2.1 million unfilled jobs by the end of the decade, and the pace of digital transformation in the industry will likely continue to redefine work for people.[37] The problem extends beyond just manufacturing. Over two-thirds of American businesses are struggling to hire.[38] Men and women alike have left the workforce.

This gap stands in the way of our country's future. It prevents companies from better serving their customers, responding to market demand, and growing. This means they aren't creating new jobs, innovating, or raising real wages for workers. The gap, in other words, inhibits the growth and dynamism we need.

There are two ways to fill it. First and foremost, we must develop American workers and create more vocational training and educational opportunities for them. Second, when the supply of American workers inevitably falls short of what is needed, we must take advantage of America's unique position as a beacon for global talent. Our economic growth, productivity, and renewal depend on it.

Invest in Americans

In my parents' generation, a strong back and a good work ethic were the keys to achieving a solid middle-class life for them and their families. Now workers need more technical skills, and they need to be able to develop new ones throughout their career. That's the ticket to the American dream for many Americans, and our country should help them to punch it.

To do so, America needs to elevate occupational training and skills-based programs that give young people the opportunity to earn a good living and improve their condition without saddling them with debt. However, this is not about preserving certain types of jobs or granting a certificate. We need to focus our workforce development programs on giving people the skills they need to be productive over time. Politicians love to talk about making college accessible to everyone. If everyone gets a diploma, the theory goes, they'll be set. But those politicians are trying to solve the wrong problem.

Workers have been hit hard by globalization and technological disruptions. If the nation doesn't help them adapt to a rapidly changing economy, they will continue to struggle. What we need to do is simple: Develop people. Help them get the skills they need to succeed in today's competitive job market, and create opportunities for them to prepare for tomorrow's. Americans deserve the best shot possible to make something of themselves and pursue their own American dream.

No one lives that standard better than my good friend Bill Strickland. Bill's a fellow Pennsylvanian, born and raised in Manchester. Growing up as a young Black man in a poor neighborhood on Pittsburgh's North Side, Bill had limited access to the same opportunities as many other Pennsylvanians. Bill didn't care much for school and figured he'd end up back in Manchester after he graduated from high school. One day, he walked past the art room in his high school and saw his teacher making ceramics. He stepped into the studio, and before he knew it, he was hooked. He started making ceramics every day.

Despite Bill's bad grades and failing the entrance exams, the teacher took him under his wing and helped him ultimately attend the University of Pittsburgh. That was the nudge Bill needed. He came to university as a probationary student and graduated with honors.

Bill's love of ceramics led him back to Manchester. In 1968, he founded the Manchester Craftsmen's Guild, a ceramics collective, to teach other kids from his neighborhood how to make pottery. Then in 1972, he took over the local Bidwell Training Center. The center, founded the same year Bill formed the Craftsmen's Guild, provided job training and opportunities. Bill envisioned it being so much more, and he turned it into a beautiful center of vocational training and education for inner-city kids.

At the Bidwell Training Center, children have the opportunity to learn how to be a pharmacy technician, a chef, or a lab tech. Moms from struggling communities come to cultivate orchids in greenhouses and sell them to help support the school. Everyone that comes to the center is welcomed with a beautiful campus and entryway and high-quality facilities. Galleries feature the students' artwork, and music fills the halls. Bill turned it into a place of learning, community, jazz, and joy.

Manchester is still a rough part of the city with high crime rates and schools with gates and bars on the windows. Yet, despite the absence of security or fences or bars on the windows, the Manchester Bidwell, where I served on the board in the 1990s, remains an oasis of calm, security, and beauty. Bill's explanation? Those who are treated with respect and held to high standards will return it in kind.

The Manchester Bidwell Corporation has now built training centers in cities around the country. Business school students study Bill's work, and he's been honored for his devotion to fighting poverty. It all goes back to that pottery room, but of course, it was never just about ceramics. In that room, Bill found someone who saw potential in him. He found the dignity of a job well done. And he found opportunity.

Bill is living proof that if we invest in people, we will strengthen the country from the bottom up. What does that mean? First, treat Americans as assets, not liabilities. If we, as Bill likes to say, "treat them as the best human beings life is capable of producing,"[39] we'll find extraordinary potential in people. Second, create opportunities for people to realize that potential. Finally, set high standards. Opportunity and personal responsibility go hand in hand in America. The best thing we can do is create the former and expect the latter. If we follow these three principles, we will begin to rebuild communities and make America more competitive. The jobs will follow.

Develop People, Create Jobs

How do we translate that into policy? To begin with, break the culture that says everyone should go to college. Aspiring college students can turn to Pell Grants, 529 savings accounts, student loans, and many other means to pay for their schooling. Graduate students can as well. Why can't Americans use the same means to pay for apprenticeships, vocational training, and other nontraditional options? Why do we waste so much time debating forgiveness of college loan debt instead of making it more rewarding to seek out a job? Let's expand the earned income tax credit to reward people who seek out work, and let's explore individualized accounts that would give federal support directly to people trying to reenter the workforce.

Next, lean on community and technical colleges. After his time in Bloomsburg, my dad became the founding chancellor of the Pennsylvania State System of Higher Education and then the chancellor of the Minnesota State Colleges and Universities. He found himself overseeing dozens of community colleges, technical schools, and expansive career and technical education programs around the state, and he made it a point to be a student of each and every one. This network of schools and training facilities formed the backbone of Minnesota's workforce development system. The same is true around the country.

These schools have elevated generations of Americans, yet we're only scratching the surface of their potential. Community colleges can quickly address near-term demands in the labor market with new programs.[40] Federal support for community colleges should increase substantially, particularly for in-demand fields, such as advanced manufacturing technologies.

However, we can start even earlier. IBM, for example, has pioneered a program called P-TECH. The initiative starts with junior high–age students, and in six years, they graduate and are ready to excel in a broad range of fields, from advanced manufacturing to medical work. It's just one program, but it's emblematic of how we can diversify education and training beyond the old education to college or to a jobs program pipeline.

Businesses ought to get more involved. During my Senate campaign, I had the opportunity to visit Lackawanna College School of Petroleum and Natural Gas in Tunkhannock, northwest of Scranton. The natural gas industry is going through the "great crew change" and could lose as many as half its workers in the coming years. So, the industry has partnered with the school to fill that gap with fresh faces. Students can graduate with a two-year associate's degree and all the technical skills needed for a career in the industry. They pay their way, but summer internships pretty much cover the cost. Then they graduate and get high five-figure jobs—right out of school.

We need more programs like this, and the government should help fund them by matching business investment in career and technical education programs and creating tax incentives for U.S.-headquartered firms to invest in American workforce development. And as discussed in the next chapter, businesses and governments—at the local, state, and national levels—also must relax their credential and licensing requirements. Most jobs don't require a college degree, and the majority of Americans don't have one. Why should they get credentialed out of jobs where they could excel?

Each of these workforce programs should be "stackable," treated not as one-time opportunities but as part of a lifelong learning process. Americans change jobs much more often than before, and all of us will have to grow and learn continually. That doesn't mean we have to go back to school over and over, but it does mean people should be able to stack degrees, credentials, and training in pursuit of new skills and techniques and the mastery of new technologies.

Finally, there are two groups of Americans who, in my experience, have been too often overlooked but who have extraordinary potential to move our country forward.

First are our veterans. Most veterans excel in society, which is why I've always made it a point to hire them. They are well-trained young men and women with a lot of potential, and they often have leadership experience and technical skills from their service.[41] But too many don't get the help they need to make a successful transition out of the service.

Fortunately, thousands of outside organizations exist to give them and their families more holistic support.

One such group is FourBlock. Founded by Michael Abrams, a Marine Corps veteran of the war in Afghanistan, FourBlock equips veterans with the skills they need to move from the military to the office. Participants in its Career Readiness Program go through courses and briefings and come out ready to sell themselves to future employers. Through corporate partnerships, FourBlock keeps the training valuable and sets these young men and women up for success. Their inspiring model lives up to Bill Strickland's standards. They see the potential in veterans. As Mike described it to me, FourBlock gives veterans a shot and then they expect them to do great things with it.

Second are women, an untapped source of energy, innovation, and economic growth for our country. I have experienced firsthand the power of female leaders, like Ann Korologos, a former cabinet secretary under Ronald Reagan who inspired me into public service, and the women in my life—my mother, my wife, my six daughters, and my close female mentors—who have shaped me into who I am. And I know I'm not alone.

Two facts are undeniably true: women are the backbone of our society and among the most underserved within it. They routinely face obstacles to education, capital, and opportunity, but, when we close those gaps and invest in them to help them become economically independent, women not only can pursue their dreams but also have an enormous, wide-reaching effect across society—as has been shown time and again in research and in practice.

In 1999, a research team at Goldman Sachs put forward that thesis for Japan. Fifteen years later, their work inspired the Japanese government to launch a "Womenomics" agenda to get women into the labor force and into leadership positions in business.[42] In six years, the labor force participation rate for women in Japan rose from 63 to 71 percent. The country has a long way to go, but the potential is indisputably there.[43]

That same research inspired Goldman Sachs to make a series of investments in women through three initiatives—10,000 Women, 10,000 Small Businesses, and One Million Black Women. Working with an extremely talented and dedicated team and the full support of the firm's leadership, my wife, Dina, built these programs as president of the Goldman Sachs Foundation and later as a member of the firm's management committee. These innovative programs helped unlock the potential in great female entrepreneurs, like Jessica Johnson-Cope, by offering private capital, business education, mentorship, and support systems.

Jessica's grandfather, Wilbert, founded Johnson Security Bureau, a private security firm in the Bronx, in 1962. Her grandmother took over when he died, and then her father took the helm. When he passed unexpectedly in 2008, Jessica gave up her own career to keep the family business going with her brother. With virtually no business experience, she brought the company back from the brink and built it back stronger than ever, creating one hundred and fifty jobs across the Bronx.

We got to know Jessica through her participation in the 10,000 Small Businesses program, and she is a shining example of the basic fact that empowering women is one of the smartest—and most necessary—investments our society can make. This has been a priority of mine in business, and it ought to be for our country. Let's encourage more programs like these and make it easier for women to start families and build their careers, particularly through child tax credits and other pro-family policies. Women shouldn't have to choose between work and family.

Politicians like to promise handouts. They like to give away money that's not their own and expect people to fall in line. They have it backwards. Americans are not problems to be solved with welfare checks. They are dignified, promising individuals who deserve opportunity and, if given it, will usually thrive. That's why I keep coming back to the mantra "invest in Americans." That's how we'll expand access to opportunity and well-paying work all around the country, not just in big metropolitan areas or coastal cities.

America's renewal also depends on the implementation of a set of pragmatic and principled policies to stem the dangerous tide of illegal immigration and take full advantage of America's unique capacity to draw skilled immigrants from around the world. Sadly, this is also one of the most contentious issues today in American politics and requires strong, tough leaders to take it head-on.

In the spring of 2021, former president George W. Bush published a collection of his paintings titled *Out of Many, One*. The book is a stirring tribute to American pluralism and all that immigrants have done to serve this country. In it, portraits of two former secretaries of state, Henry Kissinger and Madeleine Albright, appear alongside those of émigrés from faraway places like Afghanistan and Russia, and, in the case of my wife, Dina, Egypt.

Dina worked in President Bush's White House, and one day her father was visiting. President Bush noticed them as he exited *Marine One* and came over. He tells the story in his book: " 'You must be Mr. Habib,' I said. 'I just wanted to tell you that you raised a great girl. She's a very important adviser to me.' " Dina's father teared up as he said, " 'There really is no other country in the world where a man can bring a four-year-old daughter who doesn't speak a word of English and watch her one day serve the president of my adopted country.' "[44]

Stories like these fill President Bush's book, each accompanied by a portrait. Together these small tales tell a larger truth about America: we stand alone in our capacity to draw the best and brightest to our shores.

That capacity is a significant competitive advantage over other countries, especially China. Skilled immigrants have driven U.S. innovation over the years. Immigrants have excelled in science, technology, and engineering, lived the American dream, and exemplified our country's spirit of risk-taking and entrepreneurship. Roughly one-third of America's Nobel Prizes in chemistry, medicine, and physics have gone to foreign-born researchers.[45] They formed fifty of the ninety-one privately held start-ups valued at over $1 billion, and, with their children, founded over 45 percent of Fortune 500 companies, creating countless American jobs.[46]

Whether advancing the frontiers of science or energizing local economies, talented immigrants have bettered America. One Stanford study found that, from 1976 to 2012, immigrants helped produce 30 percent of American innovation, primarily through their catalytic effect on those around them: "More than 2/3 of the contribution of immigrants to U.S. innovation has been due to the way in which immigrants make U.S. natives substantially more productive themselves."[47]

Nowhere are the contributions of skilled immigrants clearer than in the national response to the pandemic. The medical professionals on the front line of treatment were disproportionately foreign-born, and two immigrant-founded firms, Pfizer (alongside BioNTech) and Moderna, led the greatest feat of lifesaving innovation in recent memory: the rapid development of multiple COVID-19 vaccines. They then furthered the triumph over disease with therapeutics and treatment plans.

Sadly, our country is neglecting the value in our ability to attract top talent.

Since 1990, the global immigrant population has grown from 153 to 272 million, and those seeking new homes are better educated and more highly skilled than ever before.[48] Canada, Australia, Germany, and even historically restrictive countries, such as Japan and China, have taken steps to benefit from the uptick in skilled people moving across borders.

We ignore this trend at our own risk. Across generations, America has stood as the land of opportunity, and newcomers have continually renewed our country's human capital. Yet our national leaders neglect that history. While we lose ground, politicians continue to lack the political will and imagination to make America's immigration laws work for the country. They stand by outdated quotas and caps and laws, which they then fail to execute faithfully. And so the beacon for talent dims.

Secure Borders and a Strategic Immigration Policy

Skilled immigration can help fill the labor gaps we are experiencing in our economy and make our nation more innovative and dynamic, but there must be three prerequisites to any policy changes.

First, we must stop the crisis of illegal immigration cascading out of control at our southern border. We can't have a functional legal immigration system unless we gain control of our sovereignty. Early in 2022, I traveled to Yuma, Arizona. Brandon Judd, the president of the National Border Patrol Council, met me and showed me around. We made a number of stops along the border, spoke with border guards and local farmers, and met with the sheriff of Yuma, who told us about the never-ending challenges they faced from cartels running people and drugs across the border. We could even see members of the cartel tucked into the hedges on the other side of the Rio Grande as they orchestrated hundreds of illegal immigrants a day crossing the border. At the end of the trip, Brandon urged me to remember what I'd seen and take those lessons to Washington. How could I forget? It was a disastrous situation, far worse than I could have ever imagined.[49]

Let's be clear, there's nothing humane about open borders. They lead to Americans losing their jobs and to terrible human and sex trafficking of those seeking illegal entry. They also enable the flow of fentanyl and other drugs into our communities, which kill over one hundred thousand Americans every year and are a burgeoning calamity in my home state of Pennsylvania.[50] We have seen all of this and more, in the past few years, and every day this crisis worsens. While it remains unaddressed, our country suffers—and, if we're being honest, the odds that Washington will develop a more effective immigration policy decline precipitously. By building a border wall system and ending the policies that incentivize people to come here illegally, the Trump administration dramatically slowed illegal immigration, but that progress was lost overnight with the reversal of policies put in place under President Biden. In 2021, Border Patrol agents had to stop nearly two million people from crossing the U.S.-Mexico border illegally, the highest number in history.[51] We need to get back to a sustainable and defensible policy toward illegal immigration, including completing the border wall.

Second, we must handle the troubling risks associated with skilled immigration. Chief among these is the security threat. Our adversaries have recruited researchers and students to acquire intellectual property and other proprietary information illicitly, or to be their mouthpieces on campuses and thereby compromise academic integrity and stifle speech.[52] However, these acts are perpetrated by a small number of bad actors and can be addressed through greater transparency about who is sponsoring researchers, rigorous enforcement of existing rules requiring disclosure of funding sources, and selective restrictions on those affiliated with competitors' militaries or intelligence services. Broadly banning foreign talent would hurt us twice over: it would slow U.S. innovation and end brain drain to the United States, one of our defining advantages in international competition.[53]

Third, as a prerequisite, we need to ensure that the inflow of legal immigrants does not stand in the way of American citizens chasing their dreams. Critics warn that skilled immigrants threaten American jobs and existing laws are too often exploited.[54] The latter concern calls for more rigorous adherence to the rules, not greater restrictions. The former is not borne out by the evidence. Only 54,000 out of 1 million green cards given in 2019 went to skilled workers.[55] This small cohort displaces American workers minimally, and targeted policies can help those affected. More important, skilled migrants create jobs through both their entrepreneurship and the demand they generate, to say nothing of their even greater impact on economic growth and innovation.[56] The bottom line is skillfully crafted policies to promote the targeted inflow of skilled legal immigration will create more jobs and economic opportunity for Americans.

If these three prerequisites are satisfied, Washington should look to high-skilled immigration to accelerate America's renewal. In 2019, the Trump administration laid out a new, merit-based immigration plan designed to prevent corporate visa abuse and raise national security vetting standards for incoming immigrants, but also to increase the number of people admitted legally due to their talents.[57] Trump's proposed reforms never came to fruition, but they can point us toward a menu of good policy options for a pro-worker, pro-growth strategic immigration policy.

First are common sense solutions, many of which have bipartisan support: simplify and accelerate visa and green-card reviews for high-skilled applicants; create a visa for well-vetted talent to support national-security-oriented innovation; and enhance protections against intellectual-property theft and technology transfer.

Second are modest reforms. These include shortening the time it takes to gain permanent residency; removing geographic quotas; and ensuring that foreign students receiving advanced degrees in high-priority disciplines can stay in the United States. Why should U.S. universities train some of the world's foremost engineers and scientists only for them to leave for lack of either an immediately available job or available green cards? Most of all, green card and visa caps should reflect our country's labor needs, not be fixed to an arbitrary number decided by lawmakers over a decade ago.

Third, we should consider more-fundamental changes to our skilled-immigration laws. Should we adopt a points system that retains numerical caps on visas and green cards but prioritizes specific skills or educational backgrounds, as Republican lawmakers have proposed? Or should we replace caps with a standards-based model that welcomes those who meet certain criteria? Should we establish a separate program for the families of employment-based green-card recipients, so that they do not take up slots that otherwise would go to workers?

In his last days in office, Reagan warned that "if we ever closed the door to new Americans, our leadership in the world would soon be lost."[58] His words resonate today. Scarred by COVID-19 and confronting the most serious challenge to its global leadership in a generation, America needs to get back in the game. We know highly skilled immigration will help. Politicians need to stop chasing comprehensive immigration reform and start fixing our immigration laws, piece by piece if necessary. They should start with stricter enforcement and border security to reset immigration. From there, start overhauling a clearly faulty system to keep the country attractive and competitive in the race for global talent.

Every day, Americans run up against barriers to the American dream. They have to deal with poor-quality schools and a complex, rapidly evolving job market. Their communities suffer, and the social solidarity that binds our national fabric together begins to fray. The great American renewal has to make life easier for people. It has to give a better start to all Americans, especially those from poorer families or struggling communities. It has to generate opportunities for everyday Americans and create the conditions for them to find meaningful work, earn a good paycheck, and pursue their aspirations. Nothing matters more to the nation's future, and nothing will do more for American renewal.

To put it plainly, *our people are our greatest strategic advantage, and we need to reimagine how we educate, develop, and expand America's human capital.* Two waypoints can guide us: First, people must be valued. They have dignity and potential, and we should put our faith and trust in them, not in bureaucratic systems or self-interested organizations. Second, education, workforce programs, and immigration all feed into one talent ecosystem. The nation's talent strategy should reform all three simultaneously.

If we do this right, the nation's engine will accelerate, but we can't stop there. We have to create the conditions for Americans to apply their talents to the big problems of the day. The remainder of the renewal agenda is designed to do just that. Increasing access to capital and data, while minimizing the role of government and big business, will empower Americans to renew our country.

CHAPTER 5

Technology: A Plan for Supremacy

We are called the nation of inventors. And we are. We could still claim that title and wear its loftiest honors if we had stopped with the first thing we ever invented, which was human liberty.

—Mark Twain, in his On Foreign Critics speech, 1890

In June of 2020, my good friend Lieutenant General (retired) H. R. McMaster invited me to speak at the Hoover Institution, a conservative think tank on Stanford University's campus. I had recently published a long paper, laying out my vision for a U.S. innovation strategy. That paper, which germinated into this book, argued that our country's traditional approach to supporting innovation was lacking.

As we talked, H. R. asked me a question that any card-carrying conservative fears: "What would Milton Friedman think of this idea?" A Nobel laureate and brilliant economist, Friedman championed economic freedom. His teachings about the primacy of markets and his vision of what makes prosperity possible shaped a generation of conservative economic thinking. From his seats at Stanford and the

University of Chicago, he advised Ronald Reagan and his economic team, profoundly shaping two generations of Republicans like me.

So you can imagine that H. R.'s question caused me to pause. I believe in capitalism. It is the greatest system for allocating capital, creating opportunity, and human flourishing, and by and large, it enforces accountability and rewards those who do right. I believe America's dynamic capital markets give it an asset no nation in history could match. I also believe that people know what to do with their money better than government ever will. No bureaucrat in Washington can ever understand the complexity of markets, much less the hopes or aspirations of individuals. All that's to say, I have a healthy skepticism of government intervention into markets.

However, I've also come to question that orthodoxy. America's technological leadership is vital to our economic and national security, but we are not doing enough to preserve it. The traditional innovation pipeline, where government-funded research turns into commercial developments, falls short of what is required, particularly amid China's rise that is backed by industrial espionage, anti-competitive policies, and forced civil-military fusion. Those tactics corrupt markets and compromise the tenets of free commerce on which our system rests, and the stakes are only increasing as emerging technologies offer both economic and strategic power.

While Milton Friedman might take issue with some of what I'm about to propose, if he were here with me today, I'd turn the question around: What would he say if he saw our adversaries outrunning us, distorting markets left and right, and employing these game-changing technologies to strip away the liberty he held so dear? What would he say about the stagnation in American society and the decline of America's innovation edge? What would Milton Friedman say is America's plan for technological leadership?

My answer is straightforward: we need a uniquely American strategy for accelerating innovation.

Three forces converged to bring us to this point. The first is the rise of China. The Chinese Communist Party wants to supplant the United States. It aspires to economic dominance and military supremacy in Asia, and it wishes to spread its ideology around the world. Its president, Xi Jinping, believes that winning the race for global technological leadership will help him reach those goals.

Xi wants China to have world-class, homegrown technology industries and to lead in everything from artificial intelligence and information technology to bioengineering. Xi's grand ambitions are matched by equally grand plans to develop top talent, to control data, and to set global technology standards. The Party enforces civil-military fusion. Ostensibly private companies partner with Chinese military developers and security agencies, whether they want to or not.

The central thrust of his plan entails massive state investment. Government-guided funds dominate private capital markets. The state, including local municipalities, is the largest single provider of private equity and venture capital funding in China, providing a third of the capital raised in 2021. And under Xi's guidance, the Chinese Communist Party ties billions in defense investment to billions in commercial subsidies to create a domestic machine of innovation and industrial production. Xi has, in other words, devoted extraordinary amounts of national resources to accomplish his goals.[1]

China has a plan for technological supremacy. What's ours?

The second is the fundamental reordering of the national innovation pipeline. During the Cold War, the U.S. government funded basic and applied research projects and developed capabilities that served national priorities, including new weapons systems and space technologies. It mostly stayed out of commercial development, leaving it to private sector entities to turn government-backed scientific and technological advances into new companies, jobs, and industries, thus contributing to America's unmatched prosperity.[2] Today, some innovations will undoubtedly follow that same path from government research to commercial revolution, but many more won't. We cannot assume that the U.S. government will be the author of game-changing innovations, since businesses are the principal funders of R&D.

Finally, and the reason that this reform is critical: America's future depends on technological leadership.

The promise of technology is extraordinary. Imagine the lives saved and families made whole if we could target specific tumor cells and treat metastatic cancers. Imagine the potential to produce cheaper, nutrient-rich crops that can resist diseases and what that would do to address hunger around the world. This isn't the stuff of science fiction. It's the emerging reality, thanks to CRISPR, the gene-editing capability developed by Jennifer Doudna and her colleagues at the University of California. Their research opened a new frontier of medical and biological development. Using it, researchers have been able to study cancerous tumor cells and may soon develop groundbreaking treatments to some of the most common and deadly forms of the disease, including breast cancer. Others are working on treatments for Alzheimer's and hereditary diseases or uncovering the evolutionary story of humanity. And this is just the beginning.[3]

Moreover, technologies coming out of commercial development blur the line between military and civilian use. Think facial recognition technologies, which can give us Face ID on iPhones but can also be used in Orwellian security states like in Xinjiang and Tibet. Moreover, these high-tech sectors are often winner-take-all, meaning a company that achieves market position can hold on to it and shut down competition.

The fight over 5G networks and Huawei, the Chinese telecommunications giant, exemplifies the new environment. Huawei received over $75 billion in Chinese state support, through subsidies and trade protections. With that boost, it became the dominant figure in 5G communications technology.[4] With the Chinese Communist Party's support, it was able to offer its 5G kits at low prices to countries all over the world. Unsurprisingly, many countries across Asia, the Middle East, and Africa, and in our backyard in Latin America accepted Huawei's overtures. Even U.S. allies initially looked to Huawei to set up their 5G networks. Eventually, we pushed back. The United States and democracies around the world blocked Huawei from their market, but it never should have come to that.

U.S. companies had been at the cutting edge of every previous generation of cellular communications. This was unfortunately not the case for 5G. We had no viable alternative to Huawei. Two European firms, Ericsson and Nokia, were in the market, but neither could compete on price alone. America's past dominance in cellular communications could be attributed in large part to Qualcomm Technologies, the industry powerhouse. It had been an industry standard in 2G, 3G, and 4G, thanks to extensive in-house R&D. However, that self-funded model couldn't keep up with China. The United States fell behind.

The Trump administration confronted Huawei and fought for fair competition. It blocked Huawei from selling in the United States and, under the leadership of Secretary of State Mike Pompeo and Undersecretary Keith Krach, created a "Clean Network" of allies and partners, which blocked sales of Huawei's kit to their countries—a concept we'll revisit later. This was a huge accomplishment and a victory for security and freedom. But, as those involved would readily admit, this was just the first step and will not on its own secure U.S. leadership in 5G or future generations of cellular communications.

Nor will this approach suffice in other sectors. Take artificial intelligence (AI), which has the potential to disrupt how businesses operate, how we consume and process information, and how we wage war. U.S. firms are at the cutting edge in AI research, and most top researchers call America home.[5] But as the National Security Commission on Artificial Intelligence warned, "China has moved more quickly and with more determination than the United States."[6] It has fostered a broad, diverse ecosystem of AI research, and the only way to ensure America remains in the lead is to accelerate innovation.

The Huawei episode should have been a wake-up call. So should the AI commission's warning. How many more warnings do we need before we put in place a more expansive, long-term strategy for American innovation?

We are caught between two extremes. At one end is the largely hands-off approach of recent decades, wherein Washington funded R&D projects but didn't take an active interest in our technological leadership. At the other end is the Chinese Communist Party's approach, exemplified by its support for Huawei. Between these poles lies a better, third way: a national innovation strategy that unlocks America's innate entrepreneurship and harnesses market forces in the name of U.S. leadership in the most strategically vital industries of our time.

There's momentum in this direction in Washington. Lawmakers, who fail to agree on anything, have crossed party lines to propose plans to advance scientific and technological development. But we should also recognize the risks: the promise of renewal could just as easily become a stalking horse for partisan agendas.

The Biden administration came into office pledging to reinvigorate American innovation and invest hundreds of billions of dollars in R&D. It quickly became clear that the administration was driven more by political motivations than by the desire for a broad-based renewal. The administration's Build Back Better agenda and all its iterations, for example, prioritized huge new social programs over investments in national security. It focused our R&D funding on green initiatives, not the broad scope of advanced technologies, which are redefining international competition.

These efforts will not spur innovation or rejuvenate the American economy. They won't make America stronger or help us win the technological race. For that, America needs to harness its fundamental strengths: its people, dynamic capital markets, and entrepreneurial ecosystem. That mission takes two parts. First is a reimagining of how the U.S. government funds national innovation. Second is regulatory reform to encourage innovation, entrepreneurship, and dynamism and to unleash the potential of all Americans.

The Conservative Case for a Technology Strategy

To win the race for technological leadership and to preserve that leadership, America needs a new way of national innovation, one that addresses the gaps in the old model but which remains true to our nation's values, and therefore is dramatically different from China's. Specifically, the U.S. government should create policies that incentivize private capital toward high-tech sectors critical to national security and our strategic interest.

There is risk in what I'm proposing. Government intervention can invite crony capitalism. Powerful lobbies will hound policymakers for their slice of the pie. Partisan ambitions can cloud judgment and lead to waste and abuse, as in the Solyndra scandal. Government investment also can distort capital markets and undermine their efficiency.

However, we have a precedent: Operation Warp Speed. The effort to develop and distribute vaccines and treatment options for COVID-19, Operation Warp Speed exemplifies how government can work with the private sector in the name of innovation. It was formed in spring of 2020 and delivered two vaccines by the end of the year—a true medical marvel.

Operation Warp Speed had certain advantages, chief among them the clarity and specificity of its purpose. Mercifully, we don't have such pressing concerns in most technological arenas, but the lessons of its success still apply. To begin with, scientific research matters, even if we can't always see its immediate value. More important, government can play a powerful supporting role. My friend Paul Mango, who helped lead Operation Warp Speed, summarizes how it succeeded: "The government provided the resources, clarity of objective, and the regulatory context for success. America's private sector brought its ingenuity and innovative spirit to the table . . . The federal government *enabled* success, America's private sector *delivered* it."[7] That's the right way—the new way—to approach innovation at the national level.

To begin, we need a significant increase in R&D funding. "New knowledge," in the words of Vannevar Bush, "can be obtained only through basic scientific research."[8] The government has an invaluable role in supporting that research, but it is abdicating its responsibility. Under Ronald Reagan, when tensions with the Soviets ran hot and the United States orchestrated its comeback and victory, Washington spent roughly 1.2 percent of the nation's gross domestic product on R&D. That's *twice* what we spend now. China will soon overtake us in

R&D funding,[9] while also graduating more PhDs in STEM programs, filing more international patents than the United States, and narrowing the gap on venture capital investment.[10] Although private sector businesses are investing more in R&D, from $2.2 billion in 1955 to over $460 billion in 2019 (adjusted for inflation), they focus on product development or applied research—the kind of work intended to achieve a specific objective—not on basic scientific discoveries.

Federal R&D spending should grow to no less than $320 billion—roughly double the current level and equal to 1.5 percent of GDP—and that figure must grow steadily with time. We must also encourage more basic and applied research in the private sector, especially by raising the R&D tax credit.

It's not enough to put more money into research. Our approach to national research must evolve too. The to-do list includes everything from "fund[ing] people not projects," as one scholar put it to decentralizing control of federal funds by block granting money to research institutions and letting them apportion it according to their best judgment.[11] Washington could also invest in research infrastructure, like a National Research Cloud, as the Stanford Human-Centered AI Initiative has proposed.[12] Finally, the scientific community must think as a community again and encourage more cross-disciplinary thinking. "Science was never meant to be narrow in purpose," write two leading funders of scientific research. "At its plainest, the purpose of science is to feed our curiosity—and to keep us alive."[13] The list goes on, but each of these steps would help expand the field of knowledge in our society. They are, however, only the first step toward an innovation strategy.

Next, Washington should use its enormous purchasing power, as it did for the COVID-19 vaccines. By guaranteeing the purchase of millions of vaccines, it incentivized pharmaceutical companies to take a big bet and invest much more up front than they usually would. The fact is, there is no substitute for cash.[14] Many start-ups fail to innovate—to commercialize basic research at scale—in part due to a lack of demand at such an early stage.[15] Government can bridge that gap, as it has for the commercial space industry.[16]

Similarly, government-backed venture funds are building a track record of success, but scale remains a problem.[17] They aren't making sufficient investments,[18] so funding should increase by an order of magnitude. Washington should also boost its support for small businesses in the spirit of promoting competition in high-tech sectors.[19]

However, the government must also find new, creative ways to harness private capital markets. Innovators need patient capital to help them go from initial concepts to proven technology to scaled product. Private capital is rarely patient. Investors want returns. They want to see products go to market quickly and have little time for longer-term R&D. There is a gap in the market, and the United States lacks a mechanism for closing it.

The American Innovation Fund

In August 2022, President Biden signed a bill that would direct more than $50 billion in subsidies to domestic semiconductor production, create tax incentives for chip development, and boost R&D spending.[20] All well intended, but the concept is both flawed and incomplete. A one-off subsidy for semiconductor production, plus limited tax relief, will not secure America's position in that vital industry nor address all the problems up and down the semiconductor supply chains—the same vulnerabilities that led to the recent chip shortage. For that, we need long-term, patient investment in chip research and design, equipment, and production. We need to overcome the market distortions caused by foreign government subsidies. And we need to diversify the entire supply chain of material and parts that go into our most vital chip sets. Government can't do that alone. It would be too expensive, and it would fail. The only solution is to incentivize private capital investment into these critical areas—and into a host of sectors of strategic importance—thereby fertilizing the soil to maximize entrepreneurship and innovation.

Part of the solution could be an American Innovation Fund (AIF), a public-private vehicle to provide low-cost capital and liquidity to firms in strategic sectors. The AIF would function as a "fund of funds." It would be the central node in a network of public-private funds that invest in critical sectors, like semiconductors, and in America's technological leadership, through equity investments, grants, and even loans. Backed initially by taxpayer money, it should be designed to attract private capital and to reinvest returns. In essence, it could take a small taxpayer investment and raise enough capital to turn it into an evergreen fund worth ten times more.

The AIF could partner with public-private enterprises like America's Frontier Fund, a mission-focused sovereign fund dedicated to, in their words, promoting "research, innovation, and investments in foundational technologies and capabilities that are critical to protecting and advancing the well-being and security of the United States."[21] Or Shield Capital, a venture fund with a similar mission to advance America's technological edge, founded by veterans, former Pentagon officials, and experienced investors Raj Shah and Philip Bilden.

This kind of fund could adopt a first-loss approach, where the government provides some portion of initial investment and accepts a significant portion of potential losses. It would also take a capped upside, meaning the returns would be even greater for private investors. China used similar funds to support AI advances, and we could use them to incentivize private investment and harness market forces, while offsetting externalities that limit R&D funding.[22]

But it would only work if paired with extensive tax reforms to make it easier to raise private capital and regulatory reforms to make it easier to hire talented people and break ground on big projects. Given the right tax environment, capital will flow into the chips industry and other high-tech sectors. Private investors will become willing partners, and there's enormous untapped potential in America's capital markets.

We could also, as others have suggested, pair grants to contracts.[23] If an agency identifies a specific technological need, such as a treatment for a new disease or a specific weapons capability for the military, it could hold a competition. The winner would receive not just a funding grant, but also a contract to produce and deliver the product over the next five or ten years. These grants could take advantage of the immense talent in our national laboratories and federally funded research centers. If a researcher comes up with an idea they want to commercialize, they could receive an approved leave of absence and a big sum to go to market. This concept would go beyond SBIR grants and be a clear signal that our nation is willing to put our money on the line to ensure our long-term security and health.

Private citizens have a role to play, too. My friend Steve Feinberg recently formed a patriotic venture that will "invest in mature and early-stage companies with special capabilities, products and services that address national security challenges and supply chain vulnerabilities,"[24] and there is a long tradition of philanthropists and investors putting up their money for their preferred causes. We can learn a thing or two from them. Groups like the MacArthur Foundation, for example, use "catalytic capital," essentially first-loss, capped-upside funds, for social impact. Why not replicate that approach for national security impact?

You may be asking, do we really need to spend more taxpayer money? Can we even afford to spend more after the profligacy of the last few years? This is a question of prioritization. If you believe, as I do, that technological leadership is necessary for sustained economic dynamism, job and wage growth, and national security, then it moves to the top of the priority list.

Getting the Balance Right

For someone like me, who is skeptical of government overreach, this concept poses obvious contradictions. On the one hand, this book warns about the growth of the bureaucracy and government, but it also calls for a new enterprise to spur innovation. Let me clarify. The purpose of these proposals is to focus our national leaders on one of the most important issues confronting our country: the race for technological leadership and its implications on our national security and prosperity.

The importance of winning the technological race increases every day, yet Washington has so far failed to take the steps necessary to achieve victory. When Congress decided it was time to fund semiconductor production, it didn't create funds to support semiconductor design, manufacturing equipment, and production. It haggled for years over how to do it, coming up with a panoply of initiatives to do so, all of which would compete with the others for federal funding.

Washington has developed the bad habit of thinking complex solutions are good solutions. It's infected all our laws. Remember Obamacare? It was a chaotic, partisan mess that drove up healthcare

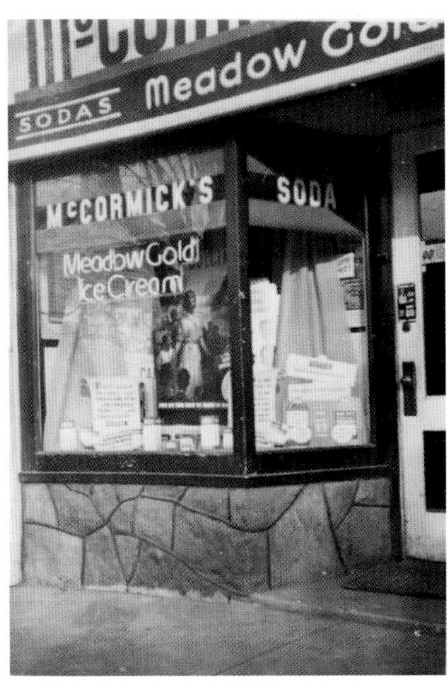

My grandfather Harold McCormick's drugstore in Plumville, Pennsylvania, circa 1950. *(Author's personal collection)*

Preparing for a hike with Dad and my brother, Doug, on the McCreary homestead outside of Blairsville, Pennsylvania, where we spent many summers as kids, 1977. *(Author's personal collection)*

The family farm outside of Bloomsburg, Pennsylvania, 2010. *(Author's personal collection)*

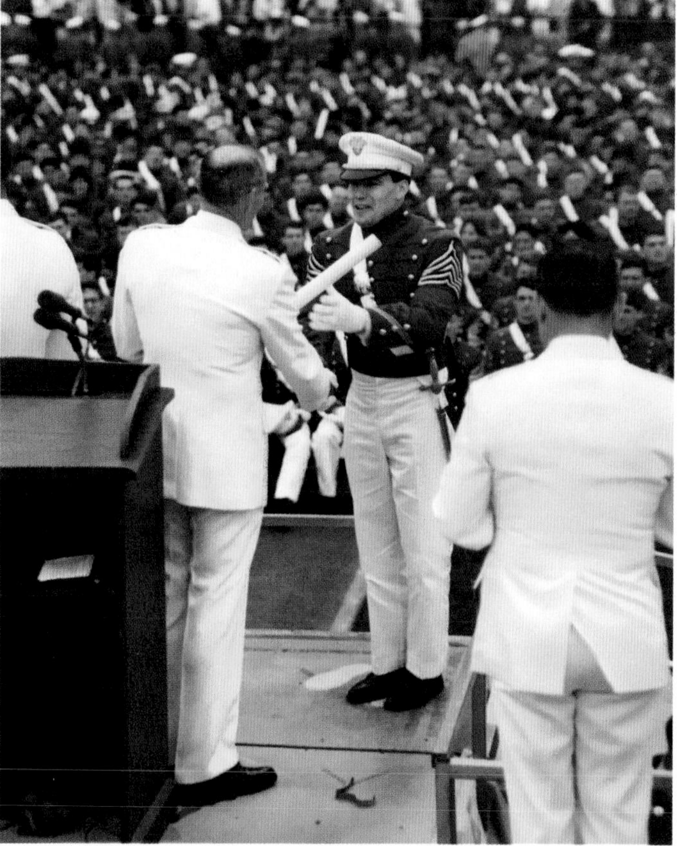

Receiving my West Point diploma, May 1987. *(Author's personal collection)*

Mom's master's degree graduation ceremony at Shippensburg University, 1988. She went on to complete her doctorate in education at Lehigh University at the age of fifty-two. *(Author's personal collection)*

Standing next to my Humvee in Iraq shortly after the launch of Operation Desert Storm, February 1991. *(Author's personal collection)*

The FreeMarkets logo was the first to occupy the Pittsburgh skyline—a sign of the Steel City's transformation in 2000. *(Paul D. Toth/Moment via Getty Images)*

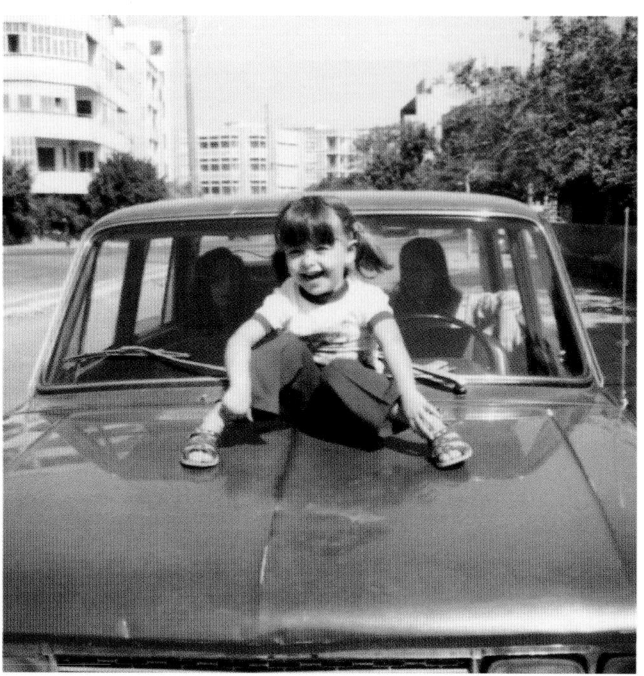

Dina as a young girl in Cairo on the hood of her parents' car, 1978. *(Author's personal collection)*

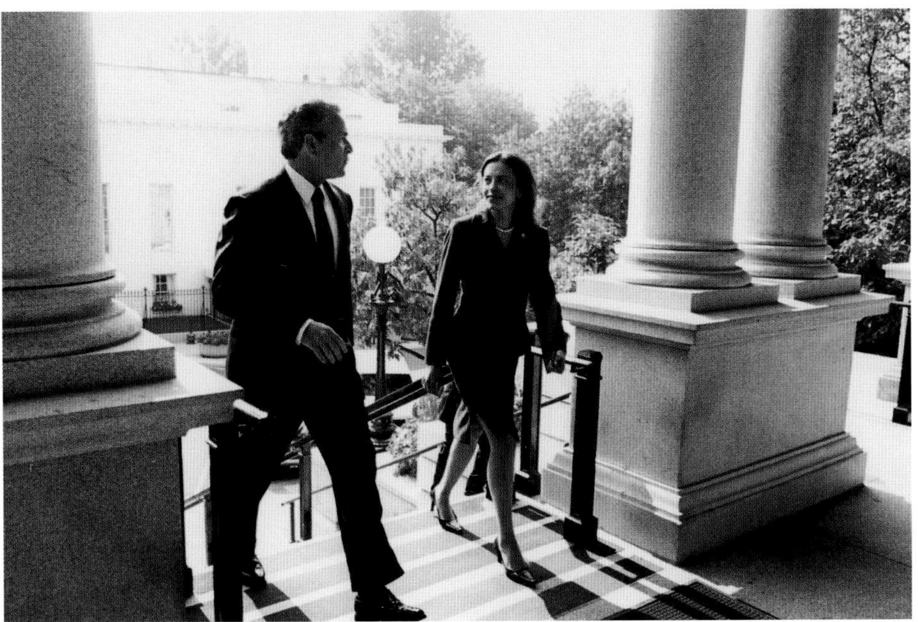

Dina walking with President George W. Bush after being appointed as the youngest assistant to the president for presidential personnel, 2003. *(Paul Morse, former White House deputy director of photography)*

Weather

Details, B10

The Washington Post

DISTRICT & MARYLAND FINAL

NEWSSTAND 50¢

Printed using recycled fiber

SATURDAY, OCTOBER 11, 2008

World Leaders Vow Concerted Action

Finance Officials Promise 'All Necessary Steps'; U.S. Stocks Flail to Worst Weekly Decline

Tiff Macklem, from left, of the Bank of Canada, Federal Reserve Chairman Ben S. Bernanke, Treasury Secretary Henry M. Paulson and Undersecretary David McCormick meet at the Treasury.

By STEVEN MUFSON *and* GLENN KESSLER
Washington Post Staff Writers

U.S. stock markets gyrated wildly yesterday as the world's top finance ministers met in Washington to hammer out a joint set of principles aimed at containing the financial crisis and restoring badly damaged confidence.

The Dow Jones industrial average fell 128 points, or 1.49 percent, to 8451, but during the day it had lurched from 7883 to 8901 — a roller-coaster ride of more than 1,000 points and an indicator of the uncertainty gripping investors as they try to figure out the severity of the economic downturn and whether various companies will survive.

Over the past five days, the Dow Jones industrial average has registered the biggest weekly percentage decline in its 112-year history, surpassing the record decline set during the Depression, in the week ending July 22, 1933.

Finance ministers from the world's seven biggest industrialized economies, in Washington for a regularly scheduled meeting, issued a communique last night vowing to "take all necessary steps to unfreeze credit and money markets" and to "use all available tools" to prop up and prevent the failure of institu-

The Washington Post reporting on a historic G7 meeting at the height of the financial crisis. I'm pictured here with Federal Reserve Chairman Ben Bernanke and Treasury Secretary Hank Paulson, October 2008. *(From* The Washington Post, *© 2008* The Washington Post. *All rights reserved. Used under license.)*

Delivering the commencement speech at Bloomsburg University, May 2, 2009. *(Author's personal collection)*

The annual family "Rocky Run" prior to the Army-Navy game, Philadelphia Museum of Art, December 2018. *(Author's personal collection)*

White House state dinner for Emmanuel Macron, president of France, hosted by President Donald Trump, April 24, 2018. *(Mandel Ngan/AFP via Getty Images)*

Family vacation in Florida, 2018. *(Author's personal collection)*

A final campaign rally at my high school in Bloomsburg, the day before the election, May 16, 2022. *(Author's personal collection)*

Greeting supporters on election night in Pittsburgh, Pennsylvania, May 17, 2022. *(Jeff Swenson/Getty Images News via Getty Images)*

costs, yet it's celebrated as somehow improving our healthcare system. When was the last time you tried to understand the tax code or decipher how America's health insurance system works? Bureaucratic complexity has become the norm and effective governance its victim.

What's proposed here is designed to cut to the chase. It would immediately increase the amount of taxpayer and, more important, private money going toward U.S. innovation, with the goal of unleashing latent potential in America's private sector. And it would force technological supremacy and innovation to the top of the priority list in Washington.

It also costs only pennies on every taxpayer dollar doled out by Washington each year but promises a radically compelling return on investment. This isn't Build Back Better or the Green New Deal, which impose heavy-handed regulations and have the government fund the projects it chooses, using taxpayer dollars. This is targeted investments, matched by tax incentives and deregulation and designed to leverage the private sector and unlock American ingenuity. This market-based approach will trigger greater private sector investment, faster technological development, and accelerated growth. The return on investment would be compelling. It would get our country moving again and put more money into the bank accounts of hardworking Americans.

This is the new way of national innovation, and it is overdue.

Principles for Innovation Investment

We must be bold and direct. But we also should remember that government cannot—must not—get into the business of trying to manage the economy.

I harbor no illusions about the dangers of government intervention, so this uniquely American way of accelerating innovation must be guided by strict limiting principles to guard against cronyism and overreach:

First, identify sectors of strategic importance. This is the most straightforward of all. We must narrow the focus of innovation funding and make bets on what sectors will matter most to our national security in the coming decade. The list should continually evolve, but it might include such obvious choices as semiconductors, AI, quantum sciences, biotechnology, and the like.

Second, develop new technologies or capabilities with unique upsides. Government funding for early-stage research activities can yield significant benefits at relatively low cost. Research areas could include metamaterials, bio-synthetics, energy storage, and bioengineering, as well as manufacturing capabilities, such as advanced additive manufacturing or innovative computer-aided design tools enabled by high-performance computing. These are high-reward, low-risk targeted investments—the sorts of projects that have produced great value for the United States in the past.

Third, support sectors with winner-take-all aspects or large first-mover advantages. Recall the Huawei example. Huawei got into the market first and locked up its prime position. Then, because we couldn't offer a good alternative to build 5G networks, we relied on other countries denying Huawei access to their markets, with mixed results. We can't afford to find ourselves in that position again. The U.S. government should promote innovation in sectors like these where the stakes are clear.

Fourth, support domestic development in sectors or technologies where foreign firms are highly subsidized by U.S. competitors. Chinese firms enjoy substantial state support, and non-Chinese firms compete on uneven ground. We face the same imbalances around the world. Considering how important high-tech sectors are and the advantages that go to the firms that make it to market first, we cannot rely on tariffs, export controls, or other trade adjustments to secure a level playing field for U.S. firms. Innovation support may prove necessary in these instances and could be coupled with complementary trade and export policies.

Fifth and final, promote competition, not companies. As someone who had worked in venture capital and the government once said to me, "we don't want to build the next Google. We want to identify what the next search engine is and help a half dozen companies compete to produce it." Some lawmakers might disagree and call for us to back specific companies. The lobbyists representing those companies would concur. But that's the kind of narrow, top-down thinking that is focused more on boosting one firm's profits than on ensuring comprehensive American innovation.

We need to have a long-term road map that positions us favorably beyond tomorrow, meaning we need to enable entire industries, rather than specific companies. To do that, we must think holistically. Firms have suppliers and rely on public infrastructure. They need a foundation of skilled and talented workers. The renewal agenda, therefore, should and must seed the ground. It should encourage business formation and support small suppliers and big producers alike. It should ensure the right tax, legal, and regulatory conditions.

To bridge the capital gap through public and private financing, the focus of such efforts should remain narrow, and these principles should constrain the government's "use cases." Any government-led effort to transform the economy will fail. Doing so is beyond the power of government. More important, it is beyond the proper role of government. It is overreach, but sadly an excess to which too many in Washington fall prey.

Instead, we must commit to identifying the highest priority sectors and making meaningful, targeted investments in them. As a former government official at the center of Operation Warp Speed, told me: its stunning success was made possible by the "audacity of its vision." It pledged to deliver a product within a set timeline, and that clarity, backed by as much as $18 billion, aligned the interests of disparate government agencies and the pharmaceutical industry. It was a big gamble, but boy did it pay off. We will need a similar approach to the other most pressing innovation challenges of our time. Though we will rarely have so clear or pressing a timeline, we will need the audacity to bet on American innovation.

Cutting Red Tape—The Energy Revolution

A central theme of this book is the primacy of people. At our best, Americans fuel innovation and drive renewal. The talent strategy, laid out in the previous chapter, is intended to help everyone in this country access that opportunity through a two-pronged attack. It lifts people up and it breaks open doors traditionally closed to too many Americans. The innovation strategy should take a similar approach. Research and innovation funding put capital in the hands of innovators. Now government has to get out of those innovators' way and let them put that money to its best and highest use. This is the third lesson of Warp Speed: create a regulatory environment that encourages innovation.

The benefits of deregulating, and the risks of overregulating, are most apparent in the energy sector. In the early 2000s, America was energy dependent. We imported over 60 percent of our petroleum supply, and we produced a historically small portion of the energy we consumed.[25] Access to foreign energy supplies was a central concern in Washington, heightened by the sense that we were depleting our oil and gas reserves at home. In fact, we would soon learn, we were only just beginning to unlock them.

America sits atop enormous reserves of natural gas, much of it produced in shale rock formations. For years, oil and gas men labored to develop the capability to access and harvest those vast reserves. To break open those formations, they devised hydraulic fracturing techniques, commonly called fracking, in which they would dig deep vertical wells, then pump high-pressure water, sand, and chemicals into the largely impermeable rock, allowing the gas and oil within to flow more easily. Horizontal drilling made it possible to access wider expanses of shale formations, and new types of drill bits sped the process. At the same time, researchers had gotten better at identifying and mapping those formations, making breakthroughs in modeling of shale beds, and, especially, in seismic imaging. With those technologies in hand, drillers could make three-dimensional maps of shale formations, which gave them eyes below the surface of the earth, allowing them to find and fracture gas-rich deposits.

Despite all this progress, Washington continued to hold back the shale gas revolution through excessive regulations that stifled the use of fracking and horizontal drilling. Finally, in 2005, Congress reined in Environmental Protection Agency oversight of those techniques.[26] Ten years later, it lifted the ban on foreign exports of crude oil. In between and beyond, Washington loosened or eliminated entirely regulations on production, land use, and transport of natural gas. As a result, America has now become a world leader in the production of natural gas. In 2019, we exported more energy than we consumed.

The shale gas revolution secured America's energy supply and put us on the path to energy independence. It freed us from dependence on oil cartels and positioned America as a central player in global energy markets. Other countries started coming to us for energy supplies, not the other way around. American workers benefited hugely, but so did the environment.

In my home state of Pennsylvania, which sits atop the fourth largest gas reserves in the world, the fracking boom revitalized old industrial counties.[27] It put people to work—over 100,000 Pennsylvanians directly and another 377,000 indirectly, by one estimate. And as of 2019, oil and gas supported roughly 6 percent of the jobs in the Commonwealth.[28] All that production and labor created tax revenue, which then supported schools, social services, and housing from Washington County in the Southwest to Wyoming in the Northeast.

Because the natural gas produced in places like Pennsylvania is cleaner than coal or the gas produced anywhere else, it did wonders for the environment. And as someone who grew up hunting, hiking, and visiting our national parks, I care deeply about protecting the natural beauty God gave this country. To me, conserving our land goes hand in hand with conserving our nation. I own more than one thousand acres on a family farm outside the Pennsylvania town I grew up in and in Colorado, with conservation easements and programs designed to protect the land. And that's why I am such a stalwart advocate for the unlocking of America's gas reserves as a means to grow our economy, advance our security, and protect our environment by reducing carbon emissions.

In 2019, our country saw a 2.9 percent reduction in emissions, the largest of any country in the world, thanks in large part to the shale gas revolution.[29] In fact, U.S. emissions have declined substantially since fracking entered regular use; greenhouse gas emissions from power generation dropped 41 percent from 2005 to 2019, while shale production increased sixfold. All the hand-wringing and regulations around the modest and manageable environmental risks of fracking miss the big picture.

Throughout the first half of 2022, I had the opportunity to visit numerous energy production facilities throughout Pennsylvania. One example was a Washington County rig operated by Range Resources, a pioneer in natural gas production and one of the first to tap into the Marcellus Shale, a massive formation of shale rock housing some of the largest natural gas reserves in the world. The land was leased from a local family and brought them life-changing income, and the rig operated with a footprint of three to four acres. Workers operated in fourteen-day shifts, with fourteen days off. For twenty-six weeks of hard labor, they made close to $100,000 a year. Some made more as they rose up the ranks. And everything was done with the utmost care for the environment; they had a complex system of liners and berms to prevent spills, erosion controls, and methane burners to reduce greenhouse gas emissions.

The site was a testament to what the shale gas revolution has given the country and, especially, Pennsylvania. High-paying jobs. Huge growth in economic activity. Tens of millions paid to landowners and billions paid to state governments. Yet, the operators still run up against walls of excessive and uncertain regulations.

Range Resources can extract the gas, but it needs to be able to move it. For that, it depends on pipelines domestically and harbor terminals for overseas shipments. On both counts, government—at the state and federal level—is getting in the way. New England needs energy resources. Pennsylvania natural gas is the best possible option. But they can't get the permits required to build a pipeline connecting the two. Likewise, our European allies need alternatives to Russia's oil and gas. We should be providing it to them, but it takes millions of dollars and many years to go through environmental impact reviews to build a gas terminal somewhere like Philadelphia.

President Biden made it that much worse, too. On his first day in office, he canceled the Keystone XL pipeline and put in place regulations restricting new gas production and raising the costs of existing production. His regulatory blanket drove private capital away from the industry by creating uncertainty and reducing the return on investment. Americans lost good jobs. Russia was emboldened to invade Ukraine.

That's what happens when government gets in the way. It doesn't just slow and misdirect innovation. It hurts everyday Americans by depriving them of better products, lower prices, more advanced medicines, and so on. It hurts the country by weakening America's standing and relative competitiveness. And it even hurts the environment. American natural gas, after all, is far cleaner and produced more safely than that which comes from Russia, Saudi Arabia, or Venezuela.

Energy is just one example. Across the country, laws and regulations impede our ability to innovate. Regulation regularly lags technological progress, preventing new ideas or capabilities from making it to market—just as the EPA hemmed in fracking. Finally, occupational licensing laws prevent people from changing jobs, moving, or starting off anew on entrepreneurial adventures. In the 1950s, one in twenty jobs required workers to have government license. Now one in four does.[30] Everyone from barbers to florists must go through training and get government approval to practice their trade. Past administrations, Republican and Democrat, have agreed that overwhelming licensing rules lead to lower wages and hurt workers.[31] They make it harder for them to pursue opportunity while the economy is driving more job turnover and forcing people to be flexible.

For the innovation strategy to succeed, we must address three primary weaknesses of the country's legal and regulatory ecosystem that are so apparent in our energy sector: the slow pace of change, distorting effects, and unnecessary work restrictions. These three simultaneously delay American innovation and undermine the ideas that make America exceptional.

Unlock Entrepreneurship, Innovation, and Opportunity

Our government has created an ecosystem that encourages passivity, discourages risk-taking, and obstructs the pursuit of happiness. That must change. In its place, let's build an entrepreneurial ecosystem in law and regulations. Such an environment would not just allow but also encourage people and firms to innovate, develop, and scale new technologies. It would embrace what some economists call "permissionless innovation,"[32] where entrepreneurs would not need approval, and liberate people to chase their ambitions and find meaningful work.

Clearly, some consumer protections in areas such as medicine and transportation safety are needed to keep Americans safe and healthy. The problem arises when they overreach and unnecessarily hinder private activity. Or when they are enacted and then become untouchable. The ledger of federal regulations grows constantly; simply slowing the pace of new rules was an achievement for the Trump administration.[33] Given this complexity, we need a few principles to act as guideposts for the never-ending campaign to restore our government to its proper place in American life.

First, Washington and state capitals should make it easier to be entrepreneurial. As is, Americans have to ask permission to start a business. Depending on what they're trying to do, they either have to apply for a permit or license from a federal agency or from their state or local government, or both. This being government, those permits take time and cost money. It gets more complicated. Entrepreneurs and small business owners continually have to interpret a complex, often changing mosaic of overlapping jurisdictions and rules. Some amount of overlap and confusion across local, state, and national administrations is inevitable in our federalist system, but it doesn't have to be this bad. Americans have to pay for the privilege of starting a business. On principle alone, this practice is hard to stomach. Why not start small and get rid of licensing and permit fees for the formation of small businesses?

Second, we ought to speed up regulatory reform to try to keep pace with innovation. Autonomous cars make for an obvious example of where law impedes technology, but they're not alone. Just look at the many potential applications of AI, the slow commercial adoption of robotics and sensors in American factories, or the availability of healthcare-affiliated technology. America may move faster than most European countries, but we can be better. It's going to take more to compete with China. Agencies ought to look for opportunities to adapt regulations or develop new, permissive environments early in the innovation cycle.[34]

Finally, we have to free people to move, work, and create. The reduction of licensing requirements for jobs that shouldn't need them—like manicurists or beauticians—is a vital step but not the only one. We must also support pro-family policies. Meaningful work and strong families should go hand in hand, not work in opposition. We should continue to expand parental leave, and we should explore how to make benefits more portable. Workers too often find themselves tethered to a job for fear of losing good insurance coverage.

They also struggle to build a nest egg when moving from job to job. These sorts of obstacles take power out of workers' hands. They make Americans less mobile and less dynamic, unable to seize opportunity for fear of hurting themselves or their families. We need to help Americans control their future and encourage taking a risk to pursue their American dream. Americans realizing those dreams are force multipliers for our nation's future trajectory.[35]

Around the time of my visit to the Range Resources rig, I also had a chance to tour the new Shell Cracker Plant in Beaver County, Pennsylvania. Set on a mile-long stretch of land along the Ohio River northwest of Pittsburgh, the facility is designed to produce plastic pellets from natural gas produced nearby in western Pennsylvania. The pellets made there will then be used to manufacture any number of plastic products.

This tour revealed that the work being done to get it up and running resulted in hundreds of Pennsylvanians back in action in well-paying manufacturing jobs. Thousands more would be employed either directly at the plant or indirectly through the transport, upkeep, and community infrastructure that's building up all around it. Backed by a massive state tax credit, it had already drawn billions of dollars of investment into Beaver County, and it would trigger hundreds of millions of dollars of economic activity in no time. An economic boom made possible by the natural gas boom.

We've seen what the first stage of the natural gas revolution did for jobs, energy security, and the climate, but this is only the beginning. As an example, Toby Rice, the CEO of a major energy investment firm, EQT, has put forward ambitious plans to maximize natural gas production across Pennsylvania and the country and in the process to accelerate reductions in emissions. Others have proposals for expanded carbon capture and storage or innovative ways to use the gas and heat produced from fracking. As he described to me, these plans would draw extraordinary levels of capital investment to Pennsylvania and create enormous job opportunities for young people across the Commonwealth and neighboring states.

And the fracking revolution is just the start. Researchers have made breakthroughs in nuclear fusion and can now generate more energy than is required to catalyze the fusion. Others are drilling deep into the earth's surface to harness the vast geothermal energy potential, and nuclear reactors are becoming cheaper, smaller, and more efficient. We've only scratched the surface of what unbridled American ingenuity and industriousness can do to ensure energy dominance and protect the environment.

These are bold reforms, but renewing America will require a courageous commitment to innovation. We will have to step across the frontier from the known into the world of the unknown. We cannot know where that step may land. It may find solid ground and propel us forward, or it may find a hole. The possibility of the latter—the possibility of failure—distinguishes the act of innovation. To quote the outgoing president of Purdue University, Mitch Daniels, "The biggest risk of all is that we stop taking risks at all."[36] If our government wants to create a genuine acceleration in U.S. technological development, it will have to expect and accept failure, as any entrepreneur can attest. Congress will have to give R&D projects some freedom to fail and learn from those failures, and Washington will have to make bets on the future.

Unfortunately, the government is not set up to do either of those things well. Structural and cultural obstacles exist across agencies and across the branches of government. They will impede the renewal agenda, particularly this innovation strategy, so long as they remain. I will address these imperatives in greater detail in later chapters, but for now, we close this chapter where it began. Americans face profound challenges, and our government has failed to address them. We need a revival of good government. In China, we see the alternative at work. We see a top-down system that treats people as a means to an end: the preservation of the Chinese Communist Party and the expansion of Chinese power.

Throughout its history, our citizens have proved to be America's greatest asset. This innovation strategy is grounded in that truth. If we do this well, we will put resources in the hands of Americans and unleash our potential to solve the challenges we face and thereby strengthen our country.

CHAPTER 6

Data: A New Source of Power

The calculus of innovation is really quite simple: Knowledge drives innovation; innovation drives productivity; productivity drives our economic growth.

—William Brody, President of Johns Hopkins University, before Congress, July 21, 2005

In May of 2009, five months after I left the Department of the Treasury, my car turned into the unmarked, tree-lined entrance of Bridgewater Associates. I wasn't entirely sure what I was doing there. You see, "finance" had never been my strong suit. As a kid, I had a paper route around my neighborhood. Every day, I'd wake up before dawn and bike through the dark, tree-lined streets, tossing papers up onto front lawns. My dad was a big believer that we should work, and I liked it well enough. It got me up and moving. But I never embraced the bookkeeping side. The point of a job, as best I figured, was to have money to buy what you wanted, and at that age, I wasn't looking to buy much. So I'd only go around to collect money when I needed a little pocket change, and I mean real pocket change; I'd just crumple up the bills and put them into the pockets of my jeans. Even then, I'd usually get so caught up chatting with the neighbors that I'd forget to collect the money. It's no wonder I pursued my graduate studies in international affairs and not finance. A financier I was not.

So you can imagine my trepidation as I pulled onto Bridgewater's campus. Bridgewater was, even then, one of the largest but least-known active macroeconomic investors in the world. Yet its office sat in a modest building in a pine forest along the Saugatuck River in Westport, Connecticut. More than an hour away from Manhattan and the frenzy of Wall Street, the quiet location was no accident.

Ray Dalio founded Bridgewater in 1975 in his New York apartment. Originally, it was an advisory firm. Ray and his colleagues studied global markets and sent out daily missives to clients. These *Daily Observations* often bucked the accepted wisdom on Wall Street because they reflected what came to be Bridgewater's unique and heralded approach.[1]

Ray believed there were fundamental and universal truths about why markets moved the way they did. The challenge lay in discovering them. Bridgewater's method was straightforward yet extraordinarily difficult: conduct extensive historical research to gain insight to discover truths and, through continual evolution and learning, sharpen those insights.

The company's unique corporate culture and thought process, which were designed to achieve that goal, often make headlines. The firm is legendary not only for its extraordinary investment success but also for its idea meritocracy and radical transparency, where the best ideas win out over the highest rank, and where everyone would continually provide direct and pointed feedback to one another to help the firm improve.

Bridgewater's process distinguished it, but so did its insights. The firm often found itself going against the conventional wisdom. Before long, Ray formalized the split from Wall Street, eventually setting up the offices in a stand of tall pines in Connecticut. Clients took notice, and Bridgewater began to manage their money as well, excelling in global bond, equity, currency, and commodity markets.

With each success and failure, the firm deepened its insights into how these markets worked. Soon Ray and his early partners came to recognize the power of "systemization"—of not just writing down the timeless and universal truths gleaned from years of experience but also institutionalizing them. The company put in place processes to guide investment decisions. They started as rules and principles written on reams of yellow legal pads. With the advent of computers, they were digitized, and the capacity for managing large data sets scaled exponentially. By the time I joined the company in 2009, an intricate set of algorithms existed, and the company's highly touted fundamental, systematic, and diversified investment process was well-established. These systems grew more complex and technologically advanced with each passing year.

That entire system runs on millions of pieces of data. Ultimately, data is nothing more than information coded into binary, digital units and stored on a server. Those ones and zeros can capture almost anything. They can articulate every entry in the *Oxford English Dictionary*, a human's genetic code, or my mom's recipe for meat loaf—any information, past or present. When accumulated, refined, and processed by machine or man, data becomes knowledge, and knowledge is the foundation of innovation.

At Bridgewater, we were highly dependent on market data and basic economic data around growth and inflation. Stock prices and investment flows from the world's largest pools of capital. Interest rates and bond yields. Commodity and currency trades. All of it was fed into the algorithms to deepen Bridgewater's understanding of markets and guide its investment decisions. Without this growing pool of data, there would be no way to understand what was going on in the markets and the world; no evolution in how we approached the endlessly complex challenge that is investing; no strategies for better managing client money and generating returns for the pensioners, institutions, and nations that depended on Bridgewater; no enhanced knowledge.

Other companies are equally dependent on data. Amazon and other online retailers depend on real-time information about consumer preferences, inventory, shipments, and transactions. Manufacturers need constant data about their productivity and production totals, as well as about the availability of materials, when suppliers will deliver necessary components, and so on. Regardless of the business, the collection, storage, and refinement of data is increasingly a prerequisite for success.

Data is at the center of global trade and global investment and now, more than ever, central to innovation. For decades, international trade in goods and services set the pace of globalization. After the global financial crisis, however, growth in trade plateaued, and in its place came an explosion of digital trade with data being shared across international borders. From 2008 to 2020, cross-border data flows increased by roughly 112 times, and the growth shows no signs of slowing.[2] In 2018, 330 million people made online purchases from other countries, each involving the cross-border transmission of data, helping e-commerce hit $25.6 trillion in sales, despite only about 60 percent of the world being online.

Digital technologies introducing data into the market now enable, and in some cases have replaced, traditional trade in goods and services. Movies, once sold primarily as DVDs, now stream on digital platforms, and news, books, and research papers are increasingly consumed online. Even physical goods come laden with digital components. Cars are no longer merely chassis built around internal combustion engines; they also house complex electronics and software capturing massive amounts of data. Trade in physical goods also comes with digital enablers, such as devices and programs that track shipping containers, which likewise generate data and improve efficiency.

What a radical break from history. Until very recently, "information has been so costly to acquire that people were often operating in the dark," writes Alan Greenspan, the former chairman of the Federal Reserve.[3] Two millennia ago, documented human knowledge was written on scrolls and housed in a few great libraries. Then, for much of the Middle Ages, monks labored in darkness to preserve the works of classical scholars and what little written record existed. The earliest universities began to promulgate knowledge, and the invention of the printing press allowed for mass production of texts. But even then, only a select, privileged few could read Aristotle's works or see Isaac Newton's writings on calculus and physics.

Railroads and telegraphs eventually connected distant people, allowing information to travel more freely, and telephones, radios, and televisions accelerated connection. Ultimately, it was the computer and eventually the internet that vaulted us into this age of data. They allowed for the mass production, storage, and transmission of data and made it available at our fingertips. They turned data from a pricey commodity to a ubiquitous resource, "like the air we breathe."[4] Data has democratized information and powered progress.

However, the digitization of our world is just the beginning. To quote a renowned German professor, "Not everything can be digitized. But everything that can be digitized will be."[5] The advent of 5G exemplifies the importance of exchanging data faster and in larger portions. The internet of things is about connecting devices and sharing data among them. When you turn on your television and go to Netflix at the end of the day, you're part of the digital transformation.

This explosion in data has huge implications for the global economy, but also for the balance of national power.

Data drives commercial success. Companies whose competitive advantages are built by aggregating, analyzing, and using data have seized top market positions across the globe. Ten years ago, any list of the ten most valuable firms included oil and gas producers, consumer goods firms, and banks. Today, technology companies that amplify data dominate the list. BHP Group, Chevron, and ExxonMobil have given way to Alphabet, Amazon, and Meta.[6] The current crop of technology leaders thrives in no small part because they transform vast amounts of data from billions of individuals and organizations into new economic value for their customers.

Data is crucial to national security, too. It drives productivity and thus the economic power that underwrites the United States' military edge. It is also a primary domain of U.S.–Chinese competition for economic and geopolitical superiority—as demonstrated, for example, by the two countries' battle over 5G technology.

Put simply, data offers incredible advantages to all who hold it, but it is also readily abused. Countries and companies that seek anticompetitive advantages try to control it. So do those that wish to undermine liberty and privacy.

China is the chief culprit. The Chinese Communist Party treats data as the vital resource it is and has laid out a disturbing vision for how to control it. Outside of China, however, data remains largely ungoverned. The current international trade and investment framework was designed seventy-five years ago, in a very different time. It is not adequate for the reality of global trade today. Confusion about the value and ownership of data abounds, and major world powers have competing visions of how to manage it.

If the United States does not shape new rules for the digital age at home and abroad, others will. China is promulgating a techno-authoritarian model that we must counter, recognizing that shaping the rules of digital power is a key component of geopolitical competition. The United States should offer an alternative: with a coalition of willing partners, it should set up a new framework, one that unleashes data's potential to drive innovation, generate economic power, and protect national security.

While data access is critical to innovation, privacy must also be protected. Big Tech has accumulated a disturbing power and autonomy over our personal data. It wields that data for profit and with little regard for consequence—social, economic, or national security. The tech titans jealously guard their hold over our data, at the cost of competition and privacy. They encourage us to turn over ever greater portions of ourselves, at the cost of our culture and souls.[7]

There is a balance to be struck. Big Tech remains a principal source of high-end innovation in this country. Google operates at the forefront of AI and quantum computing, and Amazon's cloud services, for example, are an extraordinary resource for storing and sharing data. However, we cannot continue to ignore the harm they sometimes do to economic competition, security, society, and our politics.

The data strategy, in other words, must do two things. In recognition of the power and ubiquity of data, and of China's dangerous ambitions, data must remain a free and open resource, shared across companies and countries. And in recognition of Big Tech and social media's hulking presence in our national life, competition, innovation, and privacy must be carefully balanced and protected, which includes confronting the presence of Chinese technology in our lives.

Data, the New Sunshine

In 2017, the *Economist* declared that "The world's most valuable resource is no longer oil, but data."[8] The cliché stuck: "data is the new oil." Provocative but, like most clichés, wrong. Data is not the new oil. Data is something different, something new.

For one, data is what economists call "nonrival." Nearly all goods and services are "rival," meaning their use by one person or firm precludes their use by someone else. A barrel of oil, for instance, is rival. Once the oil has been used, it's gone and no one else can burn it. But data is nonrival: it can be used simultaneously and repeatedly by any number of firms or people without being diminished. In other words, data can power innovation again and again without being depleted. As my good friend Matt Slaughter, the dean of Tuck School of Business at Dartmouth University, says, data is more like the limitless supply of sunshine than the limited supply of oil.[9]

Data, unlike oil, is also both an input and an output of innovation and economic activity. Oil can create any number of products. It can fuel the machines used to extract more oil from the ground. But when data is used, data is created. Think about the last time you used Google Maps on a long drive. You pulled up the app on your phone, plugged in the address, and then got live directions and updates along your route. Each step used data. The app used data about your location. You used Google's global positioning data to map the right path. Your phone continually pulled data from Google's servers to update your arrival time. You also created data all along the way. Google used your progress to update its real-time traffic information. Its algorithms fine-tuned themselves ever so slightly by comparing your trip to what it expected. Data consumed and data created simultaneously. That's how the global economy works too. It has become a perpetual motion machine of data: it consumes it, processes it, and produces ever more quantities of it.

The ubiquity and "nonrival" nature of data make it a tinderbox of potential innovation. Information has always been an essential input for discovering new ideas. Benjamin Franklin needed data on lightning strikes to improve humans' understanding of electricity. Gregor Mendel needed data on pea plants to discover rules of heredity. Their experiments collected data, and their genius turned that data into knowledge about how the world around them worked. But in the past decade or so, data has become inseparable from knowledge creation and, therefore, innovation. Today, a vast amount of data is needed to refine ideas into economically productive uses.

Thanks to major advances in computing power, cloud storage, and machine learning, researchers have acquired the capacity to use data at a scale far beyond the wildest imaginations of their predecessors. Imagine all the information required to train a self-driving car for the variable unpredictability of a city street. Imagine the number of images the algorithms must process; the possible permutations of cross-traffic, bikers, and pedestrians; the potential for a dog to dart off-leash into the road or a driver to lose control. It's almost impossible to comprehend, yet developers are able to handle that problem. They have the capacity to store the data, computing power to process it, and technology capable of learning and adapting. And here we are with cars capable of navigating themselves down highways and self-driving, long-haul trucks.

Or consider the Human Genome Project. In just thirteen years, the U.S.-led international public initiative sequenced and published data on the three billion DNA base pairs that constitute the human genome. This groundbreaking advance in human knowledge was made possible by data access and the capacity to handle it, with profound, positive economic and health impacts. One study estimated that from 1988 to 2010, this project led to a total economic impact of $796 billion—including over $244 billion in additional personal income from over 300,000 new jobs. To say nothing of the lives saved or made better by this knowledge.[10]

Both innovations resulted from the novel use of data, and both have been made possible by technological progress. These are just a taste of what's to come. Data is power. It is a source of innovation and competitive advantage, and its governance is a key battleground of geopolitics. We must treat it as the vital asset it is, address the enormous risk it poses, and elevate data as a top priority of the national agenda.

Getting Our Digital House in Order

The data strategy begins at home, by setting new standards of digital trust and privacy. Right now we fall woefully short on that account. The problems are legion, but chief among them are the lack of national rules on data privacy, the prevalence of Chinese firms in the United States, and the overwhelming control and abuse of data by certain U.S. technology companies.

The first problem is, effectively, legal. Our nation has no framework governing how companies collect and use individuals' data. Think about all the internet-connected devices in your home. Your phone and laptop, but maybe you also have a Nest smart thermostat or Roku smart television. Do you wear a Fitbit to exercise or have an Alexa? Each of those devices is constantly collecting data on your life—everything from your heartbeat and the number of steps you took that day to what you watch and when. Now add in the apps on your phone and the social media platforms you scroll through while waiting in line. Each of us has become a constant producer of data. We are the product that social media and other businesses sell, and consumers are helpless to do anything about it.

Second, our data is also vulnerable to Chinese predation. In recent years, the Chinese Communist Party has rapidly expanded its control over the personal data of Americans, as is documented in greater detail below. To understand the risks, look no further than TikTok, which has taken the world by storm.

TikTok has roughly 80 million users in the United States alone and more downloads than Meta and visits than Google. But it is also owned by ByteDance, a Chinese company, which raises serious questions about whether every one of those Americans logging into TikTok risks handing their data over to the Chinese Communist Party.[11] If ByteDance can access users' data, the Chinese Communist Party likely can too. Some might say this doesn't matter for national security, but even the most innocuous seeming information can be used for nefarious purposes. Just a few years ago, for example, a twenty-year-old Australian revealed the previously hidden locations of U.S. troops in Syria by tracking Fitbit data online. Others followed and identified troops' jogging routes in Somalia, Afghanistan, and elsewhere. Military command restricted Fitbit use afterward, but the damage had been done.[12] We don't know yet how others will use our personal data, but that's also beside the point. Imagine if Washington suddenly declared it could see all your personal data? That's a true invasion of privacy, and according to reports, user data is already being accessed from China.[13]

There's also the question of reciprocity. China blocks U.S. social media and apps, but TikTok operates freely here. Again, even if the user data doesn't matter much for national security, its acquisition by the CCP would be a violation of our basic standards and our privacy. For that reason, and "[i]n light of repeated misrepresentations by TikTok concerning its data security, data processing, and corporate governance practices," the top Democrat and Republican on the Senate Intelligence Committee have asked the Federal Trade Commission to investigate TikTok.[14]

This is a benign example, but the problem goes well beyond one company. Across sectors, U.S. data flows to China into the hands of the Communist leaders. Chinese data never flows back. China is, effectively, siphoning U.S. data and private information about us, our businesses, and our lifestyles, and it's using it to fuel its dangerous geopolitical ambitions. We must fight back.

Finally, we have the challenge of Big Tech and social media companies. Again, many of these companies have produced invaluable products and drive innovation in society. There's no denying that the Google search engine and Apple products have improved our quality of life, and Instagram and other platforms bring joy to millions of users. However, Big Tech, especially Amazon through online sales and Apple through its App Store, possess unrivaled intelligence about the markets in which they are competing. That knowledge gives them a leg up over competitors and allows them to move to limit competition.

Social media companies have also designed products that feed on attention, push toxic and controversial content, and deepen partisan divides, and these companies exert unrivaled control over political speech.[15] Shortly before the 2020 election, when the *New York Post* broke the story that Hunter Biden's laptop had incriminating evidence about his family's ties to foreign countries, Twitter shut down the *Post*'s account and prevented users from sharing the story.

The *Post* hadn't violated any of Twitter's standards. The story mattered to a presidential election. The initial reporting proved accurate, and the FBI even opened an investigation into Hunter Biden's activities later. But Twitter deprived the public of the truth out of a clear political bias.[16] It was an unprecedented insertion of bias into the election.

It's not just Twitter. For a time, Facebook silenced discussion of the possibility that COVID-19 had originated from a laboratory in China. When the Biden administration changed its tune and called for serious investigations, Facebook dutifully followed and allowed discussion again. YouTube also stifled views that differed from the acceptable Centers for Disease Control and Prevention narrative, including removing a roundtable hosted by a sitting governor.[17] Google has likewise been accused of manipulating search results in favor of Democratic politicians and going after right-wing news organizations.[18] And Amazon has downgraded or even stopped selling books by conservative authors.[19]

Many in Big Tech often demonstrate little regard for American interests. Some, like Microsoft, have been admirably willing partners of the Pentagon. But in Silicon Valley, partnering with the military isn't quite so popular, as evidenced by Google backing out of its work on a military AI project after some employees protested.[20] Meanwhile, many Silicon Valley firms are happy to expand their businesses in China—and in some cases look the other way from their human rights abuses.[21] For example, Apple has become a willing a partner of the Chinese Communist Party's ambitions and surveillance state, turning over data to the CCP, removing apps upon request, and reportedly cutting a deal worth $275 billion to help China develop leading technology, including through workforce training and commitments to buying Chinese-made components.[22]

Big Tech Needs Fixing

If data can open new doors to innovation, it also opens dangerous windows into our lives. We need to give American citizens greater control over when those windows open and who gets to look inside.

To begin with, America needs the passage of national privacy and transparency laws to create nationwide standards for how companies handle consumers' data, ensuring transparency into their practices and basic protections for consumers.[23] As is, users end up signing away much of their personal data when they click "accept" on a website's or app's terms. But who reads that stuff? Who has time to comb through legalese to order some food to be delivered? Even if you wanted to opt out, it's not like there are alternatives that don't invade your privacy. Consumers should be able to see readily what data is being and has been collected and to know where that data is going: What third parties purchase it? How are the platforms processing that data? Users should have to agree to share their data before it is collected, rather than opt out as is the current standard. Data encryption, as supported by HIPAA, would help protect against data breaches or hacks as well.

At the same time, we ought to build up our own stores of data. Washington ought to create an open-source data infrastructure that makes anonymized information, for example data collected by government-funded research projects, public for use by students, researchers, and innovators.[24] It could also incentivize companies and academics to create open data sources, such as by allowing them to write off the work and infrastructure costs.

We must also address China's abuse of U.S. data. The government should demand reciprocity in data rules from China. The Communist government may never open their metaphorical data ports. If so, we should limit their access to ours. Chinese companies would pay for the Party's intransigence, but what choice do we have? We can't let China continue to take advantage of us and exploit American data. Likewise, we must take a hard look at Chinese companies like TikTok and subject them to greater scrutiny than American companies.

Even if we pass national privacy laws and deal with China, we still must take steps to protect our society against the corrosive and censorious effects of Big Tech's power. We should begin by defining what *good* looks like. What would it mean for social media companies to become better stewards of their position as the dominant platforms for discourse and political speech in America?

Three principles should be front of mind for policymakers as they address the risks of Big Tech and for leaders in the technology sector as they consider self-governing actions they might take:

First, they should reduce the insidious social and political effects of social media. We can't let social media platforms continue to steal our sons' and daughters' attention, self-esteem, and happiness, and we can't let them inflict their political agendas on an unsuspecting nation. It is critical that we take full measure of the social and political cost of these companies.[25]

Second, they should not promote the interests of authoritarian states or compromise our national interest. Companies shouldn't be able to fund China's strategic technologies, military buildup, or genocide. At the same time, companies should embrace working with the Pentagon and designing and developing technologies or industries critical to our national security and the competition with China.

Third, they should enable free speech and expression within their enterprises and across society. As two conservative economists put it, a healthy society "should place the creation and diffusion of ideas at center stage."[26] That doesn't mean we shouldn't have standards.

Good sense and the law dictate that certain virulent or illegal content should be restricted. However, political speech must be protected. Its stifling has repercussions well beyond any one election. It diminishes the health of our republic.

In practical terms, these goals would be accomplished through a set of legislative actions and rules. We can start small: limit endless scrolling on platforms like Instagram; give users more control over what they see; curtail autoplay features; and make the algorithms of social media platforms, like Facebook and Twitter, public. Each action would reduce the social costs of these platforms and advance transparency and free expression.

We also need to have an honest debate about how large social media platforms uniquely inform and distort political debate in America. They amplify a few voices; by one estimate, 90 percent of tweets come from 10 percent of the users, the majority of whom lean to the progressive side.[27] And they silence others. We need transparent data on political algorithms—how many conservatives do they ban versus liberals?

We could go a step further by reforming Section 230 of the Communications Decency Act of 1996. Section 230 contains two key provisions on this issue. The first protects online platforms from being held liable for the content posted on them. The second protects those service providers from liability for moderating or removing content. The law covers not just social media but also online news sites and other platforms that host third-party content—collectively called "interactive computer services." But in the case of social media platforms that dominate the public square, Section 230 effectively empowers some of the most powerful companies in the world. It gives them cover to avoid responsibility for what happens on their platforms while also claiming control over what's allowed on those platforms. We ought to revisit it to find the best way to make social media platforms responsible for the content they share, or don't share, as the case may be.[28]

Finally, we might consider breaking up Big Tech's control over information. As Senator Tom Cotton put it in 2021, "Google controls more than 90 percent of the search market, Amazon controls 80 percent of the e-book market and a huge share of cloud services, Facebook controls a majority of social media, and Apple—along with Google—shares total control of the App Store market."[29] TikTok may have encroached on Meta's position in the social media market, but Google, Amazon, and Apple remain dominant, which endows them with tremendous power.

Many in Congress have proposed bills to "break up Big Tech," but few agree on what that would mean. The most promising approach, I believe, would be to address the overwhelming monopoly in market intelligence of many Big Tech companies. That would mean limiting Amazon's ability to prioritize its own wares on its own platform or requiring Apple to allow users to purchase apps with something other than Apple Pay. These existing practices stifle competition and innovation and limiting them would advance the renewal agenda and protect American speech.

This isn't a simple story of big bad companies or good companies doing bad things. These same technological giants also drive much of American innovation. In the race for quantum computing mastery, for example, Google, Intel, and IBM are keeping the United States toe-to-toe with a Chinese-government-backed consortium.[30] We have to be careful. Excessive, heavy-handed regulation is a tax on innovation, competition, and opportunity—and a subsidy for the rich and powerful. Whatever we do, we can't do that.

Yet two things are indisputably true: first, the status quo must change, and second, we must not give the government powers that we don't want it to have. As a conservative, I'm wary of the three horsemen of government intrusion: overreach, failure, and unintended consequences. All three are very real concerns when it comes to Big Tech. Republicans should not forget that while technology companies possess unnerving power, government wields the ultimate power. We must not let the zeal to take on Big Tech give way to an embrace of federal overreach. Nor should we let it endanger our national security. The headlong rush to "break up Big Tech" could, in the words of President Trump's national security adviser, Robert C. O'Brien, "hurt the U.S. and strengthen the hand of our greatest geopolitical rival, the People's Republic of China."[31] The great irony is that these companies are central to addressing the threat of technological inferiority posed by China. We must balance these competing demands—but technology executives, and their employees, have a duty as well.

These are American companies, many founded by immigrants or the children of immigrants who came to our shores because of the unique promise of America. Our way of life and talent made their enormous success possible. They thrive in the open space created by American law and strength. They should comport themselves in ways that acknowledge and protect this privilege.

The Competition for Data

With our house in order, we can turn our eyes abroad. Today, there is no agreed-to set of rules for how to manage the flow of data between countries or how to protect users' privacy. In that vacuum, the fight for leadership in the digital age has begun.

Europe's approach, the General Data Protection Regulation, is predictably heavy-handed. It impedes innovation and stifles the free flow of data in the name of privacy and government control—and makes the user experience terrible, considering you must accept cookies on every website you open. Those rules may not appear all that bad, but they exist to serve the interests of the European Union, not Americans. Far worse is China's tyrannical, Communist model that disregards privacy and seeks outright control over people's data and lives.

The Chinese Communist Party has a vision for dominating the digital age, and it starts with control of data. Xi Jinping sees data as central not only to innovation but to China's national rejuvenation. He has made clear his intention to "give full expression to the advantages of mass data,"[32] and the CCP has built a massive governing and technical infrastructure to that effect.

In the earliest days of the COVID-19 pandemic, even as it dissembled about the nature and origin of the virus, the Chinese Communist Party turned to data to augment its quarantine and lockdown policies. Every night, Chinese citizens had to enter their health information, including their temperature and any symptoms they had, into an app. They would then receive a color-coded QR code. Green meant they were cleared to leave their homes. Yellow usually signaled a few more days of lockdown. Red meant extended quarantine. Almost overnight, hundreds of millions of Chinese lived at the whim of that little QR code on their phone.[33] Of course, they had no right to question it. Of course, the Communist rulers kept all the data. They had expanded their digital panopticon over the country, but it was just the latest step in their campaign for digital control.

The CCP's techno-totalitarian vision began over a generation ago with the "Great Firewall," a combination of laws and technologies that restrict the flow of data in and out of China, in part by blocking foreign websites. Under Xi, the Communist government then mandated that the government could access all data generated in the country. Be it a conversation on WeChat or transaction records from a mobile payment app, no data is exempt. Even the most prodigious Chinese companies, like Didi and Alibaba, aren't safe. Beijing has further forced state-backed companies to store data on Party-approved cloud servers and walled-off the transfer of data out of the country. Communist China is not concerned about protecting users from the overreach of its own Big Tech; it is concerned about control, and it's made clear there are few limits on its reach.

Communist China's ambitions do not end at the water's edge. It seeks to spread this model beyond China's borders and become, as two former Trump administration officials put it, "the world's most powerful data broker."[34] In the past year, the Party passed a raft of new laws and regulations giving the Party access to data held by Chinese companies operating abroad and by foreign companies operating in China. No one doing business in or with China is exempt. Meanwhile, Chinese companies keep expanding their reach around the world. Huawei's 5G equipment may have lost favor, but its cloud services, which pose just as great a security threat, are now in use in over forty countries.[35]

China also used the 2022 Winter Olympics to launch its digital currency. The digital yuan, as it's been called, would give the CCP another vehicle for monitoring and controlling information about individuals' habits. Any purchases made would undoubtedly be recorded and made available for CCP data analytics. More concerning is the power it gives Beijing to restrict payments and transactions and to evade U.S. sanctions. If its digital currency could reach broad circulation, the CCP would be positioned to set up its own payments system, and the United States would be measurably weakened.

All of this gives Beijing functional control over such a quantity of data that it can further fuel innovation and expand its repressive system of control and surveillance—even beyond its own borders. Chinese agencies have built the capacity to collect foreign data from places like Twitter and Facebook and use it to hunt down and punish critics all over the world.[36] And the Communist Party seeks to spread its model of data governance and expand its access to data by building internet infrastructure abroad and boosting digital trade. This is just the above-aboard policies. There's no greater perpetrator of data breaches or industrial espionage than the Chinese Communist Party and no greater victim than the American people.

The United States, in other words, cannot ignore the Chinese data threat. It cannot pretend that handling our business domestically will be enough, or that China's reach does not expand beyond its own borders. And we must not look the other way while China promulgates an evil, totalitarian campaign of digital control. We need a vision for the digital age that protects privacy and maximizes the free flow of data so that we can continue to innovate and grow. And we need to realize that vision quickly. There's no time to waste with Beijing on the march.

An American Vision for the Digital Age

FreeMarkets, the company I ran in Pittsburgh, operated at the vanguard of the digital age. We created an online marketplace where buyers could put out tenders for products and suppliers could answer with prices. It was real-time data exchange, via the early internet, the kind of business model that could not have existed even earlier that decade. It spurred competition and drove prices down for U.S.

businesses. And in doing so, we built a thriving business, employing hundreds of people in and around Pittsburgh.

FreeMarkets was proof of two concepts. First, when data can flow freely between businesses and across borders, it can generate market-changing innovations and good jobs, and it can spur dynamism in our country. And second, there are costs to the free flow of data. Some quickly became evident; there's no denying that the digital economy hurt some American producers and put people out of work by opening up overseas markets. Some costs became clear with time. Many countries don't want a level playing field; they want to game the global market to their benefit. And while businesses may readily want to share pricing data online, not all data is fit for public or corporate consumption. It will be vital to protect user privacy, for example, while still encouraging innovation-enhancing uses of data.

China's vision for the digital age places each of those costs on American shoulders. It creates unfair trade and business environments. It seeks to undermine American businesses and jobs, and it sees privacy as an obstacle to be overcome, not a right to protect. The America vision must counter China's illicit intentions, and it must build a network of trusted participant countries, who agree to three binding principles.

First, maximize the flow of data. Given that the quantity of data a country can access will likely result in a sustainable edge in innovation and productivity, and therefore security, and given our size disadvantage relative to China, we should focus on maximizing flows. *Second, the free flow of data cannot come at the cost of privacy and security.* Contrary to what some think, it doesn't have to; a wealth of so-called privacy-enhancing technologies is at our fingertips. *And third, we must help those whose livelihoods may suffer from the creative destruction that data can trigger.* American workers ought not to be left behind in the race to out-innovate China. These three principles should become the basis for a data governance regime, led by the United States.

There is already a powerful example of such agreements. In 1996, dozens of countries accounting for nearly 95 percent of world trade in information technology ratified the Information Technology Agreement, a multilateral trade deal under the WTO. The agreement ultimately eliminated all tariffs for hundreds of IT-related capital goods, intermediate inputs, and final products—from machine tools to motherboards to personal computers. The agreement proved to be an important impetus for the subsequent wave of the IT revolution, a competitive spur that led to productivity gains for firms and price declines for consumers. Likewise, the U.S.–Mexico–Canada trade agreement negotiated by the Trump administration codified strong data standards, and in 2019, the G-20 leaders, guided by Japan, produced the Osaka Track vision for "data free flow with trust," an initiative to produce a coherent international data framework. The initiative held up many of the same principles that I propose here but never moved beyond the words on the page.

The internet auctions we hosted at FreeMarkets were grounded in these same trust principles. They worked a little like eBay, except the purchaser would put out requests and suppliers would bid against each other to get the job. One of our clients was the U.S. Navy. In their first auction, they sought bids for an ejector seat component used in most naval aircraft. Navy officials watched as offers rolled in and prices tumbled down. After less than an hour, the contract went to a California-based company at an excellent price for the taxpayer. It was just one of numerous auctions that saved our users, many of whom were government agencies, over $1 billion.

At the time, the internet wasn't exactly a trusted platform for doing business. The idea of buying and selling with customers halfway around the country or even the world, without ever meeting face-to-face, spooked some old-fashioned businessmen. They questioned whether they could rely on—and trust—those on the other end of a transaction. Yet the Pentagon, which has some of the most rigorous standards for who it uses as a supplier or service provider, trusted FreeMarkets' platform and its network of suppliers.

We were on a path to building what Keith Krach calls a "clean network." In 1996, Keith cofounded Ariba, a business-to-business e-commerce company that was a close cousin to FreeMarkets, and Ariba acquired FreeMarkets in 2004, under the leadership of then-CEO Bob Calderoni. I stayed on the team as the president of Ariba until 2005. Ariba's strategy was all about trust between the company and its users.

Keith brought that trust-based mind-set to the Trump administration when, in 2018, he took over the State Department's economic bureau. He jumped into the middle of the burgeoning technological competition with China, and under the direction of Secretary Mike Pompeo, Krach orchestrated the U.S. response to Huawei selling its 5G hardware around the world.

Together, Pompeo and Krach developed a concept for the "5G Clean Network"—a consortium of countries, companies, and civil organizations that would agree to keep Huawei out of their networks. The premise was that Americans needed to be protected from foreign surveillance and predation when communicating at home and abroad. That meant no Chinese equipment, but also no snooping by other countries. So they dug back into the trust playbook and began building "a network of partners *based on trust* and rooted in internationally accepted standards."[37]

It was an undeniable success. It brought allies and partners on board and reversed Huawei's momentum. As such, it exemplified the right approach for America's data leadership: start with principles, add partners who embrace them, and then build out a network where all members trust each other and therefore can cooperate and communicate seamlessly. No other country but the United States has the wherewithal, will, or standing to build a trusted digital network like this. But many would welcome it. We should start with our closest allies, especially the United Kingdom, Canada, Australia, and Japan. Deep bonds of trust already exist among us. Why not deepen them around data sharing? From there we can expand.

Principally, we can build secure telecommunications networks, as was the goal of the Clean Network. There's no place in our data coalition for Huawei's 5G technology or any other Chinese-made telecom network. In the near term, we'll need to use trusted tech from allies—such as Ericsson and Nokia. In the long run, we need to get back in the driver's seat of network technology, as discussed previously.

We can also use the privacy-enhancing technologies that surround us. We have, for example, the capacity to anonymize medical data and then use it for the development of new treatments, drugs, and procedures or to train machine learning algorithms without creating databases of user data.[38] We also have blockchain. Known mostly as the technical basis for cryptocurrencies, blockchain can best be understood as a record of exchanges. Usually these will be financial transactions, but they could also record the transfer of data packets from one entity to another, be it a person or an organization.

Each block in the chain records the most recent exchanges, and complex cryptography secures the chain. Once a block is set, the data stored in it cannot be manipulated or accessed in secret. Moreover, authority within a blockchain comes from participants, not from a centralized figure. Whereas a bank might oversee and record all transfers in and out of accounts held with it, in a blockchain, the participants manage the ledger by consensus. Blockchain technology, in other words, is a "trust machine," to quote the *Economist*.[39] It has a ways to go to prove its value and reliability, but it could be a valuable tool for free and private exchange of data.

The weak link in the chain is the participants themselves. If they are trustworthy, the network would be as secure as possible. If not, vulnerabilities arise. That's where Keith's trust network concept is essential. If we advance this vision for a free and prosperous digital future and assemble a network of trusted partners, we can build a new framework for handling the digital age that would help ensure the United States has access to the sort of data that drives innovation. We can build a new network of trusted partners to offset China's built-in advantages. And we can build a new frontier for American leadership on the global stage.

This data strategy has two key elements. First, America must set clear domestic rules for the management and use of data, address China's abuses of our open market, and confront the corrosive power of the keepers of most data, Big Tech. Second, we should take leadership over the digital age and build a trusted network, and international framework, that encourages free flows of data, protects privacy, and counters China's techno-authoritarian vision.

I have no illusions about how extraordinarily complex achieving this will be. Each dimension of this trusted network addresses a different problem and requires a different set of expertise and leadership to bring to fruition. However, each piece fits together, and each serves the same overarching goal: accelerating American renewal.

Opening the arteries of data flows with friends and partners will give innovators access to vital information and collaborators. Building open data infrastructure at home will likewise give students and researchers a critical tool to pursue their work and push the frontiers of science and technology. Opening the technology industry to greater competition and innovation is an investment in what America does best: start, build, and prosper. And salving the social wounds opened by Big Tech will help heal our society.

There are costs to what is proposed here. Open data flows may take a toll on some American businesses, just as free trade did. We must learn our lesson from those past failures and ensure any negative impacts, whether job losses or reduced wages, are offset through strong programs to help affected workers adapt to the digital economy, such as those outlined in preceding chapters.

Yet the potential benefits cannot be ignored. This is a chance to reset our relationships with our friends to make sure we're putting our most sacred principles and interests first, chiefly privacy, liberty, and economic opportunity. More pressing than that, we have an opportunity to reassert American leadership and to confront China. The Chinese techno-totalitarian model is an affront to what we hold dear and a grave threat to our way of life. We cannot concede to a world where Communist leaders in Beijing dictate the rules of the road for anyone trying to do business. By moving forward aggressively in the race for data supremacy, we can guard against that ever happening.

PART III

Leading Renewal

CHAPTER 7

Confront China, Secure America

If we want to have a free twenty-first century, and not the Chinese century of which Xi Jinping dreams, the old paradigm of blind engagement with China simply won't get it done. We must not continue it and we must not return to it.

—Secretary of State Michael Pompeo, at the Richard Nixon Presidential Library, July 23, 2020

I first visited China in the spring of 1992. After leaving the Army, I set off on an eight-month trip around the world, which eventually took me to Beijing. During my travels, I had read a book by Paul Theroux called *Riding the Iron Rooster*, cataloging his journey through China in the 1980s. His stories of travel aboard the "Iron Rooster"—the network of dilapidated old trains connecting city to city—captivated me. I decided I had to see it for myself.

From Beijing, I rode south to Nanking, then to Shanghai, Guilin, and finally to Guangzhou before crossing over to Hong Kong. The more than two-thousand-mile, multicity trek allowed me to witness firsthand the urban centers of eastern China as well as the vastness of the countryside in between. It was a very different country then. The streets of Shanghai and Beijing were chock-full of bicycles; there were few cars, and just a small number of skyscrapers dotted the skyline. There were two currencies, one for locals and one for visitors. I remember taking early-morning runs through the city parks, surrounded by elder Chinese practicing tai chi. My presence was as foreign to them as theirs was to me. I felt so disconnected one day in Shanghai that I sought out the famous Peace Hotel just to find an English newspaper and learn what was happening at home.

Roll the tape forward just over a decade, and I returned to Beijing, this time serving as a U.S. government official. We arrived outside the city in one of the most modern airports in the world, then headed downtown. As our procession of vehicles careened down China's ten-lane highways, I looked out onto a transformed city. The quiet bike-laden roads I remembered from my earlier travels had been replaced by skyscrapers, cranes, and cars.

I probably visited China a dozen times between 2005 and 2008, often traveling on U.S. aircraft, first as the undersecretary of commerce for export administration and then later as part of the delegation with Hank Paulson, then secretary of the Treasury.

It was remarkable to me how much China had changed and how quickly. I had seen it first as this country on the verge of modernity. Now it had arrived. It was the most significant up-and-coming power in the world—and a serious threat to America.

In June of 2006, Saint Vincent College, a Catholic college near Pittsburgh, invited me to speak about the rise of China. At the time, most in Washington and the business community were salivating at the prospect of penetrating the massive Chinese market, convinced that China's accession to the World Trade Organization (WTO) a few years earlier would render it a "responsible stakeholder" in the international community, as the administration called it. But in my position at Commerce, I saw the threat of the Chinese Communist Party.

In my remarks to the Saint Vincent community that day, I issued an early warning about China's pervasive theft of intellectual property.[1] Roughly 90 percent of Chinese software had been acquired illicitly from other countries and mostly from the United States. China's flouting of IP law undercut American innovators. Over the course of the year, I continued to raise alarms about China's dismal human rights record and its use of U.S. technologies to advance its dangerous military buildup.[2] To guard against misuse, I pushed for aggressive controls on tech exports to China to guard against these three overriding concerns: IP theft, human rights abuses, and military expansion. We made incremental progress, but the status quo in Washington persisted.

In 2006, when I served on the National Security Council staff, Secretary Paulson kicked off the Strategic Economic Dialogue, which was his attempt to strengthen the U.S.-China relationship in a manner that advanced U.S. strategic objectives.

Specifically, the initiative was intended to be a lever for applying pressure on China to open their economy and further embrace free market principles, since it had so far failed to live up to the commitments it made upon joining the WTO. The administration came in with a specific agenda, laying out the market access needed across industries and its desire for them to end their currency manipulation and enforce greater intellectual property protections. However, while the dialogue created a place for conversation, it objectively failed to achieve our goals. The administration was, in retrospect, rearranging the deck chairs on the *Titanic* in U.S.-China relations, and soon the global financial crisis superseded it.

During one of my trips to China the following year, at the height of the financial crisis, there was a large ceremonial meeting between the U.S. delegation and the Chinese Communist Party President, Hu Jintao. Amid all the pomp and circumstance, Secretary Paulson and I, along with a single interpreter, ducked into a small room behind the great hall for a quiet discussion of the financial crisis with Hu. We laid out our plan to stabilize the U.S. and global economies. Hu reassured us that China would be a stable counterpart as we maneuvered through the crisis, and they were.

Yet, despite this moment of critical cooperation, it was increasingly clear that the administration—and the bipartisan consensus that it represented—was wrong on China. The Bush administration aspired for China to become a "responsible stakeholder" in the international system. As I came to see, China had no intention of following through on this aspiration. The writing was on the wall as early as 2005. Even then, while it pursued an aggressive plan for military modernization, China regularly reneged on its commitments to economic reform, whether around the role of state-owned enterprises, market access to key industries, or intellectual property protections.

I saw the Chinese Communist Party's malfeasance firsthand. As the Commerce Department official in charge of protecting sensitive goods, I worked to restrict sales of U.S. tech to Chinese military-affiliated organizations and warned of the dangers of China's technological ambitions.[3] I worked to do the same while at the National Security Council and then at the Treasury, where I regularly found myself face-to-face with my Chinese counterparts. It was in those meetings with Chinese officials and in my perch in the administration that I and others began to perceive the growing risk of China.

Despite a growing number of warning signs, America continued down the wrong path over the decade plus that followed, long after I had left the government. When Xi Jinping ascended as general secretary of the Chinese Communist Party and president of the country in 2013, he declared his intention to lay "the foundation for a future where we will win the initiative and have the dominant position."[4] Xi then committed the nation's resources to that goal. The CCP accelerated its military modernization and built a massive missile arsenal and the world's largest Navy and presented a ten-year plan—dubbed Made in China 2025—which committed massive state subsidies to achieve Chinese leadership in the most important high-tech industries, like information technology and aerospace, and stepped up R&D and innovation support.[5] On top of that, this mandate required companies operating in China to turn over their proprietary technologies to Chinese partners, and what it couldn't obtain "legitimately" through state-mandated technology transfers, it pirated and stole—often from U.S. companies.[6]

Xi also launched the Belt and Road Initiative to further its economic activity through trade and investment abroad. At Xi's directive, the Party began to throw its weight around in Asia. It built islands in the South China Sea and threatened America's allies with military and paramilitary troops. Australia, Japan, and others weathered repeated economic threats and coercion. Meanwhile, we lost hundreds of billions of dollars' worth of intellectual property and state secrets to Chinese espionage as Beijing continued to fall way short of what it had committed to and what we had hoped. As Aaron Friedberg put it, "Instead of a liberal and cooperative partner, China has become an increasingly wealthy and powerful competitor, repressive at home and aggressive abroad."[7]

Sadly, while all this happened, America's stance toward China barely evolved until the Trump administration broke the status quo in 2017. It redefined China as an adversary and competitor and, led by U.S. Trade Representative Robert Lighthizer, highlighted the raw deal that the United States had gotten in its bilateral economic relationship with China. The centerpiece of the president's agenda—a shift to fair and reciprocal trade—was overdue, and his stance on China earned bipartisan support. Congress also did its part to help protect American technologies from Chinese theft and cooption.[8] These steps are just the start.

It bears repeating that our dispute is not with the Chinese people but with the Chinese Communist Party. The CCP subjugates the people. It violates human rights and abuses its neighbors. It has set the country on its current course, and its actions and intentions are to blame for the heightened competition—not the intentions of the Chinese people or, crucially, of the United States. From 1979 until 2016, the United States made every effort to work with Communist China, help it develop, and bring it into the fold of law-abiding nations. America shifted from engagement to competition only after it had become clear that the CCP had no intentions of reforming or becoming anything but a bad actor.

The aggression, abuses, and ambitions of Communist China make it the greatest external threat to American renewal. The threat exists on two timetables. In the near term, the CCP could move to seize Taiwan out of fear that China's extensive internal weaknesses could soon render it incapable of doing so. This is principally a military and political threat, so to deter it, America must strengthen its military position immediately and make it clear to Xi Jinping and the CCP that we take the threat seriously. We must sprint to ready ourselves, for we have no time to waste.

In the long run, we face a marathon competition for supremacy but lack a plan to compete and win. China's leaders believe we are in decline and desire to keep it that way. However, China's economic and political problems far exceed our own. While I'd take our position in this race over theirs any day, victory is not assured. For that, our nation needs a comprehensive strategy to compete and win against China in the economic and technological domains.

Comprehensive strategies are hard to develop and harder still to execute. For one thing, the federal government simply is not organized for our era of technological competition and economic warfare. Unless we reform how Washington makes and implements policy in those arenas, we're in for a rough ride against China. For another, the China challenge is so complex, so far-reaching, that it will stress the entire federal government, as well as the private sector. We'll need to step up militarily, politically, economically, and technologically, and we'll need to fight for liberty and individual dignity in a way we haven't since the Cold War. That will require unprecedented levels of coordination and vision across not just government but our entire country. In other words, it will take leadership at the pinnacles of power to confront China and make it possible for America to renew herself.[9]

The China Strategy

An economic strategy for confronting China should consist of five parts. First, we must extend the Trump administration's model of fair trade. Second, we must reduce our dependence on China and secure our supply chains. Third, we must stop funding China's military modernization, technological ambitions, and human rights abuses. And fourth, we must stand up to the CCP by protecting American innovation and holding China accountable for its abuses. Finally, we should also look abroad—to our friends and allies—to help advance our goals of technological supremacy. By working with our allies, we will be better able to accomplish our shared goal of preserving a free and fair world economy.

Protect Fair Trade

For many years, I advocated a balanced trade agenda that would, as I said in a speech in Philadelphia in 2008, advance the "competitiveness and success of the U.S. economy...and take steps to mitigate some of [the] negative consequences of dynamic global competition."[10] Getting China right was central to that.

I never agreed with the naive hope, held by some in the Bush and Clinton administrations, that trade would make Communist China democratic or reduce tensions. I did, however, see the potential for fair trade governed by strict standards of reciprocity to deliver cheaper goods into U.S. households and for China to become an enormous emerging market for American know-how and goods, which would help grow American businesses and create jobs at home. But it would only be possible if China had the necessary incentives to follow the rules or would otherwise be held accountable for its failure to do so.

Unfortunately, my worst fears about China came true. In the end, Americans did gain access to lower-cost products, and the world economy did become an extraordinary web of buyers, sellers, suppliers, and makers. But the costs were enormous. Enticed by cheap labor and the CCP's policies designed to attract them, companies moved production lines to China. American communities were gutted as a result, especially industrial towns where local factories were the biggest employer. Moreover, China never adequately or reciprocally opened its market, so American manufacturers, businesses, and workers never got an opportunity to reap the rewards of the relationship. Ultimately, America became dangerously dependent upon Communist China for critical supplies, components, and materials. China violated every rule, and efficiency and cost savings for consumers came at the cost of resiliency for American industry and jobs for American workers.[11]

Now we must rebalance our trade relations around three concerns. First, trade should be conducted under fair conditions that help American businesses grow and create American jobs. Second, the desire for fair trade does not mean that every industry deserves subsidies or handouts. And third, as Robert Lighthizer put it, "A sensible trade policy strikes a balance among economic security, economic efficiency, and the needs of working people."[12] That is, the impact of trade on our communities matters and must be considered equally alongside any benefits of free trade.

The commitment of Lighthizer and his colleagues to this notion of fair trade ruffled some feathers in Washington, but they were returning us to a proper, balanced approach to global commerce. Our trade policies should seek to increase market access and lower the costs of imports, but they also must ensure, to again quote Reagan, "free and fair market conditions" and should raise the real incomes of Americans.[13] That's what fair trade means, and we should not lose sight of it again.

The Chinese Communist Party rejects this concept of fair trade. It violates the terms of the WTO, places levies on U.S. goods and commodities, and gives subsidies to its own companies—all with the goal of undermining the competitiveness of foreign companies. So long as those practices continue, we should continue to employ tariffs in priority sectors where China distorts the market.

We also ought to investigate why China keeps getting such favorable treatment in global organizations and in global markets. How is the world's second largest economy still drawing loans from U.S.-funded and founded institutions like the World Bank? Why does the WTO allow China to self-identify as a "developing" economy, thereby enjoying benefits and preferential treatment that should be reserved for actual developing countries for whom such benefits were intended?

The CCP plays the system to its benefit, and to our detriment. American innovators, businesses, and workers cannot be expected to compete with a country that twists the rules to its advantage, exploits every conceivable loophole, and steals trade secrets, allowing it to get ahead without putting in the work or investment. If we are serious about restoring America's competitiveness, we will have to confront these challenges.

However, as I learned firsthand in my negotiations with Chinese leaders at the Department of the Treasury, the CCP will never hold up their end of the bargain unless compelled to by us. They will continue to steal our technologies and jobs, then turn around and ask us for trade concessions. So we must be tougher and more vigilant than we have been in the past.

Enforcing reciprocity is key. Chinese companies like Tencent, the gaming titan, can do business freely in the United States and even own large portions of America's gaming industry, with minimal review. No U.S. company could do the same in China. The relationship is fundamentally lopsided, and it must change. We should review Chinese companies' presence in the United States to identify the critical sectors in which American producers are not getting a fair shake—then move to redress the imbalances in the relationship.

Reduce Dependency and Decouple Strategically

It would be impossible and unwise to disentangle our economies completely. China is America's largest trading partner. Our country exports roughly $125 billion worth of goods to China every year, supporting over one million American jobs.[14] However, we can no longer depend on China for goods critical to our economy and national security. We must decouple strategically.

In practice that means moving critical supply chains out of China.

Imagine a set of concentric circles. At the center are the things we absolutely must have at home for our own security and necessity. In the second circle are our most trusted friends and partners, like the United Kingdom, Australia, and Japan. We can trust these nations as sources of vital goods, things like semiconductors, pharmaceuticals, and next-generation telecommunications equipment. The next circle includes reliable trade partners—the countries that we trust to produce critical goods but would hesitate to depend on solely. Further out are other dimensions of nonstrategic trade, with countries like China included.

However, even as we reduce our vulnerabilities, we must be strategic. China has spent three decades building leverage over America and her allies. The ideas presented here so far are intended to break that hold. At the same time, ongoing trade relations with China are inevitable. Why not make them work in our favor? Take natural gas as an example. China needs energy, and we have it. States like Pennsylvania should export gas to China. Doing so would not only create good jobs and boost the Commonwealth's economy but also build leverage and strategic advantages of our own.[15]

We should also be smart about what's strategic and what's not. I grew up riding motorcycles and bought a new Harley-Davidson about a decade ago. It's a great machine, made by a great American company. Recently, Harley started building and selling motorcycles in China, and I can't see anything wrong with that.[16] This move allowed Harley-Davidson to expand its business and its jobs in the United States, which also means it can contract with more local suppliers at home. One such shop is KLK Welding in central Pennsylvania. KLK provides welding and assembly services to Harley-Davidson, but it also operates its own welding school, creating a solid job pipeline for young men and women in Hanover and York. It's just one of hundreds of small businesses that benefit enormously from U.S. exports to China. In fact, every year,

Pennsylvania exports over $2.5 billion in goods to China. It's the third largest foreign export destination for my home state.

We must be strategic. Harley can sell bikes in China. Starbucks can sell lattes. The Gap can fabricate shirts and shorts there. But American businesses and their investments in China cannot harm our national security. There is no reason the United States should fund the CCP's advanced technology programs, its military buildup, or its genocide in Xinjiang and widespread human rights abuses. That's where strong and tough-minded investment review comes into play.

Stop Funding China

As is, U.S. dollars finance Communist China's most egregious acts and ambitions. U.S. investors back Chinese semiconductor companies.[17] They also support hundreds of AI developers that work closely with the Chinese People's Liberation Army and even support the party's techno-totalitarian regime.[18] This kind of active investment in China must stop.

Active investment occurs when U.S. firms take a direct stake in a foreign company through vehicles like private equity or venture capital. In the case of China, these deals often serve the CCP's interests, undermining America's security.

Congress should establish a committee to review and curtail such deals. An outbound investment review committee could follow the mold of the Committee on Foreign Investment in the United States (CFIUS), which reviews inbound investments into the country that could threaten the nation's security. As I saw in government, CFIUS is a proven, effective forum; it should be replicated for outgoing investments, too.

This new committee could address active, or direct, investment by requiring firms to report potential investments that meet two conditions: first, that they would be in countries of concern, which the committee would name, and second, that they would involve a technology of concern. The list of countries should be short but include at least China, Russia, Iran, North Korea, Cuba, and Venezuela. The list of technologies could be longer, encompassing the same set of strategic technologies identified for capital investment. As of this writing, lawmakers are negotiating the creation of just such a committee.[19] Let's hope they succeed but do so wisely. The committee must prize efficiency and quick reviews, meaning it must be overseen by someone with the wherewithal to keep things moving, and it must ensure companies cannot evade review simply by moving part of their business overseas. With clear rules, specified countries, and a consistent enforcement, the committee could have an immediate and powerful effect.[20]

However, active investment is a straightforward issue compared to the breadth of so-called portfolio investment in China, wherein American investors take a small, passive stake in a broad portfolio of Chinese stocks, bonds, and other assets. Derek Scissors, an expert on the Chinese economy, found that "American spending on Chinese stocks and bonds reached $1.15 trillion by the end of 2020."[21] The reason is simple: the CCP's subsidies and tax breaks make Chinese companies a good investment, and many American money managers see investing in China as a way to diversify and hedge against a market downturn in the United States—even as they understand the risks in doing so.

We struggled with this tension during my time at Bridgewater, when the firm built out its business in China. Though that business amounted to only 2 percent of our assets by the time I left the firm at the end of 2021, it drew headlines and attention. I understood the criticism, and it is one that most CEOs of large U.S. companies face today. For years, I had butted heads with our founder, Ray Dalio, about our very divergent views on China's direction and the threat it posed to America.[22]

From a business perspective, I worried about the regulatory uncertainty but also the costs to our reputation and our integrity. So, we worked hard to balance our duties to generate high returns for our global investors, who were demanding access to fast-growing markets, particularly China, with the political and substantive dangers of investing in China, given the aggressive posture of President Xi and the Communist Party. From my perspective, we managed our fiduciary responsibilities and the risks reasonably well, but they're unavoidable. The tens of thousands of U.S. businesses that export to China and all the investors holding over a trillion dollars in Chinese assets struggle with the same thing.[23]

They need guidance from Washington.

To begin with, the Securities and Exchange Commission should scrutinize Chinese firms that list on U.S. stock exchanges.[24] If they will not follow the same disclosure rules as every other firm listed or otherwise don't follow our laws, they should be delisted from our exchanges. From there the outbound investment review committee should require investors to report who their counterparties are, if their investment rises above a minimum threshold, and to provide annual disclosures about how much they have invested in China and where. Firms often cannot trace where the money they invest ends up, but the committee could investigate those deals to determine the end point and risk. Start small, restricting direct investments in a few high-risk sectors like semiconductors and genetic engineering and screening portfolio investments for links to those sectors.

Some might say that if U.S. capital doesn't support these Chinese companies, other countries will. Therefore, the argument goes, we ought to stay the course and at least reap the return on the investments. If that's the case, then why aren't we seeing a huge influx of capital to China from other countries? Why aren't venture firms in

Europe or in oil-risk Gulf states leading the charge? Because there is no substitute for U.S. capital.

Whatever excuses may be offered, the truth is inescapable: We cannot honestly say we are competing with China if we are funding their targeted efforts to defeat us and our way of life. New laws and the outbound investment committee will help us change course, but business leaders must take responsibility too and show sound leadership in how they engage with China.

Hold China Accountable

Likewise, we must also address the reality that Communist China remains the greatest source of industrial espionage in the world, and its abuses and aggression have only increased. The Chinese Communist Party's economic warfare is the greatest external threat to American innovation. They steal hundreds of billions of dollars in intellectual property, illicitly acquire U.S. technological secrets, and use investment to control American companies.[25] As a result, we have suffered what FBI Director Chris Wray called, "Chinese theft on a scale so massive that it represents one of the largest transfers of wealth in human history."[26]

Congress has taken the legal steps needed to protect U.S. technologies and secrets, but the bureaucracy hasn't followed through.[27] The Commerce and Treasury Departments need to get their act together. However, playing defense is not enough. We have to go on offense against China's predations.

We should sanction the perpetrators of intellectual property theft, but also the beneficiaries of it, including companies and Chinese Communist Party officials that support and enable it. And we should ensure that no U.S. researchers are working on behalf of the Chinese

Communist Party—it's too often neglected that many students and professors at U.S. universities take money from the Chinese military or affiliated groups. We're only just beginning to come to terms with this threat, and we can't let up.

We also have to hold the Chinese Communist Party accountable for its genocide in Xinjiang, its complicity in the fentanyl epidemic destroying American communities, and its responsibility for the COVID-19 pandemic. Over one million Americans have been killed by the virus, which came out of China and which the CCP lied about and covered up for months, at the expense of countless American lives. We should demand reparations for the deaths and suffering brought on by their mendacity and carelessness.

Likewise, when speaking with the men and women at treatment facilities in Pennsylvania struggling with the opioid and fentanyl crisis, and with the law enforcement officials who are day in and day out fighting this epidemic, it is clear the magnitude of the human cost is overwhelming. China is the primary source of these drugs, and we must sanction all involved in their production and trafficking. We should do the same to Chinese officials responsible for committing one of the worst human rights abuses in recent memory in Xinjiang.[28]

Companies should also be held to account. Not a dime of federal innovation support should go to any firm or entity that engages in joint ventures or research with, shares IP with, or gets investment from the Chinese government. Semiconductor fabricators should not, for example, receive capital from a public-private entity if they are also expanding their business in China, with the CCP's support. Likewise, companies that hide or misrepresent their ties to the Chinese government or military, as many have, ought to face swift retribution from the Justice Department—as should researchers who do the same.[29] The goal isn't to shut companies down but to force transparency. That's the least we can ask of the business community.

Innovate with Allies

As undersecretary of the Treasury during the global financial crisis in 2008, I led negotiations with our European and Asian partners. For months, I lived on the road, going from capital to capital to coordinate a plan to stabilize markets and currencies. They may have been among the most challenging months of my life, but they paid off. Even the Chinese agreed to support the coordinated global effort.

No country other than the United States, including China, could have orchestrated that response. None can claim such a strong network of allies, friends, and would-be partners who trust their leadership, and none can form coalitions or muster the combined trading and market power of advanced economies like the United States. In the words of the Trump administration's National Security Strategy, the "invaluable advantages that our strong relationships with allies and partners deliver"[30] are some of our greatest assets. Those relationships can, as already noted, help us build more resilient supply chains, and they are fundamental to the data strategy. But the advantages need not end there. Our allies should be key partners in helping us win the race for technological leadership.

To begin with, we should build on what already works. The United States, for example, maintains something called the National Technology and Industrial Base. In theory, it facilitates joint research, development, and production of dual-use technologies and weaponry with the United Kingdom, Canada, and Australia. In practice, a web of restrictions undermines it. If we eased those rules, such as the State Department's International Traffic in Arms Regulations, we could open new avenues for multinational innovation.[31] Similarly, why not include Japan in this and other trusted partnerships? Let's expand our innovation efforts beyond the water's edge.

Ultimately, this is a question of trust. We trust Japan deeply on military matters. We trust the United Kingdom and Australia on high-level intelligence sharing. Could we not trust them on innovation? We could, for example, collaborate on and jointly fund research in critical capabilities like quantum sciences. We could also work together to set standards for the adoption and use of emerging technologies. China is committed to twisting international technical standards to their techno-authoritarian vision.[32] We have to counter them. Whichever country sets the rules for which technologies get adopted globally gets fast-tracked to innovation leadership and market access in high-tech sectors.

With trust comes accountability. In the past, some of our allies have not lived up to their commitments. President Trump put NATO on the spot for its indolence, but they aren't the only ones. As we move forward, we have to make sure everyone's doing their part and hold them accountable if not.

Such efforts go hand in hand with American leadership in the digital age. Like the data strategy, these multinational initiatives would be built on trust. They would create space for Americans to collaborate with reliable, committed partners.

The Future of the Global Economy

In the end, all the dimensions of the U.S.-China economic competition proposed here come down to one thing: American leadership. The era of unfettered globalization has ended. What the future looks like hangs in the balance.

The Chinese Communist Party wants to reshape the world in its image. Its strategy to do so is well documented, both here and elsewhere. But the CCP has adopted what it calls a "dual-circulation" model. It intends to become the world leader in critical new technologies and supporting industries, from AI to semiconductors, and therefore to reduce its dependency on all other countries. At the same time, in the words of Xi Jinping, it aspires to "tighten international production chains' dependence on China."[33] To accomplish these goals, the CCP melds massive subsidies, trade barriers, data controls, and industrial espionage with debt-trap diplomacy, infrastructure investments, economic coercion, and a concerted effort to set the rules of the road for new technologies. Effectively, this strategy would place China at the center of the global economy and make it the preeminent technological force.

The world America made welcomed individual liberty and democracy. It promoted prosperity, trade, and the rule of law. Our nation had its share of missteps and abuses, but it believed in the sovereignty of nations. We demonstrated patience and benevolence. We had to watch supposed partners flirt with our adversaries and listen to endless criticisms from countries that depended entirely on our benevolence for their defense. Yet that was the price of peace, and we bore it.

Communist China has no such patience. In 2021, Lithuania dared to allow Taiwan to open a de facto embassy under its own name, not Chinese Taipei, the CCP's preferred euphemism. For that heinous offense, China restricted trade to Lithuania and blocked imports. A similar story played out with the National Basketball Association (NBA), when Daryl Morey, then general manager of the Houston Rockets, dared to criticize China's human rights record. The NBA traded market share for principles and swiftly condemned him. They knew Communist China's playbook: follow their rules; say what they want you to say; and accept their demands, or you suffer harmful punishment. There's no space for freedom or disagreement, for sovereignty or independence. That's what the world will look like if the CCP achieves its aims.

Such an outcome seems almost certain unless America steps up and lead. No other country can stand up to the might of the Chinese Communist state. No other nation will defend our way of life. We must lead the way by offering an alternative, uniquely American vision, marked by free and fair trade; respect for property, IP, and the rule of law; and access to the most vibrant economy in the world—one where people and companies can operate safe from government control. That's something all freedom-loving people can get behind.

America has the potential to correct its relationship with China and implement a broad, ambitious strategy to form a new economic status quo that favors our most precious national interests. But absent reforms and stronger leadership, Washington will inevitably struggle to get it done.

In 2005, my role as commerce undersecretary in charge of overseeing export controls was a lonely redoubt at the intersection of national security and economics. Most of the federal government was organized around big spheres. The Treasury and Commerce Departments dealt with economic affairs. The State Department handled foreign policy. The Pentagon looked after the nation's defenses, but no department or agency accounted for this intersection. Despite the increasing importance of export controls, a small team with minimal institutional support was all there was.

The longtime bureaucrat and administrator Rufus Miles once wrote that "where you stand depends on where you sit."[34] In other words, you tell me what office someone comes from, and I'll tell you what they'll argue. Miles's Law, as the saying is called, held true across my experience in public service. Officials from the trade and commerce side lobbied on behalf of U.S. business interests. Pentagon and intelligence community representatives prioritized security. My role at the Commerce Department put me in the middle. I was viewed as too hawkish and security-minded for the economists and business interests. More often than not, the final decision represented an uneasy compromise between business and national security considerations.

Later, at the National Security Council and at the Treasury, when I was dealing with issues like foreign investment in U.S. companies and innovation, it became clear these problems were indicative of a deeper gap in the executive branch. Policy questions with major implications for the nation's security, trade, technology, and prosperity had no natural home in government. Minimal top-down vision for how to balance what were often viewed as competing priorities, much less for dealing with a rapidly changing world, compounded the issue.

For years, my old friend and mentor, Bob Kimmitt, who had a distinguished government career culminating as deputy secretary of the Treasury, advocated to make the Treasury secretary a formal member of the National Security Council to address this gap. "The concept of national security has broadened considerably since the NSC's early decades, elevating economic and financial issues to crucial elements to our nation's security," he wrote in 2012. The solution, "the Treasury secretary...should be at every meeting to advise on how economic and security issues intersect, and to ensure that the United States is using its economic and financial strength in the most effective way."[35] Six years later, Congress listened. It was a big step in the right direction, but problems persist.

After a disastrous U.S. withdrawal from Afghanistan and economic appeasement of Russia and Germany over the Nord Stream 2 gas pipeline, Vladimir Putin believed he had leverage over the West and invaded Ukraine. While the United States and its allies mobilized to sanction Russia in response, their response still came too slowly and incrementally. And that was against Russia and its weak, relatively disconnected economy. China is a different ball game. Imagine if we had to conduct such a coordinated game plan against a country so central to the global economy. Imagine the leverage Beijing could pull against us, so long as we rely on them for critical goods and supply lines. We would need to have a far more decisive, cohesive, and internationally coordinated response—and frankly Washington is not up to the task.

The executive branch just isn't organized for this kind of economic and strategic competition. On China, policymakers still waffle over whether Americans should be funding the CCP's technological and military ambitions and whether companies should be allowed to receive taxpayer money and still expand their presence in China. And on the technology front, it is captured by the same tired exchanges debating between heavy-handed government subsidies and hands-off free market orthodoxy.

It's time for Washington to meet the moment. It would be easy to say, "Forget it. It can't be done." But as we've seen throughout our nation's history, when circumstances demand it, our government can evolve. Now's one of those times.

Reforming Washington for the China Competition

For most of the nation's history, military affairs took place in the "War Department," essentially the Army, and in the Department of the Navy. The State Department took care of diplomacy. That arrangement continued all the way through World War II. Coming out of the war in 1947, President Truman and Congress recognized foreign and defense policy were inseparable but, in the words of the NSC's official history, "No institutional means for the coordination of foreign and defense policy existed."[36] Combined with the dawning recognition that the Soviet Union posed a long-term threat, that fact prompted an overhaul. We adapted.

The National Security Act, passed in July of that year, created the National Security Council and the Central Intelligence Agency. It merged the War and Navy departments with the newly formed Air Force to create the Office of the Secretary of Defense, and it established a network of other councils and committees to facilitate national security policy. The national security state, as we know it today, was born. Over the years, it grew and changed. Every president organized the National Security Council in his own way, and cataclysmic events have triggered the creation of new entities, like the Department of Homeland Security's formation after 9/11.

Now it's time for another reform. Like Truman and his congressional counterparts, we stand at an inflection point for our country. A new rival threatens us. A new era of geopolitics is upon us. We must find a way to unlock our nation's potential to win the race for technological leadership and to out-compete China at the intersection of economics, national security, and technology. To do so, Washington will have to recall the lesson of Operation Warp Speed: "The federal government *enabled* success; America's private sector *delivered* it." That should be the mantra for reform. Catalyze private sector innovation; don't mistake government as the source or progenitor of that leadership. Unlock what makes America great; don't try to transform it.

Put simply, the executive branch needs to reorganize for this new era of competition. The mess of committees, agencies, and offices dotting the landscape is overwhelming. At best, they stay out of each other's way. More often than not, they work at cross-purposes, and their infighting spills out into the public. What they need is vision and guidance from the top—from the White House.

Bureaucratic reforms could help provide that guidance. A National Innovation Council, for example, could take its place alongside the National Security and National Economic Councils (the NSC and NEC respectively), with responsibility for coordinating policy in areas of technological and economic competition. An ambitious proposal, it would have the virtue of elevating this competition to the same level as national security and economic policy in the government's hierarchy—a long overdue prioritization. The downside is there's still no natural home for the business of economic and technological competition, no agency or department tasked with carrying out policy. We have ways of addressing that gap, such as an outbound investment review commission, as noted already, but that's a solution to a discrete problem. More will be needed, but the adding of a new layer of bureaucracy to an already bloated executive branch is a risky business.

The federal government has become a behemoth run by unelected officials—what some call the "administrative state."[37] Congress has delegated and deferred much of its constitutional duty to the executive branch. Most new laws and rules are made by regulatory agencies from the Environmental Protection Agency to the Department of Transportation, not by elected officials, and the executive has become almost uncontainable and ungovernable.

In the words of conservative scholar Christopher DeMuth, this state of affairs "is problematic not just as a constitutional matter but also as a practical matter."[38] The federal government is getting too big and too complex to solve the very real problems of everyday

Americans. There's an old line that the ship of state turns slowly. Well, the ship of state has started sinking under the weight of its own registry. It's no wonder government more often finds itself slowing innovation than spurring it.

We have to get the administrative state under control, and there is no easy fix for that. One intriguing path, taken by the Trump administration, is a rule requiring two regulations be removed for every new one put in place. Ultimately, however, Congress must reassert itself. We need legislators strong enough to hold the executive branch accountable and principled enough to uphold their constitutional duty, as the founders imagined.

That is one of the reasons I decided to run for the Senate. In our republic, the most powerful form of accountability is elections. Voters get to pass their judgment in the ballot box, but then elected officials have to fulfill their promise to the voters. They must go to Washington and represent their constituents honorably in Congress. Sadly, not enough representatives live up to that end of the bargain.

All of this, ultimately, is a question of leadership. What are the goals of competition with China? What is the broad strategy to achieve those goals? How do we plan to turn that strategy into action? Only the most senior leadership in our government can set a clear direction for the nation's China strategy and for its economic statecraft. Only they can make the execution of that vision a top priority, above the endless list of competing interests. It will likewise take serious leadership to rein in the administrative state and to reform government for our generational confrontation with China. Nothing short will suffice.

The need for leadership extends well outside of government though. Everything I've written so far—all of the strategies and blueprints—deals with the hardware of American strength, with the practical things that make this great nation exceptional. Far more important in the long run is our national software: the spirit within every American.

National renewal will require a revival of that spirit, and that in turn requires us to rebuild our core institutions. Americans, to quote Alexis de Tocqueville, "constantly unite." We gather in political associations but also in institutions of "a thousand other kinds: religious, moral, grave, futile, very general and very particular, immense and very small." Through these, Americans pursue "in common the object of their common desires."[39] Our institutions, in other words, are the structures of our society through which we accomplish our goals. Through them, we give form to our goals and aspirations—to our spirits.

The American spirit reveals itself through our institutions, big and small, but that spirit is now under assault from the most powerful organizations in our society. Their cultures increasingly stifle and corrupt the spirit of all who work through them. We need to undo the damage. We need to replace their decayed cultures with new cultures of innovation that foster and channel the American spirit. Only then will America regain her confidence, be capable of confronting China, and recommit itself to exceptionalism.

CHAPTER 8

Revive Our Institutions

Good leaders organize and align people around what the team needs to do. Great leaders motivate and inspire people with why they're doing it. That's purpose. And that's the key to achieving something truly transformational.

—Marillyn Hewson, former chairman and CEO of Lockheed Martin, August 15, 2013

My first day at West Point, my fellow plebes and I were led into a large auditorium, where a speaker asked how many of us had been valedictorians in high school. Hands shot up all around me. He asked how many of us had been their class president. More hands. My hands never moved. Finally, he asked, "How many of you were captain of your football team?" My hand flew up.

Western Pennsylvania may be most famous for producing the steel that built America, but it's also what one sportswriter called "America's Football Factory."[1] Over the years, that area alone produced one-fourth of the quarterbacks in the National Football League's

Hall of Fame. George Blanda, Johnny Unitas, Joe Montana, and Dan Marino—the greats. The legacy continues with players like Curtis Martin in the early 2000s and Aaron Donald today. Both proud graduates of the University of Pittsburgh.

Maybe it's something in the water, but I like to think it's the institution of football—the traditions, culture, training, and coaching—in small towns all across Pennsylvania, like my hometown of Bloomsburg.

When I was a kid, football was a way of life. On Sundays, we watched the Steelers. These were the dynasty days of the Steel Curtain and Terry Bradshaw. My friends and I would sit in front of the television every week and cheer as Mean Joe Greene put a beating on whatever team stepped foot in Three Rivers Stadium. I'd watch every play Jack Lambert made and will forever remember watching Franco Harris's immaculate reception as he scooped the ball inches off the turf to beat the Raiders in the 1972 playoffs.

I loved football and couldn't wait to play when I got to high school. The problem was... I wasn't very good at it. My first two years of high school, I mostly rode the pine, seeing limited playing time only when we were winning big or losing badly. But I worked my tail off nonetheless to take advantage of every second on the field.

What happened next changed the path of my entire life.

In between tenth and eleventh grades, our school hired a new football coach named Tom Lynn. Coach Lynn was your stereotypical high school coach—tough, mean, and took no guff from anyone—but he understood how to coach young men like me and how to get the best out of us.

Before training camp that year, he called me into his office and told me that based on his review of all the previous game films, he thought I had real potential and could be an important player and leader on the team. I just had to work for it. That's what I did. I worked as hard as I could in the lead up to camp and all through it, staying after practices for additional drills and doing an extra set in the weight room. At the end of camp, to my complete surprise, he named me cocaptain—as a junior.

Our team struggled in the first couple games that first year under Coach Lynn, but we got better every game we played and solidified as a team. I clearly remember one game, roughly halfway through the season. It took place under a torrential downpour. I played poorly in the first half, was knocked around by their big men up front, missed tackles, and misread plays. It was ugly.

During halftime, Coach Lynn lit into us. I listened like everyone else.

Then he went after me.

He ran through everything I'd done wrong. He called me out for not preparing well enough, for not fighting hard enough, for getting complacent and lazy and believing the favorable press about me in our local newspaper from the preceding week. It was brutal but deserved. Coach Lynn had put his confidence in me. He had put me in a position of responsibility, and I had let him and the team down.

It was rough. I wanted to get out of there. I wanted him to go after someone else. Except that's not how leadership works. I had become one of our captains because of hard work and expectations, and Coach Lynn was right to hold me, as our team's leader, to an even higher standard. I promised myself at that moment never to get comfortable with my role as cocaptain or starter. The only acceptable standard was excellence, to get better every day, and to never again disappoint my teammates.

The next week and next season we continued our winning ways and eventually made it to Pennsylvania's Eastern Conference championship, where we lost a heartbreaker in the final seconds. It was a tough loss, but looking back, I'd already had the real victory. By putting his faith in me and holding me to high standards, Coach Lynn had elevated me in my own eyes. He had changed me. He had made me tougher and taught me what good, accountable leadership looked like and helped me see something in myself that I hadn't seen before. Thanks to him, I was named All-State linebacker my senior year and could stick my hand in the air and know I belonged at West Point.

My high school football team was one of thousands of small, beautiful institutions that Tocqueville described as scattered across our vast society. But its effect on my life was undeniable. It taught me confidence and humility. It strengthened my spirit, and I know I'm not alone.

You've likely had a similar experience. Maybe it was a high school coach, like Coach Lynn, or maybe it was a teacher who inspired your love for math or history. Maybe it was Sunday Mass or Tuesday-night pancake dinners at the local VFW. Or maybe it was boot camp and military training or years spent working your way through a company. The institutions in our lives—and the people who fill them—make us who we are.

In his brilliant book *A Time to Build*, the political scientist Yuval Levin writes, "Our souls and our institutions shape each other in an ongoing way."[2] When operating well, institutions inculcate a virtuous character in their people, and the "exercise of these virtues, in turn, helps our institutions flourish." He calls this the virtuous cycle. On the other hand, when institutions decay and lose sight of their purpose, they foster misplaced values and "undermine a free society"—the vicious cycle.

Every institution, however big or small, has a role to play in our society. For some, like a fire department or local charity helping the homeless, the role is easily understood. For others, say a big multinational company or the federal government, it's still there but more in dispute. That doesn't mean institutions should go unchanged. Quite the opposite. They must keep evolving to better fulfill their role and accomplish their mission. It's the duty of their leaders to make sure that happens, and they do so by fostering cultures dedicated to their respective missions.

That's what Coach Lynn did at Bloomsburg High School when he created a culture of constant improvement, excellence, and accountability. Everyone who put on the uniform understood they would outwork and out-prepare every opponent and that hard work would be rewarded. We also knew becoming a starter or a team leader brought greater responsibility and higher expectations. This culture elevated and developed us simultaneously. And it vaulted us from mediocrity to the conference championship game in just one season.

Every successful institution I've ever been a part of has followed a similar pattern. They had strong cultures that unleashed the potential of the people within them and molded them with the kinds of habits that led to constant improvement and helped the institution accomplish its mission.

This book is an ode to the American spirit. That spirit, which fills our national character with courage, ambition, and creativity, is one of our greatest strengths. However, that spirit needs to be cultivated. Like a football team bringing out the best in its players, our institutions must shoulder that burden. They must create virtuous cycles wherein people can unleash their potential in service of a shared mission and through which people's hard, honest work and ingenuity are rewarded. When that happens, the American spirit flourishes.

Sadly, the major institutions of American life—our government, big business, the media, and the like—are going in the opposite direction, caught in the vicious, self-defeating cycle of decay. They have lost sight of their core missions and are proving incapable of innovation and growth. They are stifling the individualism and spirit of Americans and dividing our country along lines of partisanship and other identities. Therein lies the greatest obstacle to American renewal.

The solution comes from within the organizations themselves. It begins with leaders reorienting their organizations to their proper mission—their true north—then aligning culture, people, and process to that mission. Across every institution, however big or small, leaders must foster virtuous cultures of innovation in service of their mission; attract and reward the kind of people who will carry on that culture and help accomplish the mission; and ensure the institutions operate in a way consistent with the culture and mission. If this happens, institutional renewal will follow, and with it, we'll see a revival of the American spirit, working through the organs of American life.

The Vicious Cycle

Our major national institutions have deviated from their missions, caught in a vicious cycle. They have been captured by bureaucratic and elite interests and by politicization, at the cost of them not fulfilling their role in society. As a result, their cultures and our country have suffered.

The first and most obvious form of decay is bureaucracy and elite capture. When bureaucracies or entrenched interest groups—often one and the same—take hold, they twist institutions to protect their interests. In doing so, they corrupt them. Few institutions can rival the federal government on this score. As Milton Friedman said, there's nothing so permanent as a temporary government program.[3] One of the reasons why is that once the federal bureaucracy gets ahold of something, it's almost impossible to reverse it. In fact, the bureaucracy will obstruct changes that do not simply add to its authority. I ran up against that wall every day when I served in government. The problem extends outside Washington to big business, the military, and beyond.

A close cousin of bureaucratic overgrowth is elite capture. That is the way in which entrenched interest groups take hold of a place and make it work for them, not for those it's meant to serve. Teachers' unions are the perfect example. They dominate K–12 education and prioritize what they want—like keeping schools closed during COVID—over what the students need. The grip of bureaucracy and elite capture explains why many of America's schools struggle to offer a good education and why the federal government seems incapable of addressing even the most basic national problems.

The second and most pervasive sympton is politicization. Our nation is more divided than ever, and politics has found its way into institutions that shouldn't be doing politics. The mainstream media, for example, has deviated from their mission of simply telling people the news. Museums, medicine, and even the military are going woke as well.[4] But college campuses have become the epicenters of the woke revolution. Intellectual uniformity has replaced the free exchange of ideas, especially at the most elite schools like Harvard, where 80 percent of the faculty report as left-leaning.[5] On top of that, cancel culture stifles the debate and free exchange of ideas that are vital to education—and to a healthy republic. Political crusaders have turned these nonpolitical institutions into political entities. They have ventured outside their lanes, to the detriment of the people they serve.

The problem is particularly pronounced in the business world. In the last few years, corporate America has become consumed with

Environmental, Social, and Governance (ESG) initiatives wherein businesses use their positions to achieve political and social objectives. I understand the intention. I have long worried about what I see as soulless examples of corporate leadership driven solely by profit and loss statements, balance sheets, and all the impersonal metrics of success and profitability. I also understand the demand. The public and would-be employees pressure executives to speak out on these issues, so corporate leaders feel the need to be responsive in order to attract the best people and keep their businesses competitive.[6] And I agree with Milton Friedman that "it may well be in the long-run interest" of a company to invest in its surrounding communities.[7]

Examples of positive corporate initiatives abound: The Home Depot's guarantee of continued employment to military spouses that move bases; Walmart's global learning programs, which pay for employees' education and offer training and leadership courses; and Microsoft's $500 million investment in affordable housing in its home base of Seattle, to name a few. Each is motivated by the understanding that the quality of opportunity available to a business's employees and the well-being of its customers and the ecosystem in which it operates have significant effects on the business's productivity and success.

The challenge comes in doing so while remaining principled and focused on their mission. By that standard, the current trend goes much too far and has, in the words of the *Economist*, "morphed into shorthand for hype and controversy."[8]

My greatest concern is that the ESG push will undermine our merit-driven, capitalist system by driving corporate leaders to lose sight of their commitment to their shareholders and customers and make decisions for political purposes, which would in turn diminish America's dynamism and its security. Performance in the market and shareholder returns are the ultimate enforcer of accountability, and those standards force executives to drive innovation and continually evolve their organization. Losing or even weakening them would be disastrous, not only to each company but also for our entire capitalist system. I likewise fear that, in their commitment to social agendas, business leaders could drift from the notion of merit as the key principle driving decisions, whether relating to personnel choices or business strategy. As an example, some corporate leaders are adopting hiring quotas that explicitly reject basic ideas of merit and competency.[9]

There's also a tendency to favor fashion over substance. Essentially, companies can call their practices "ESG friendly" or "climate friendly" or claim they have some special social value, regardless of whether they do or not. It's often little more than virtue signaling—companies posturing for partisan points at home, while gladly doing business with oppressive regimes abroad—but this kind of "ESG-washing" also takes more subtle forms.

Finally, companies like BlackRock use their ownership stake in companies to push their own political agendas. The people who entrust them with their money—people like you and me or anyone with a 401k or pension—don't get a say in what those standards are. We become party to a partisan campaign we may or may not support, often at the expense of our retirement and savings.[10] And now the government bureaucracy is aiding this practice, with the Securities and Exchange Commission requiring funds to disclose their ESG compliance, a clear precursor for future regulation.[11] In our political system, the public gets to define the public interest through the democratic process. But under this cultural shift, I fear that big companies will increasingly circumvent that process to enforce their own definition—at enormous cost to our democracy.

Others share my concerns. Some conservative politicians and

business leaders decry the ESG trend, and many states are taking steps to limit it. Companies have been formed in opposition to these ideas, and even ESG's greatest advocates, like BlackRock, are stepping back a bit. However, this worrying trend isn't going away.[12]

I wrestled with these tensions throughout more than a decade in senior leadership positions at Bridgewater, and they accelerated with time. Beginning in 2017, my co-CEO and I made diversity and inclusion a priority with the goals of ensuring equality of opportunity but also of creating a high-performing team with diverse backgrounds and perspectives.[13] From my earliest days in the Army, I had proudly spent my entire professional life recruiting, developing, and promoting great women and men of diverse backgrounds. However, in recent years, I experienced relentless pressure from outside the firm and sometimes from within to make whatever changes were needed immediately to assure "equal representation," without consideration of business implications or merit.

I discovered what leaders of many other organizations have, that building a more diverse workplace without sacrificing merit is a knotty challenge. Even with the best intentions and strong execution, it takes time. Yet the growing force behind the amorphous concept of ESG pressured us to do it overnight, which wasn't realistic.

We also faced significant pressure from our biggest clients to develop a new ESG investment strategy, which would allow them to invest in ways that met their ESG goals in line with their fiduciary responsibilities. We developed one, but with strict guardrails. It followed the same proven investment methodology of our other strategies and represented a standard of quality we could be proud of, and we never moralized to our clients about the need to invest in this way. More than that, we encouraged them to determine what ESG meant to them then helped them build a portfolio to achieve their goals. It was completely market-driven and client-driven. It was up to them to decide if and how they wanted to make ESG a part of their strategy. It was a fine line, but one we navigated with moderation and wisdom, and in doing so remained true to our purpose.

The third, and most virulent, is corruption or the loss of institutional integrity. You may remember the famous case of Johnson & Johnson and the tainted bottles of Tylenol. In late September of 1982, seven people died from taking Tylenol pills that had been laced with cyanide. J&J faced a dilemma. Pull Tylenol from the shelves and temporarily lose the product that accounted for almost one-fifth of the company's income? Or try to win the public relations battle and hope the police could figure out who had tainted the pills? The chairman, James Burke, chose the former. The recall cost Johnson & Johnson over $100 million but saved its reputation.

Too bad more institutions don't follow that example. The stories of corporate double-dealing and scandal are endless. There's Purdue Pharma, which perpetrated widespread fraud in the name of creating an opioid-addiction crisis across the country. There are the Silicon Valley unicorns, like Theranos, and the faces of corporate fraud, like Enron. Corruption takes many forms. Washington is rife with it, from special interests pleading their cases to lawmakers earning profit thanks to the power granted them by their position.[14] There are too many instances to list here, but in every case, the corruption turns institutions away from their rightful roles and reorients them to the whims of the selfish not the selfless.

The Wages of Decay

Here's the thing about the vicious cycle: it not only damages the institution itself but also society at large. The historian Niall Ferguson has written that the quality of a country's laws and institutions are the principal determinant of its success. Their strength in our country explains why America fared so much better than dictatorial, backward, and corrupt nations over the past two centuries. But now their "degeneration" explains how we ended up in our current state of sclerosis.[15]

Our country depends upon a self-governing, dynamic citizenry that always strives for something more. Activity, adventure, and engagement in civic life are the hallmarks of our national history, as is the free exchange of ideas. That's how a messy, pluralistic society like ours became what it is. But America is now living through what Bari Weiss called "a revolution of culture."[16] Free speech and expression are smothered by political reactionaries infiltrating the major national organs, and stagnant institutions perpetuate passivity by discouraging risk-taking and encouraging people to stay in line, not rock the boat.

Captured institutions also protect bureaucracies or elites by suppressing the innovative spirit and ambition of those within them, which has profound effects across society. For two years of the pandemic, Americans heard endless messages of fear and isolation, and the basic capacity to assess risk and make informed judgments went out the window. This came on top of our kids being coddled for years, which suppressed the chaotic yet energetic spirit that naturally powered this country.[17] The evidence is all around us: young people today are getting married less, having fewer kids, starting businesses less frequently, even driving less.[18]

All this is made worse by a fever of disunion, continually fed by the politicization of America's institutions. Not long ago, I saw a poll that found almost half our fellow citizens report feeling "like a stranger in my own country."[19] Core American values of liberty, opportunity, and individualism are under assault. There's no single explanation for how we got to this point, but surely politics has played a part.

In a nation as diverse and spread out as ours, shared experiences—found through institutions—and a communal patriotism bind society together. We will always disagree on the questions of the day, often vehemently, but our republic gives us institutions and spaces to hash out our differences: in Congress, at the ballot box, in the square of public debate. Beyond that, most things should be apolitical. National monuments, concepts of patriotism, even the national pastimes of baseball and football should be just what their names suggest: national. They should be enjoyed and celebrated by all, regardless of party affiliation. But when politics intrude, they turn into arenas of political combat, instead of the bastions of common aspiration they ought to be. They divide America in the places where it should be most unified.[20] Without institutions to bind us, polarization is on the rise, and our society is coming apart.

Finally, corruption has the most obvious and often the most profound cost. If leaders have lost their integrity, how can we expect them to operate faithfully in a free society? How can we expect them to cultivate virtuous people? How can we trust them? Corrupt institutions have lost their true north, and their crooked timber eventually rots.

Americans can see how entrenched elites have taken hold of government, businesses, and the media. They can see how self-interested leaders have twisted otherwise apolitical entities into tools for partisan warfare or political indoctrination. They know there's no accountability. So they've lost trust in our country's institutions and leaders.

According to a long-running Gallup poll, only one-third of Americans have confidence in the central institutions of American life.[21]

Another survey, this from Pew, found just a quarter of the public trusts the government.[22] The decline in trust and confidence applies across institutions. That same Gallup poll reported 28, 7, and 11 percent confidence in public schools, Congress, and television news respectively.[23] Only the military, police, and small businesses enjoy the majority's support, but even that is slipping. The trust deficit extends across society. Just 55 percent of Americans trust their fellow Americans.[24] A stunning 83 percent of Americans are worried the next generation will be worse off than they are![25]

Today, institutional decay is impeding innovation, dividing our union, and smothering the American spirit. It is the single largest impediment to renewal. The legendary economist Adam Smith foresaw this exact phenomenon in *The Wealth of Nations*. He warned that a caste of elites could co-opt institutions to their own benefit, not the nation's, creating a "stationary state."[26] This state would stop growing and stop evolving. Its engine would grind to a halt, and hopes of innovation would vanish. Division would take hold. Eventually, it would decline. It all sounds eerily familiar, but we can't lose hope.

The Virtuous Cycle

The challenge before us is straightforward but mighty. We must reverse the vicious cycle of institutional decay at work across the country. In its place, we must begin the virtuous cycle. That starts with the question of purpose.

All institutions, at their best, are similarly mission driven. They serve a distinct role within our free society, and their culture is aligned to that purpose. West Point exemplifies this model. Its mission is to educate and train future military leaders and instill them with the integrity to operate with the utmost honor in service of the country. And it does so exceptionally because it embeds in every graduate the virtues enumerated in its motto of "Duty, Honor, Country." I—like generations before and after me—benefited enormously from the school's clarity and integrity.

Though I attended church as a kid at my parents' insistence, my faith became stronger when I arrived at West Point in 1983—and has sustained me since. I will never forget a sermon on Psalm 121 one humid evening during that first plebe summer, after a long day of training. The Psalm reads, "I lift up my eyes to the mountains—where does my help come from? My help comes from the Lord, the Maker of heaven and earth." After that sermon, whenever I walked across the plain between those bronze statues of Eisenhower and MacArthur, surrounded by those rugged mountains that frame the Hudson Valley, I thought of that psalm. I gathered strength from it then—particularly on those challenging West Point days when one is prone to second-guess oneself—and I gather strength from it still, like many millions of Americans who find comfort and purpose in their faith.

Indeed, in difficult times, that Psalm and that perfectly manicured plain and beautiful backdrop always come back to me. Early in December 2008, when I was working at the Treasury Department during the financial crisis, I flew to West Point with President George W. Bush for his final address to the Corps of Cadets. These were fearful, chaotic days. I remember vividly, as our helicopters landed on the plain in front of the superintendent's house, among those old granite walls, looking up at those magnificent mountains—and feeling a deep sense of calm and connectivity to the certainty, the consistency, and the timelessness that is West Point.

Not every institution possesses such constancy nor such clarity of mission as the Church or West Point. Even so, they can stand for something. A news service can value honesty and impartiality in its reporting. A school can aim to create an environment dedicated to learning and moral development. A company can sell good products at a good price and treat its employees fairly. Whatever the setting, all can possess a sense of mission. From there, they must create cultures that will help them achieve it continually; attract and promote people that embody the cultural values; and preserve those cultures in policy, rules, and norms.

Institutional Cultures Understood

It's easy to think of institutions as static structures: organizational charts and processes populated by employees and customers. But, to quote Yuval Levin, "Often what matters most about them is what that sort of thinking leaves out: their mission, their ethic, their ends, their ideals." He continues, institutions "are more than organizations. They embody our aspirations. They are the forms animated by the spirit of our society. They stand for something, so that, by acting through them, we can stand for something too."[27] Institutions are, in a way, living constructs of American society. The people, facilities, offices, equipment, and the like comprise the hardware, but culture is the software. It sets the place's values and determines whether it lives up to its mission.

An organization's culture, in the words of a management guru, is its "learned patterns"[28]—the inherited traditions and values that guide how its people behave. More simply, I like to think of it as its *way of being*. It's the unwritten rules that guide how people are with each other, how they make decisions, and what they value most.

Bridgewater Associates, for example, is known for its culture of "radical truth and radical transparency," conceived by Ray Dalio. Everyone is expected to be honest with each other about what they're thinking and to listen to other people's ideas, whether you're an analyst, a senior investor, or the CEO. In fact, it sees these things as a duty that all share because they help the institution best perform and achieve its goals. As CEO, I viewed the preservation of that culture as perhaps my chief responsibility. I wanted to ensure that we protected an "idea meritocracy," as we called it, where the best ideas won. I understood that it was the secret sauce that enabled Bridgewater to understand markets well, take care of its clients, and generate good returns for them.

I'm reminded again of my high school football team. Cultural restoration, guided by the coach's leadership, turned the program around. The culture Coach Lynn built focused our minds on the team's mission—winning football games—and fostered in every player the habits and virtues necessary to accomplish that goal honorably. That is the virtuous cycle: *mission driving culture and culture in turn serving the mission*. It is the success equation for institutions and the most powerful force of organizational change there is. But how do you change culture? Through people.

Building Winning Teams

Throughout my career in business, I considered the hiring and development of people to be the most important part of my job. I always looked for *interesting*. I wanted people that I'd enjoy working with every day and who would bring some unique perspective or background to the job. At Bridgewater, despite being a world-class investment firm, we had a reputation for hiring philosophy majors and engineers, not just economics or finance students. We went after veterans and entrepreneurs, and I was so proud when employees would leave Bridgewater to start their own firms. It told me we had aspirational, innovative people in our midst, the kind of people who would keep the firm going. The right kind of people.

There's a great line in the 2004 movie *Miracle* about the U.S. men's hockey team beating the Soviets in the 1980 Olympics. The U.S. Olympic Committee gathers dozens of prospective players in Colorado Springs for tryouts, and before the first day is over, Herb Brooks—the coach—hands his roster picks to his assistant coach. When pressed about leaving off some big-name players, Brooks responds, "I'm not looking for the best players... I'm looking for the right ones."

People are the number one reason any organization succeeds. More precisely, it's the mix of people—the composition of attributes and capabilities—and their suitability to the organization's mission that determines how far it can go. A hockey coach like Herb Brooks might be looking for a team with goal scorers, tenacious defenders, a goalie with the killer instinct, and veteran leaders. In a software start-up, you lean most heavily on creative developers and a few experts in business, sales, and management, while an established business might rebalance things.

Teams, like culture, should be downstream of mission: an organization's objectives and responsibilities should guide what kind of people it attempts to recruit and develop. Getting the right people in the job is the single most important thing that leaders can do to have immediate and undeniable effects on their organization, and it's the only way to change an institution's culture.

Military Culture and Innovation: A Case Study

We can see how people, culture, and mission work together by looking at the troubling examples of institutional decay and stagnation in the United States military.

Early in his administration, President Trump asked me to serve on his Defense Policy Board, an independent committee established to advise the secretary of defense on the full range of issues on his plate. Joining the board gave me access to detailed information about the state of affairs in the Pentagon. It did not give me confidence.

Even the long-respected U.S. military has been caught in the vicious cycle of excess bureaucracy and resistance to change, and it is whipsawed about by politicians looking to advance partisan agendas. These forces distract the military from its central missions—to deter our enemies and defend our freedom—and, as a result create a culture that depresses the innovative spirit of the men and women in uniform and makes their jobs harder.

The Vicious Cycle in the Military

A few years ago, a friend of mine visited the U.S. Army's huge training installation in Bavaria, Germany, to observe a major NATO training exercise. In a big exercise like that, the allied units face an "opposing force" (or opfor) made up of a large contingent of U.S. soldiers that are stationed at the training grounds. The troops going through training wage a multiweek campaign against the opfor using a mix of live-fire munitions and laser targeting—kind of like the world's most advanced game of laser tag.

The opfor flew small drones over allied units to identify targets then unleash devastating artillery barrages. The participating soldiers couldn't figure out how to protect themselves other than moving constantly, which was exhausting and hurt their ability to fight back. Then an enterprising warrant officer had an idea: big Styrofoam triangles spray-painted green. By placing them on important equipment, like mobile command centers or tanks, they could confuse the opposing force's drones. It was undeniably effective. Except for one problem: Army regulations prevented the soldiers from using the panels.

It's an all-too-common story: innovation in the ranks, stifled from above. The military is full of smart, innovative young men and women who come up with creative solutions and workarounds to everyday problems. But that innovative spirit gets snuffed out by overweening rules and regulations made in the endless halls of the Pentagon or Congress.

The problem extends to the strategic level. In March 2020, the new commandant of the Marine Corps, General David Berger, released his vision for how to evolve the Corps for the most pressing military challenge of our time, China. Dubbed Force Design 2030, the plan called for cuts to infantry and tank units and reductions to traditional heavy weapons, like artillery and attack helicopters.[29] The proposal triggered an immediate backlash. Some of the most prominent retired Marine officers lobbied against it in public and behind closed doors.

There are legitimate questions about the wisdom of the plan and the way in which it was developed, but the speed and volume of the criticism was breathtaking. Marine Corps leadership had, for years, warned that the service needed to evolve. Their view was backed by serious analysis, yet the old guard of the Corps waged, as one writer had it, an "intellectual civil war" out in the open.[30] Experts on the Marine Corps can best determine whether Force Design 2030 is right or not, but I can see the virulence and publicity of the pushback for what it is: the manifestation of a culture that instinctively resists change.

The problem is compounded by an excess of bureaucracy, administrative responsibility, and, simply put, busywork. Ask any military officer and they'll tell you *time* is their most precious resource, but the unrelenting cycle of training, equipping, and deploying their unit and a never-ending checklist of administrative tasks mean they never have enough of it. It's all they can do simply to be ready to go when their number is called.[31] After the tragic accidents of the USS *Fitzgerald* and USS *John S. McCain*, the Navy found systemic problems of overtasking leading to sailors being ill-prepared to perform their core responsibilities.[32] And in the absence of a vision of what the Navy is for and how it should be used, the service seems destined to continue spirally down this path.[33]

Excess regulation and administrative pencil-pushing lead the military services to incentivize risk-aversion and a "zero-defect mentality," creating a culture of fear and stagnation. Personnel policies, for example, discourage ambitious officers from taking risks in their career choices.[34] And the former Secretary of the Navy John Lehman has even warned that the great naval leaders of the past would never have made it in today's Navy.[35]

The exceptions prove the rule. Special operations forces tend to prize adaptability, new ideas, and experimentation, but, as they profess, "cannot be mass produced"—nor, in all likelihood, can their model.[36] Likewise, when the Pentagon wants to innovate, it creates hubs, such as the Air Force's innovation accelerator, AFWERX, or the Army's Futures Command. These may be hotbeds of creativity but have minimal effect on the department. At worst, they amount to what the innovation guru Steve Blank calls "innovation theater," which creates "*activities* rather than deployable *solutions* that can be used on the battlefield or by the mission."[37]

Even the Pentagon can't escape woke pressures. Its leadership put the force through a sixty-day "stand down" to discuss extremism and racism, and those serving in the building will tell you that the goals of diversity, equity, and inclusion have taken center stage—to the detriment of our military might. To make matters worse, politicians keep co-opting the military to advance their political agendas. Some, for example, want the military to focus on climate change, so the Army developed a strategy to reduce its carbon footprint and fight climate change before the Pentagon even had a National Defense Strategy.[38] Others want to divert military funding to take on COVID and future pandemics—neglecting the fact we have other agencies designed for and dedicated to that task.

Climate change and pandemics are serious issues that deserve attention, but they aren't the military's problem to solve, especially with China breathing fire down our backs and Russia and Iran stirring chaos.[39]

All this, along with an incredibly competitive labor market, has contributed to a recruitment crisis in the military. Every service cannot recruit enough young men and women to wear the uniform. The Army will even have to shrink by as many as 28,000 soldiers because it can't fill its ranks. This is a national security crisis. Fewer than one quarter of young people are eligible to serve due to obesity, criminal records, and other obstacles. Fewer still express any interest. A tight labor market always makes it harder to recruit, but the politicization, wokeness, and cultural drift sweeping the armed forces undoubtedly are to blame as well. They have undermined public trust in the military and reduced the honor and prestige of the force.[40]

Each year of inaction worsens the situation. The U.S. military is overstretched. Its equipment is old. Creative ideas fail to progress. And its people are tired and overworked. The nation asks it to do more than it can afford.

Meanwhile, China poses a danger unlike any since the Soviet Union, and the People's Liberation Army—the Chinese military—now rivals the U.S. military in both size and capability. As a result, the U.S. military, long the most advanced and dominant in the world, cannot credibly claim to be the most powerful force in the Pacific, and our ability to defend our allies, deter Chinese attacks on friendly democracies, and preserve the peace is fading during the most consequential period in a generation. Experts on both sides of the aisle warn that the United States could lose its next war.[41]

Two members of Congress, who served in the Marine Corps, put it well: "We don't have time for incremental change. China is rapidly modernizing, and a Chinese invasion of Taiwan could happen before 2030."[42] Yet our nation continues putting off much-needed weapons acquisitions and accepting relatively flat defense budgets, and the uniformed military continues to innovate too slowly. There are many reasons, but at its root, the problem is one of culture.

Fostering Innovation in the Military

When I was a young lieutenant in the 82nd Airborne, my battalion commander would take all the officers to battlefields around the country as a staff training exercise. Being paratroopers, we'd jump in, walk the battlefield, have a big dinner, then fly back to Fort Bragg the next day. One trip took us to Gettysburg, not far from Harrisburg, where my parents were living at the time. It was my first chance to have my parents see a jump. I arranged to be the first man out of the plane and called my mom to tell her what was happening. She and my dad loaded into their station wagon and parked by the field outside Gettysburg, on a farm that we'd arranged as a drop zone.

As we flew in low over Gettysburg, I stepped up to the open door of the aircraft. The jumpmaster slapped me on the back, and I jumped. My parachute deployed immediately, but then something went wrong. I looked up and saw the boots of another paratrooper through the thin silk of my chute. The second man out of the plane had come in right on top of me.

My chute collapsed. I began to free-fall. After the longest two seconds of my life, the chute unfurled and caught the air. I leveled out and came in hard into the Pennsylvania soil, a little spooked but unhurt. After collecting my gear, I jogged over to my parents. They were in tears.

Some thirty years later, I was back in Gettysburg for an Adams County straw poll during my Senate campaign. These were some major Trump supporters, who spoke out against the establishment and globalists. And initially they didn't give me a warm reception. But as I got to talking with them, I told this story. Before long, we were swapping war stories and other tales of our common Pennsylvania upbringings.

Those voters were serious about partisan politics, but they were even more serious about their patriotism and their respect for military service—and that transcends party and ideology. For them, and for most of America, the U.S. military remains a shining example of integrity, duty, patriotism, and honor. Most warrior-citizens who wear the uniform feel called to serve and spend their lives devoted to their nation. Likewise, the military usually holds itself accountable—with Congress's help—and the strength of its inherited culture and traditions perseveres. The military stands alone among America's institutions, which makes the vicious cycle even more concerning.

That story highlights another truism about the military: war—and the preparation for war—is a dangerous business. For the men and women training for combat, taking risks can be uniquely perilous, and those who command others in combat must be schooled and experienced in the war-fighting competencies. Likewise those of us on the outside have a duty to care faithfully for the men and women we send to fight our nation's battles. We cannot take that responsibility lightly or treat the military as a laboratory for open experimentation.

We need to honor those who serve by not allowing the military to stagnate. My love for the Army and for the armed forces makes me want to help it grow and improve. And the values and habits and cultural drift decried above stand in the way. They obstruct the continual adoption of new technologies, concepts, and doctrine and therefore endanger both those in uniform and those of us at home.

Correcting course—and building a better culture of innovation and war fighting—will require the military services to redefine and set a new ethos for what it means to be a war fighter and to invest much more aggressively in new concepts and weapons of war.

To change the way those in uniform behave, the services should change what they value among their personnel and set a new standard for excellence based around prudent risk-taking and innovation. And they should put those values into policy by promoting and rewarding the men and women who embody that ethos.

There are many ways to accomplish that goal. They could establish units dedicated to innovation and experimentation. They could create an entirely new career field built around innovation and rapid capabilities development and promote officers who rotate between these and traditional commands.[43] They could also reward time spent in roles defining new operational challenges, working in rapid innovation offices, or other innovation-focused work and adopt "up and stay" career models that allow service members with valuable skills to remain in the military without being promoted.[44]

The services should also inject some fresh thinking into the force by encouraging officers to take private sector fellowships or to spend material time in industry, and by allowing more people to move laterally from the civilian world into midcareer roles in uniform.[45] And the Pentagon could also hold regular competitions where teams compete to solve a known operational challenge, then give the winners time and institutional support to pursue their idea.

Finally, the Pentagon needs to invest in military innovation. At the most basic level, we desperately need better technology within military offices, headquarters, and the Pentagon.[46] But that's just the start. There's a saying in defense circles: "divest to invest." The theory is we need to get rid of outdated, legacy weapons systems in order to buy new ones. There's some wisdom in it, but it's usually just an excuse to spend less on defense. Mothballing old weapons without buying new ones isn't innovation; it's surrender. Our country needs to spend more on defense and use it to buy and field new weapons as quickly as possible. There's no greater signal of military commitment to innovation than that.

Together these reforms would begin to inculcate a new way of being in the services—one fit for the era we live in. They would encourage the men and women in uniform to think differently about their roles, but also allow them to apply their full breadth of talent to the task of defending the nation. Over time, as innovative officers and service members worked their way up the ranks, they would begin to change the military from the inside out. Their services would take on their complexion and values. Those men and women would become the new exemplars of excellence, and the standard they set would inspire those below to push harder. In time, innovation would become more than theater—it would become integral to what the Pentagon does. This virtuous cycle would reenergize the institutions that need it most.

Kick-Starting the Virtuous Cycle

The armed forces have their idiosyncrasies. Some of them support the building of innovative cultures, including the innate sense of mission and duty within the men and women who sign up to serve. Others get in the way: the rigid hierarchy, the bureaucratic overlay that comes with it being an arm of the government, and the input of Congress, the White House, and other political entities around Washington. This is not to say the military runs just like a business. It doesn't. It shouldn't. However, the principles for how to rebuild cultures and kick-start the virtuous cycle apply from the general's office to the boardroom.

First, integrity is vital, but easy to lose. Integrity is won with time and consistency but lost in a moment. Failure does not necessarily undermine integrity if it comes in the honest pursuit of a good end. What matters is trust and the reputation it confers. The military, thankfully, has by and large preserved its reputation, but it cannot take it for granted. The more politics infects it and the more its leaders lose sight of their mission, the closer the armed forces come to a breaking point. Most other major institutions have reached that point already. They must rebuild their integrity and preserve it if they hope to remain upright, valuable parts of our national fabric—and if the nation is to renew itself.

Second, culture shapes people, but people change culture. This is the central truth of institutional cultures. They are constantly in flux, formed by the spirit and values of the people within them. So if you want to change the way of being within your institution, promote people that embody the virtues you need most.

Third, trust people. The military reforms outlined here are grounded in the belief that the men and women in uniform are more capable and innovative than they are allowed to be. They are, in other words, an untapped resource. The same is true across our country. Americans possess extraordinary potential, but the inclination to control them has permeated our society. We need to trust Americans to do what's best, while also expecting them to live up to the standards of citizenship. We must take responsibility for our own actions and live honest, patriotic lives.

Fourth, make innovation the standard. The best, most innovative institutions expect their people to take risks and try out new ideas. There is little punishment for failing ethically and prudently. In fact, it is better to try and fail than to never try. By contrast, a "zero-defect mentality," which we see in regulators encouraged to shut down anything new or risky rather than shepherd it to success, is shortsighted. Worse yet, it is poisonous to innovation and renewal.

Fifth, the best teams are diverse. When I talk about diversity, I don't mean hitting quotas of ethnic backgrounds, genders, or any other superficial metric. I mean that the best teams are composed of people with differing experiences, thoughts, and opinions, all working together toward a shared mission. Research supports this, and so does my own experience.[47] That's why my doctoral dissertation almost thirty years ago called on the military to promote people with a more diverse set of experiences and expertise.[48] And that's why I've tried throughout my career to promote, develop, and mentor outstanding women at FreeMarkets, in the Treasury, and at Bridgewater, including important leaders and colleagues like Robyn Shepherd, Tracey Yurko, and Karen Karniol-Tambour. I disagreed with them and others on the team frequently, but that's the point. High-quality debate and disagreement are the ticket to smarter ideas and better outcomes.

Sixth, put your money where your mouth is. If there's one thing I learned in business, it's this: what you invest in is what you value. At Bridgewater, when the pandemic struck, we understood we needed to give people the capability to get their work done at home. Fortunately, guided by our chief technology officer, Igor Tsyganskiy, we had already invested heavily to upgrade our technology, including both laptops, phones, and other personal equipment, as well as our firm's world-class network and technological platforms. We had the foundation necessary to support remote work. From it, we were able to set up Amazon Business accounts for everyone to get big-screen monitors, webcams, and other desk technologies, build fully networked outdoor meeting spaces, and hardly miss a beat.[49]

Some employees, mostly within our security team and trading operations, were required to work in the office throughout the pandemic, and when it was safe to do so, we began to bring the rest back. But during the worst of it, we wanted our employees to continue working well, maintain their innovative instincts and keep our culture intact, even under such terrible circumstances. We made the investments needed to make that happen. It was expensive but allowed one of the largest investment firms in the world to navigate through a time of enormous uncertainty and volatility.

Every institution, from high school sports teams to the agencies of the executive branch of the federal government, must find its own blueprint. But, guided by these principles, they can begin to reverse the vicious cycles that have taken hold and to create virtuous cycles in their place. Critically, these principles, like the specifics I recommend for the U.S. military, are intended to empower people and to revive the spirit of those in their reach. If institutions follow them, the national renewal agenda will be written into the software of American life. And that's the duty of leadership.

When I first laid out this vision for military cultural reform, late in 2021, I was flooded with messages from friends in national security circles.[50] Most were positive, but some friends in uniform had reservations. They worried that what I was saying would get in the way of the military doing what it's supposed to do. The general response was "Hey, that's just not what the military does." And you know what? They're right.

Military officers don't get any time to think about new ideas and innovate. They're just running full speed to keep up with their day-to-day demands and the unrelenting pace of operations, so innovation becomes a side project done in hobby shops across the force, not a central element of the military's activities. And that approach isn't working. It contributed to the loss of America's military supremacy and leaves us underprepared to deter or even win a war with our greatest adversary, China. That's why the military needs to change.

The reforms I've just outlined could set the conditions for the continual technological and doctrinal breakthroughs that military superiority requires. However, they will not happen without the impetus of the Pentagon's leaders, the buy-in of Congress, and a concerted effort to match defense budgets to the nation's strategy.

But it's not just the military. There is a desperate need for principled leadership across the galaxy of institutions that dot our country, but especially among those entrusted with the public's charge, who bear the greatest duty to care for America.

Richard Nixon once wrote that "leaders are often judged more by the stridency of their rhetoric and the coloration of their politics than by the success of their policies." As a result, "too many people have gone to bed at night with their ears full but their stomachs empty."[51] I don't know about you, but my ears are ringing. Our nation needs those in positions of power to stop pounding the pulpit and making empty promises, to start standing up for American values, and to get on with the business of renewal.

CHAPTER 9

A Time for Leaders

It is not the critic who counts; not the man who points out how the strong man stumbles, or where the doer of deeds could have done better. The credit belongs to the man who is actually in the arena.

—Theodore Roosevelt, address at the Sorbonne in Paris, April 23, 1910

On May 17, 2022, a record turnout of roughly 1.35 million Pennsylvanians cast their votes in the Republican Senate primary—one of the most watched elections in the country. It was a beautiful day in Pittsburgh. With hardly a cloud in the sky, Dina and I went to our local polling site on the campus of Chatham University and visited with voters and volunteers around the area. I was confident we would win.

That evening we held a small election-night party in East Liberty, a neighborhood on the northeast side of the city. Polls closed at 8:00 p.m., and I took an early lead over Mehmet Oz. Around 10:00 p.m., my campaign team came into the conference room, where I was talking with Dina and a few close friends and advisers. "We are likely to win this," they told me. "It's time to prepare the victory speech."

About an hour later, they came back. "You're going to fall behind in half an hour," they said. More votes were coming in from the Philadelphia area and surrounding counties, Oz's purported stronghold. He would soon take the lead, but based on remaining absentee ballots, we would ultimately prevail.

Dina and I went out to greet and thank the supporters gathered there that night. With tens of thousands of absentee and military ballots left to count, we wouldn't have resolution that night. So I told them what I believed. "When all the votes are counted, we're gonna win this campaign."

Seventeen days later, in that same room in northeast Pittsburgh, with the difference of just hundreds of votes between us, I conceded. While there are a few aspects of being a candidate that I'd like to forget, the experience was for the most part exhilarating and humbling because of the incredible people I met along the way.

Throughout the campaign, in every campaign stop at diners, VFWs, and fire halls, people were worried. They were worried about the huge spike in illegal immigration, the surge of fentanyl and other drugs into their communities, the radical ideas being taught in classrooms, and the wave of crime sweeping across the country. They were worried about America's place in the world as Afghanistan and Ukraine descended into chaos. They were worried about being able to fill their gas tank and put a meal on the table at the end of the day.

They lived with the fear that their children would inherit a worse country than they had. The America they knew was slipping away. They were scared and angry. And they wanted to know what I was going to do about it if elected.

For too long, politicians in Washington, both on the left and the right, have ignored men and women like those I met every day on the campaign trail. Instead of addressing the real problems that Americans face every day, progressives set their sights on grand crusades to remake America or political battles to defeat their opponents. The Biden administration looked at rising inflation and in response spent four and a half trillion dollars more to fundamentally remake the nation's economy and energy industry. Others looked at mass rioting and crime and argued for defunding the police. Their response to bad schools and COVID lockdowns robbing kids of a good education? Abolish advanced math programs and indoctrinate children with a distorted history of America.[1]

But it wasn't just the left. My own party has been far too slow to realize that the old Republican orthodoxy wasn't cutting it. Globalization may have brought cheaper goods, but it also destroyed the livelihoods of entire communities and towns. It left America dependent on and vulnerable to our greatest adversary, China, for vital pharmaceutical supplies, computer chips, and other critical goods. Instead of fighting to create opportunity and good jobs for all Americans, Republicans too often put corporate interests first, at the expense of working families and minority communities. We talked too much about making the stock market—not workers' wages—rise. And many, myself included, idealized America's role in the world, without tending to the domestic sources of strength that make our global leadership possible.

The 2016 election opened the eyes of many on the right to the inadequacies of their beliefs and set off a fight over the future of conservatism. The fight was long overdue, but so is its conclusion. A brighter future awaits. Who will lead us there?

The Project of Renewal

Our nation faces profound challenges that will not go away and for which we currently have no answer. We are caught in a spiral of stagnation and decline. We confront a Communist power dedicated to destroying the world we made and our way of life. Every day, failing schools deprive our children of the opportunity promised them. Every day, workers struggle against excessive regulations and confront a woke culture that undermines meritocracy. Every day, the values we hold most dear—that make this nation exceptional—are under attack. We must take on these challenges and renew our country.

These pages have laid out some basic tenets of an aspirational vision for the future of America. This vision moves beyond the bitter ideological warfare and the backward-looking tendencies of both parties to address the most pressing problems before our country: the opportunity gap denying people a chance at the American dream, the stagnation stifling our potential, and the rise of China and decline of American power. It is, in other words, focused on what's most needed in our moment.

The national renewal agenda may push the boundaries in many areas, but it remains anchored to three timeless and universal principles that we must hold dear: that America exists to preserve our liberty, that the American dream is the promise we pass on to each generation, and that America is exceptional.

The first principle, described in the opening chapter, holds that liberty is the God-given right of each and every one of us, and its protection is the chief purpose of our government. We must not forget these truths. Conservatives, in particular, must defend them; that is, after all, what we're struggling to conserve. We must always remember that our nation was, to quote Abraham Lincoln, "conceived in liberty," and fight to preserve that inheritance.

The second principle reaffirms that with liberty comes opportunity. America is best when all within it have their shot at the American dream. That is why I have put people first in this book. The national renewal agenda is designed to create space for each and every American to unleash the unquenchable fire that burns deep within. But the American dream does more than promise opportunity; it also bestows the solemn duty to preserve it. That means we as a country must care for the people left behind by globalization and create opportunity for them and all those too long denied it. It means we must create good jobs here at home and build a more resilient economy, to ensure America is not subject to the whims of dictators or the winds of fate.

The third principle asserts that the creed of liberty and opportunity makes our nation exceptional, and that exceptionalism gives us a unique role in the world. America has misused and wasted its power in frivolous foreign expeditions, yet no other country has done so much to advance freedom or prosperity. In our absence, none can fill our shoes. No country has the desire and capacity to promote fair trade, respect for property rights, the sovereignty of nations, or the natural rights of man. No other country will be able to stand up to Communist China, which wants to build the world in its image, to make workers in every corner of the world serve at the pleasure of the Chinese Communist Party. The only bulwark against that dystopia is American strength.

That's what is most frightening. China has a plan for global supremacy. What's ours?

The national renewal agenda is my answer to the question of what we must do next. It does not solve all the problems before us, but then again, no grand plan could. What it offers is a set of policies that are anchored to those three principles but fit for the unique moment in history in which we find ourselves. These policies give us a path to victory in the races for talent, technology, and data supremacy, and in doing so will begin the process of rebuilding the pillars of American power, restoring the American dream, and preserving American leadership. As laid out in this book, the agenda has three parts.

First is the talent strategy to improve the quality of education through school choice, STEM programs, and a commitment to American values; create opportunities for workforce development; and reform immigration to protect our sovereignty and serve the needs of America. Doing this will create opportunity in all corners of the country and make it easier for all Americans to pursue their dreams and realize their full potential.

Second is the strategy for technological leadership. Washington must take a more active role in promoting American innovation continually. It can do so principally by creating public-private investment vehicles—such as the American Innovation Fund—that can operate as the central conduit of federal funding for innovation in critical sectors. Seeded with taxpayer money and driven by or designed around market-based principles, it would attract private capital and invest in funds and innovative firms dedicated to preserving America's technological leadership. At the same time, Washington must cut the red tape and get out of the way of private citizens and firms trying to innovate. If we do this right, we will not only secure America's position at the forefront of game-changing technologies but also create entirely new companies, industries, and, therefore, good, well-paying jobs.

The third and final piece is a strategy for winning the race for data leadership and getting Big Tech under control. It would protect Americans' privacy and the public square, and it would put our country in a position to lead in the most dynamic and important industries of the future.

The national renewal agenda will not be possible without leadership. Leadership in government to ensure the United States stands up for itself in the world, confronts and decouples from China, builds new coalitions of willing partners, and reasserts leadership in this new era of geopolitical confrontation. And leadership across the core institutions of American life to revive the American spirit—the restlessness that comes with liberty and the ambition born of access to the American dream.

If we can accomplish all that is proposed here, there is no doubt America would launch an extraordinary rebirth of opportunity and confidence in our society.

All citizens would receive a better start in life and a fairer shot at the American dream. We would win the race for technological development. Greater business formation and corporate innovation would accompany that victory and create more well-paying jobs. People would have the training and support they needed to flourish in those roles. We would all be freer to live, work, and dream, knowing our privacy was protected in our online world. We would usher in a new era of American leadership, and our nation would be more secure against the predations of the Chinese Communist Party. Our government would finally wake from its doldrums and start meeting the moment. Businesses, schools, and all other institutions would refocus on their core missions. Our nation would break out of the cycle of stagnation that mires us now. America would get moving again.

However, there is a final ingredient of renewal, more important than any other: transformational leadership. None of this—the agenda nor the needed change in Washington and our institutions—is possible without it.

Transformational Leadership

My life has taken me from the rolling hills of northeastern Pennsylvania to the desert sands of Iraq, from wood-paneled boardrooms to the marble-floored halls of our nation's capital. It has exposed to me so much of what this great country has to offer, and it continues, every day, to teach me what it means to be a leader.

Leadership is a funny thing. So much has been written on it, yet good leadership remains such an amorphous concept.

Few have defined the role of leaders during times of national crisis better than Henry Kissinger in his recent seminal work, appropriately titled *Leadership*. Nations, he writes, are ever in motion, transiting from the past into an uncertain future. "Along this route, leadership is indispensable: decisions must be made, trust earned, promises kept, a way forward proposed."[2] In moments of great transition, when a country's future appears even more shrouded than usual, great men and women must rise to the occasion and lead the way.

We find ourselves in such a moment. As we consider the hurdles before us and what it will ask of our country, we must look for leaders with the vision to set the course, the courage to act decisively, the humility to improve continually, and the selflessness to serve their institutions and country. These four virtues define transformational leaders in every arena, whether they be an elected official, a corporate executive, the director of a local community group, or the head of state. As an observer and a practitioner, I have always found them to be essential and have continually, often unsuccessfully, tried to embody them. I hope our nation's leaders—be they in business, government, or any other institution of American life—will too.

First, leaders must be able to see through the fog and chaos of the moment and to envision the path forward. This was the genius of Ronald Reagan. His plainspoken vision for the country set him apart, and the clarity of mission he brought to Washington empowered his deputies to execute his agenda and to bring about meaningful change. But I know how challenging it can be.

When I arrived at Bridgewater in 2009, it was hugely successful but still functionally a founder-led boutique. Ray Dalio was omnipresent, and the firm was molded in his image. He had the foresight to recognize the need for a management and governance transition, and he charged me with that mission when he named me co-CEO in 2017.

Working closely with Ray and other key partners, my job was to orchestrate the transition of Bridgewater into a fully formed institution that would remain a world-class investment firm long beyond its founder—and for that we needed a vision for the company.

This was a founder transition, one of the most notoriously difficult undertakings in business.[3] Like most founder-led boutiques, Bridgewater had developed management structures, ways of operating, and cultures centered around Ray. Those attributes made it extremely successful, but some had to change. The challenge was knowing what to change and what to keep.

We had to protect the core of our culture of radical truth and transparency that had worked so well under Ray but also evolve it. Bridgewater needed to foster the next generation of leaders and hire diverse talent, while maintaining an unflinching commitment to meritocracy. At the same time, we had to preserve Bridgewater's fundamental, systematic, and diversified investing approach, while also becoming far less focused on the genius of a single person and fulfilling a broader set of client needs.

Most founder transitions struggle with the questions of money and control, and ours was no exception. But, despite deep disagreements, years of good and bad investment performance, changes to our leadership, and then the stresses of the pandemic, the senior team and I refined and executed a vision that balanced all of these considerations.[4] When I left the firm at the end of 2021, the difficult work of the founder transition was largely done. I am deeply proud of what we accomplished. Bridgewater remains the best at what it does. The new leadership team is in place. It is serving its clients better than ever before, and the business is performing excellently. With hard work and a little luck, we succeeded where so many founder transitions had failed.[5]

We never could have achieved it without the support and leadership of an incredible group of colleagues and advisers, particularly Greg Jensen and Nir Bar Dea, who were steadfast in times of turmoil. But the experience crystalized for me that no one else could have provided the vision. It's not always easy to find your bearings. Lord knows I've struggled with it. The dial on the compass sometimes seems to spin without stopping, but it's the leader's duty to rally the team, set the direction, bring others on board, and accomplish the mission.

Second, virtuous leadership takes courage. When we think of courage, our minds tend to go to extremes. We think of the soldiers landing at Omaha Beach or climbing Pointe Du Hoc or of the policemen and firefighters running into the towers on 9/11. Without a doubt, theirs is true courage. Their example should inspire us and remind us, as one of the men at Omaha would later say, "in the face of crisis, men rise above themselves to accomplish great things."[6] But courage is not just found on the battlefield or in the face of physical harm. It takes courage to pursue a strong vision and, especially, to change course when needed.

That kind of courage can be found in every corner of the country. I see it in my friend Mary Barra, the chair and CEO of the great

American car company General Motors. Like her father before her, Mary got her start working in a GM plant. She began right out of high school through a GM work-study program that allowed her to get a bachelor's while working. Her managers saw potential in her, so the company paid for her to get a business degree at Stanford. For years, she helped build cars like the Pontiac Fiero. Now she's pushing GM into the future. The auto industry is rapidly changing. Customers want more electric vehicles, more technology in their cars, and lower emissions, and Mary's committed to delivering best-in-class products, even if it means leaving behind the kind of work she grew up doing. She has a bias for action. Innovation and evolution to serve the customer better are the North Star for her.

I can think of so many others who have forged their path with courage. The men and women I worked with at the Treasury during the global financial crisis, for example, had the fortitude to stand in the ring in a time of national crisis, take responsibility for their actions, learn from mistakes, and do what they saw as right for the country—even when I may not have seen eye-to-eye with them.

Hopefully, our leaders will have that same courage of their convictions to fight for what they see is right and to be willing to change and adapt to an ever-changing world. For that, they will also need humility, a close cousin to courage.

As a young man, Benjamin Franklin listed thirteen virtues he hoped to follow to better himself. Among them was humility. Here was a man who would go down in our history as the father of American innovation and the sage of our republic. Yet, he knew that he, like all of us, was fallible. From his earliest days, he knew that he needed to see the world as it was, not as he wanted it to be.

Humility gives people the capacity to recognize their own shortcomings, learn from their mistakes and failures, and improve. This is invaluable for a leader. As I've seen throughout my life, when you get into a leadership position, it's hard to know what's really going on and what people honestly think of you and how you're doing. So, you have to recognize and embrace the fact people aren't always telling you the truth. You have to acknowledge mistakes, seek input from others, and learn from them. To do so, you have to be open-minded. To grow and develop, leaders have to recognize they may have the wrong answer or an incomplete picture.

I learned this the hard way at Bridgewater. A few years after starting there, Ray Dalio asked me to become co-CEO. I'd served in leadership roles since my arrival. I'd been a successful CEO before at FreeMarkets, and I'd been through the crucible in the Army and government. I felt ready to take on the role. Except in Ray's mind, I was soon failing because I had not driven change fast enough. So, a little more than a year into the job, he fired me as co-CEO and asked me to take on a lesser role within Bridgewater, working closely with our biggest clients on their most strategic problems. For the next five years, I logged the most miles of any Bridgewater executive while leading the charge to deepen our relationships with clients around the world and dramatically grow our business. Then the opportunity arose to become CEO again in early 2017.

The firm needed a leader with the proven ability to work with others to solve the thorny issues the company faced, to wrangle the many strong personalities to agree on a future strategy, and to complete the final phase of Dalio's transition. This time I was better prepared.[7] By learning from my mistakes, I gained confidence in my capacity to draw on the conflicting opinions of others as input for my own independent judgments. This helped give me the clarity and self-assurance I needed to lead successfully. In a way, Ray did for me that day what Coach Lynn did that rainy night almost forty years earlier:

he stripped me of any pretense, showed me in clear and convincing terms my shortcomings, and then let me go back out there and prove to myself and others that I could evolve and do better.

I'll admit I disagreed with his decision to fire me, then and now, and I thought hard about whether to leave Bridgewater. But I'm forever grateful that I didn't. The experience taught me more about myself than any victory could. It reinforced that everyone, even someone who thought they were as capable and prepared as I did, needs to grow. Humility of this kind is not the absence of kindness but a true sign of it. It can be a superpower that lets you walk into any conversation open to hard questions and harder answers and which allows you to improve and learn constantly. And self-improvement, as I'm continually reminded, is what keeps leaders strong.

It's also what keeps America exceptional. During her time in the Bush administration, my wife, Dina, traveled often to the Middle East with Condoleezza Rice, then the secretary of state, to meet with the leaders there. Once, one of those leaders grew heated and questioned how Dr. Rice could preach about democracy and human rights, given America's own track record. "America isn't perfect," she answered. "My ancestors were slaves, and it wasn't that long ago that my own country considered my value as only three-fifths that of a man's. So in no way can I preach to you, because I come to you with great humility." Yet in America, she said, "We desire to build a more perfect union by giving our people a voice."[8]

The ability to acknowledge our national shortcomings and to work publicly to address them has distinguished America. It has made us a better, stronger place. I hope all our leaders will share Dr. Rice's humility and speak openly about our nation—good and bad—all in the name of strengthening and advancing the American experiment.

Finally, and most important, is selflessness. Leadership is not about you. Almost four decades ago, when I was just a young man at West Point, I read a book that would forever change my view of what it means to serve. The book was *Once an Eagle*, by Anton Myrer. It tells the story of two Army officers, Courtney Massengale and Sam Damon, and their journey up through the ranks, from the early 1900s through World War II and into the 1960s. Courtney is a self-interested careerist interested only in getting promoted and getting stars on his shoulders. Sam, on the other hand, is a quiet, duty-bound soldier and leader, committed to the men he serves. Despite their differences, both men rise through the ranks. Both ostensibly find success over and over again, but it often comes more easily for Courtney. Yet Sam remains true to his code, and, in the end, that is what matters most.

When I was in the Army, the book was practically required reading, and I still return to it because it gets to the truth as only fiction can: True leadership is not about you. It is about selfless service to others and to the mission. Everything else—all the accolades and power that come with leadership—are a distraction from that simple truth.

There's a saying in the Army that "leaders eat last." The officers and noncommissioned officers I looked up to mostly lived by that mantra. At the end of a long march during my time as a platoon leader in the 82nd Airborne Division, every member of my platoon would check their feet. The platoon sergeant and I would go and check on each soldier to ensure no one was developing blisters or dealing with unresolved injuries. Trekking for hours with a heavy pack can do some damage, and even a single blister can become a debilitating infection for a paratrooper. Only after we were sure everyone else was in good shape, would he and I finally sit and take off our boots.

Great leaders always make sure the men and women in their

command are taken care of first. Great leaders focus on the mission and those along with them in that mission, not themselves. Great leaders rally people through vision, courage, humility, and service.

Our nation needs leaders like these to spearhead the great American renewal, and nothing trains leadership like the opportunity and honor of serving the country. But where and how can we find such leaders when our country remains so divided?

A Call to Serve

The legendary conservative writer William F. Buckley once described American citizenship as the union of privilege and responsibility.[9] "Privilege," because to be an American is to be blessed with liberty and opportunity. "Responsibility," because as Americans we have a duty to preserve the republic—to serve our nation.

National service is a controversial notion. Critics see it as a government works project. They have a point; I know some who have called for national service for precisely that reason. Other critics call it a boondoggle set up to place Washington even more prominently at the center of public life. I see it differently.

My paternal grandmother died young. Before she passed, my dad made her a promise. Every year on Memorial Day, he would visit her grave and all the cemeteries where his family is buried. For over fifty years, he has kept his pledge. Come late May, he and my mother fill up their car with flowers and drive across western Pennsylvania, planting flowers at every grave.

I tagged along as a kid until I left for college, but then participated in the tradition again more than thirty years later, in 2018, when my dad invited me to join them. Down winding country roads, my parents regaled me with stories of their lives together, of their parents, and of the generations long past. And when we came to a family plot, we'd get down on our knees, dig a small hole, and plant the flowers.

It was fitting to do it on Memorial Day because we weren't the only ones at the cemeteries. Everywhere we went, families and volunteers were out planting flags at the graves of those who'd served. I was struck by how many flags I saw in these small towns. I started to read the headstones. These were veterans of World War I and II, or Vietnam and Korea, and even of Iraq and Afghanistan. Some had made the ultimate sacrifice. Most had gone on to long lives of privilege as Americans. All had served the nation as brave citizens of our republic.

I grew up among people like the men and women interred in those cemeteries. I went to school with them and served with them in the Army. And everywhere I went on the campaign trail, I talked to people who had served or who had loved ones who served.

But there's a disconnect in our society.

During my time in government and business, I would often be the only one in the room who had worn the uniform. At times I was the only one with any family connection to the U.S. military at all. It was a completely different world. This reflects a truism. Those in positions of power in America are mostly disconnected from the military. For example, only 17 percent of the members of Congress in 2021 were veterans, the lowest level since before World War II.[10]

Not too long ago, most people had family or friends who had served in the military, but that's changing. A Pew poll from the early 2010s reported that only a third of young people had any family ties to the military.[11] Another survey found over 80 percent of elites didn't have family members who served after 1991.[12] But those in the military tell a different story. The vast majority of new recruits have parents or close relatives who are veterans, and they come disproportionately from areas thick with military families. The military, in other words, is becoming a family business, and that's dangerous for our military—as the current recruiting crisis shows—but also for our society.

The disconnect between the military community and the rest of the country is just one of many already documented divisions. The important question is what's causing them, and in my mind, our society is coming apart in part because we've lost sight of the responsibilities of citizenship: the preservation of the American experiment.

I wish everyone could have the same opportunity I had to wear the uniform—to feel the sense of duty, teamwork, and selfless service that it demands. That's not realistic, but some form of broader national service is. It would ground us all in our civic responsibilities.

To be clear, national service shouldn't be mistaken for a new Civilian Conservation Corps or other public works project. Instead, it should be defined broadly, to include work with philanthropies, charities, churches and other faith-based institutions, and, yes, the armed forces. I recognize that it would be nearly impossible to implement a form of mandatory service. We have to start small, with programs and incentives like those proposed by the Cultivating Opportunity and Response to the Pandemic through Service (CORPS) Act, a bipartisan service bill, which I supported vocally.[13] But the more widely practiced it becomes, the more our society would heal.

In my mind, my parents' Memorial Day tradition is a small but noble act of service. By fulfilling my dad's promise, they honor his mother. By planting a flower at each grave, they honor all those loved and lost. And by passing the rite on to my brother and me, they inspire gratitude for the past, inspiring us to keep our family's memory and history alive.

Our nation needs similar rites of service. We need to restore gratitude for our national inheritance and the sense of duty to preserve it. Doing so would have a profound effect on our society. It would bring us together in common cause. It could salve petty differences and remind us that most of our disagreements grow small in the context of our shared patriotism. Taken together, the gratitude and communion won through hard service would begin to overcome our nation's divisions, heal our society, and create a firm foundation for national renewal.

All these leadership traits were on my mind as my Senate race neared its end. A week before Primary Day, the public polls had us in third place. President Trump's endorsement, rally, and attacks on me had both buoyed Dr. Oz and pulled voters from me to a third candidate, Kathy Barnette. Pretty soon the two of them were the story, but polls, as any politician will tell you, don't win elections.

Though some in the media appeared to lose interest in my campaign, on the trail, the energy was electric. In the final weeks, my supporters gathered for raucous rallies in places like Harleysville, Carnegie, Wilkes-Barre, and Lititz. Then the day before the election, we held a rally in my hometown, in my old high school.

I took the microphone and, flanked on either side by old banners from my football and wrestling careers, looked out on an incredible crowd of friends and supporters. I'd come full circle to where it all began for me. Memories flooded back, and I was suddenly filled with an immense gratitude for all Pennsylvania and America had given me and an incredible optimism that we could pull off a victory in the race—and more important, that our country had brighter days ahead.

That feeling stayed with me through the roller coaster that followed. When Election Day proved inconclusive, we fought for seventeen days to ensure every vote submitted on time would be counted. We supported Pennsylvania's legally mandated recount, during which every county went back through and counted their ballots again.

While we thought we could make up the difference in the recount, by Friday, June 3, 2022, the outlook changed. More than fifty of sixty-seven counties, representing about 60 percent of the vote, had reported the results of their recount. Those results, combined with feedback from my election observers on the ground in the remaining counties, made it clear to me that, though I had won the majority of the sixty-seven counties, the needed votes simply weren't there.

It was deeply disappointing to lose such a close race, but the decision about what to do next was clear. Particularly during the recount, Dina and I experienced the dysfunction and incompetence of the electoral processes across Pennsylvania, from polling stations running out of ballots on Election Day to the secretary of state misreporting the number of absentee ballots to completed ballots being lost then recovered in Philadelphia precincts. We understood as well as anyone both the distrust and the desire for much-needed electoral reforms. But we also saw how the seeds of mistrust and lost confidence in elections across all levels of our society are undermining the very foundations of our democracy. For that reason, we believed it was vital for me to lead by losing with honor and grace and not fall prey to the politics of grievance and victimhood.

That night, I thanked my supporters for their friendship and sacrifice and thanked the 419,000 people who voted for me. Then I told them that, with a razor-thin margin of just nine hundred votes, we had a nominee. Earlier that afternoon, I'd called Mehmet Oz and congratulated him on his victory. Pennsylvania voters had made their will clear, albeit by a whisker, and that's what the democratic process is all about.

There's nothing like sports to teach you about the agony of defeat. When the national anthem ends and the kicker boots the ball downfield, it's game on. You fight like hell, within the boundaries of the rules, to win the game. Wrestling's even tougher. You literally summon every ounce of strength and will to dominate and pin your opponent. But when the whistle blows, you're done. You help your adversary to his feet. You walk off the mat.

The sportswriter John Feinstein tells the story of Jim Cantelupe and Andrew Thompson, the respective defensive captains of the 1995 Army and Navy football teams who played each other four years in a row, with Army winning each game. In the final game they each played, Army engineered a ninety-nine-yard, game-winning drive to win by one point. Afterward, Cantelupe slipped out of the Army locker room to go see Thompson. He found him in front of his locker, head in his hands. They stepped outside. "We're brothers now," Thompson told him. Still wearing their opposing jerseys, they embraced.[14]

Particularly today, though most political opponents don't share the bond of two young men headed into military service, we can all relate. There's a time for fighting and a time for coming together. A time for anger and disappointment and a time to find common ground. A time to be beat down by the winds of fortune and a time to turn our eyes to the future.

It is time for us, as a country, to begin the hard work of renewal. It is time to heal the partisan wounds that have for too long divided our country. It is time for leaders to step up and for the men and women charged with the public trust to leave past grievances behind and lead America forward.

We are at a pivotal moment in our nation's story. Behind us we see a grand legacy of victory and failure, ingenuity and war, decline and renewal, all of which have brought us to this point. Ahead of us lies a great uncharted territory. It is up to us to choose the path. And it is up to our leaders to guide the way, uniting us once again around the creed of liberty and opportunity that binds our national fabric.

This is the exceptional American story—we get to the edge of the cliff, then pull ourselves back. If we hope to do that now, we need, to borrow from the historian Wilfred McClay, "to believe in ourselves again... to understand that a world without America will be immeasurably diminished, both in material and spiritual terms, and that we have no choice but to live up to the responsibilities that come with our many blessings."[15] In other words, we must believe America is worth renewing, and we must believe we can succeed.

I didn't run for the Senate because I think of myself as any more special than the next person, but because this country is special. America can renew itself with a rebirth of liberty, opportunity, and American power, but we all must do our part to fulfill that promise.

Americans are a resilient bunch. They know how to take a punch, and no matter how many times they get knocked down, they always get back up. Though times may be tough, they believe in America. They believe we can do better. They believe we can revive our nation and achieve America's promise. Their faith is the rally point I return to when my own fails, and it fills me with an unerring confidence that we can and must meet the moment.

ACKNOWLEDGMENTS

This book began with an idea, that the source of American renewal could be found where economics, technology, and national security intersect. I first enunciated that idea in the *Texas National Security Review* and developed it in the pages of the *Financial Times*, *Fast Company*, *National Review*, *Foreign Affairs*, and elsewhere. I am grateful to the editors of each publication and especially to my coauthors on those early works.

Work on this book started at Bridgewater Associates, and I thank my former colleagues and friends there who made it possible, especially my trusted team. Work continued when I decided to run for office, and I am grateful for the support of everyone who worked on and contributed to my campaign and to this book. Finally, I extend my thanks, in particular, to scores of old friends and colleagues who shaped my thinking on these questions, read the earliest essays from which this book was developed, provided invaluable insight, and reviewed book chapters. I owe you all a deep debt of gratitude.

I have been fortunate to work with Alex Pappas, our editor at Center Street, and Anthony Mattero, my agent from CAA. Their professionalism and good humor have made a trying process more endurable and rewarding. Likewise, my friend and mentor Bob Kimmitt has offered unfailing aid and friendship along the way, from our days in the government until today.

This book would not have been possible without my close collaboration and intellectual kinship with my friend and colleague James Cunningham. I have been blessed throughout my career to work closely with scores of exceptional young professionals, but James is uniquely capable in both talent and collegiality. I am grateful that he has joined me on this unexpected journey.

I would not be the man I am today without my parents. They have been lifelong supporters of everything I've done, and they, along with my dear family friend Janice Fitzgerald, took a special interest in this project and helped make it better.

Finally, to my remarkable and beloved wife, Dina—thank you. You have stood by me as I left my job, took to the campaign trail, and upended our lives. Your faith in me has made all the difference. I love you, and I'm eternally grateful.

NOTES

Introduction

1 Meredith McGraw, Daniel Lippman, Holly Otterbein, and Natalie Allison, "Pennsylvania Republicans Eye Top Investment CEO for Senate Primary," *Politico*, November 4, 2021, https://www.politico.com/news/2021/11/04/pennsylvania-republicans-investment-ceo-senate-519606.
2 My two advisers at Princeton were Aaron Friedberg, a protégé of Samuel Huntington, and John DiIulio, Jr., a student and protégé of James Q. Wilson, the legendary social scientist. Both are great scholars and friends.
3 David McCormick, "Let's Roll Against Saddam Hussein," *Los Angeles Times*, February 28, 2002.
4 Salena Zito and Brad Todd, *The Great Revolt: Inside the Populist Coalition Reshaping American Politics* (New York: Crown Forum, 2018), 10.
5 Zito and Todd, 10.
6 Lawrence Delevingne, "Bridgewater executive McCormick Declines Defense Department Role," Reuters, January 10, 2017, https://www.reuters.com/article/us-usa-trump-mccormick/bridgewater-executive-mccormick-declines-defense-department-role-idUSKBN14U2ST.
7 Ernest Hemingway, *For Whom the Bell Tolls* (New York: Scribner, 1940), 467.
8 One example is my friend and former colleague Ray Dalio in his recent book. Ray Dalio, *Principles for Dealing with the Changing World Order: Why Nations Succeed or Fail* (New York: Avid Reader Press, 2021).
9 Samuel P. Huntington, "The U.S.—Decline or Renewal?" *Foreign Affairs* 67, no. 2 (Winter 1988): 90.
10 "News Conference by President Obama, 4/04/2009," National Archives and Records Administration, April 4, 2009, https://obamawhitehouse.archives.gov/the-press-office/news-conference-president-obama-4042009.

11 Eric Levitz, "American Exceptionalism Is a Dangerous Myth," *New York Magazine*, January 2, 2019, https://nymag.com/intelligencer/2019/01/american-exceptionalism-is-a-dangerous-myth.html.

12 Terry Ahner, "McCormick brings Senate campaign to Lehighton," *Times News Lehighton*, February 26, 2022.

13 Henry Kissinger, *Leadership: Six Studies in World Strategy* (New York: Penguin Press, 2022), xvi.

14 For a great account of the Army-Navy rivalry, see John Feinstein, *A Civil War: Army vs. Navy Tag—A Year Inside College Football's Purest Rivalry* (New York: Little, Brown and Company, 1996).

15 Abraham Lincoln, "First Inaugural Address" (Speech, Washington, DC, March 4, 1861).

16 Ibid.

Chapter 1

1 Their story is told in John Ismay, "America's Dark History of Killing Its Own Troops with Cluster Munitions," *New York Times Magazine*, December 4, 2019.

2 The ordinance disposal at Khamisiyah stirred up controversy. It turned out some of the munitions may have contained nerve agents or other chemical weapons. There was a big investigation, and a number of the guys in my unit suffered the symptoms of what came to be known as "Gulf War Syndrome." Thankfully I never did.

3 Charles Krauthammer, "The Unipolar Moment," *Foreign Affairs* 70, no. 1 (1990): 23–33.

4 "How It happened: Transcript of the US-China Opening Remarks in Alaska," *Nikkei Asia*, March 19, 2021, https://asia.nikkei.com/Politics/International-relations/US-China-tensions/How-it-happened-Transcript-of-the-US-China-opening-remarks-in-Alaska.

5 "China Set to Surpass U.S. as World's Biggest Economy by 2028, Says Report," *CNBC*, December 25, 2020, https://www.cnbc.com/2020/12/26/china-set-to-surpass-us-as-worlds-biggest-economy-by-2028-says-report.html.

6 Nicholas Eberstadt, "China's Demographic Prospects to 2040: Opportunities, Constraints, Potential Policy Responses," in *A Hinge of History: Governance in an Emerging New World*, eds. George P. Shultz and James Timbie (Stanford: Hoover Press, 2018).

7 See Michael Pettis, "The Only Five Paths China's Economy Can Follow" (Washington: Carnegie Endowment for International Peace, April 2022); James Kynge, Kathrin Hille, and Jonathan Wheatley, "China Reckons with Its

First Overseas Debt Crisis," *Financial Times*, July 21, 2022; and "China's Gen Z Is Dejected, Underemployed and Slowing the Economy," *Bloomberg*, July 24, 2022, https://www.bloomberg.com/news/articles/2022-07-25/xi-s-covid-rules-and-tech-crackdown-push-gen-z-in-china-to-bailan.

8 "The 2021 Long-Term Budget Outlook," Congressional Budget Office, March 2021, https://www.cbo.gov/system/files/2021-03/56977-LTBO-2021.pdf.

9 Robert Shackleton, "CBO's Economic Forecast: Understanding the Slowdown of Productivity Growth," Congressional Budget Office, September 1, 2020, https://www.cbo.gov/system/files/2020-09/56531-NABE.pdf; "Federal Policies in Response to Declining Entrepreneurship," Congressional Budget Office, December 2020, https://www.cbo.gov/system/files/2020-12/56906-entrepreneurship.pdf; and Oren Cass, "Is Technology Destroying the Labor Market?," *City Journal*, Spring 2018, https://www.city-journal.org/html/technology-destroying-labor-market-15829.html.

10 Jim Inhofe, "Combined China and Russian Defense Spending Exceeds U.S. Defense Budget," *RealClearDefense*, May 3, 2021, https://www.realcleardefense.com/articles/2021/05/03/combined_china_and_russian_defense_spending_exceeds_us_defense_budget_775323.html.

11 Courtney Kube and Molly Boigon, "Every Branch of the Military Is Struggling to Make Its 2022 Recruiting Goals, Officials Say," *NBC News*, June 27, 2022, https://www.nbcnews.com/news/military/every-branch-us-military-struggling-meet-2022-recruiting-goals-officia-rcna35078; and Mike Pompeo, "We Must Reject Wokeness in our Military," American Center for Law & Justice, May 13, 2022.

12 David Ochmanek, Remarks, "How the U.S. Military Fights Wars Today and in the Future," hosted by the Center for a New American Security, Washington, DC, March 7, 2019.

13 See *Providing for the Common Defense*, report of the National Defense Strategy Commission, November 2018.

14 "Freedom in the World 2022: The Global Expansion of Authoritarian Rule," Freedom House, February 2022, https://freedomhouse.org/report/freedom-world/2022/global-expansion-authoritarian-rule.

15 U.S. Const. pmbl.

16 Richard Brookhiser, *Give Me Liberty: A History of America's Exceptional Idea* (New York: Basic Books, 2019).

17 Richard Wike and Katie Simmons, "Global Support for Principle of Free Expression, but Opposition to Some Forms of Speech," Pew Research Center, November 18, 2015, https://www.pewresearch.org/fact-tank/2016/04/19/5-ways-americans-and-europeans-are-different/.

18 Richard Wike et al., *European Public Opinion Three Decades After the Fall of Communism,* Washington: Pew Research Center, 2019.

19 Rich Lowry and Ramesh Ponnuru, "An Exceptional Debate," *National Review*, February 18, 2020, https://www.nationalreview.com/magazine/2010/03/08/exceptional-debate/.

20 "2022 Index of Economic Freedom," The Heritage Foundation, accessed April 2022, https://www.heritage.org/index/.

21 Abraham Lincoln, *Collected Words of Abraham Lincoln* (Ann Arbor: University of Michigan Digital Library Production Services, 2001), vol. 4, 203, https://quod.lib.umich.edu/l/lincoln/lincoln4/1:319?rgn=div1;view=toc.

22 Raj Chetty et al., "The Fading American Dream: Trends in Absolute Income Mobility Since 1940," Working Paper 22910 (Cambridge: National Bureau of Economic Research, December 2016).

23 Edward Glaeser, "How to Fix American Capitalism," *City Journal*, Autumn 2020, https://www.city-journal.org/end-insider-privileges-of-socialism-to-fix-american-capitalism.

24 Don Peck, "How a New Jobless Era Will Transform America," *The Atlantic*, March 2010, https://www.theatlantic.com/magazine/archive/2010/03/how-a-new-jobless-era-will-transform-america/307919/.

25 Ben Casselman, "Pessimism About the Economy Is Growing, a U.S. Poll Shows," *New York Times*, June 30, 2022.

26 Tim Malloy and Doug Schwartz, "Vast Majority of Americans Say Ban Russian Oil, Quinnipiac University National Poll Finds; Nearly 8 in 10 Support U.S. Military Response if Putin Attacks a NATO Country" (Press Release, Quinnipiac University, March 7, 2022).

27 Lee Rainie, Scott Keeter, and Andrew Perrin, "Trust and Distrust in America" (Washington: Pew Research Center, 2019).

28 David Brooks, "America Is Having a Moral Convulsion," *Atlantic*, October 5, 2020.

29 See Stephen Wertheim, "The Price of Primacy," *Foreign Affairs* 99, no. 2 (March/April 2020); and Sohrab Ahmari, Patrick Deneen, and Gladden Pappin, "Hawks Are Standing in the Way of a New Republican Party," *New York Times*, February 5, 2022.

30 Alexander Hamilton, "Remarks on Equality of Representation of the States in the Congress at the Constitutional Convention," in *The Papers of Alexander Hamilton, January 1787 – May 1788*, ed. Harold C. Syrett, vol. 4 (New York: Columbia University Press, 1962), 220–223.

31 Thucydides, *The Peloponnesian War,* Book 5 (New York: E.P. Dutton, 1910), chapter 89, 1.

32 One of the clearest statements of the Chinese Communist Party's ambitions can be found in Xi Jinping's speech at the 19th Congress of the Communist Party of China. Xi Jinping, "Secure a Decisive Victory in Building a Moderately Prosperous Society in All Respects and Strive for the Great Success of Socialism with Chinese Characteristics for a New Era." Remarks, 19th National Congress of the Communist Party of China, October 18, 2017.

33 Mancur Olson, *The Rise and Decline of Nations: Economic Growth, Stagflation, and Social Rigidities* (New Haven: Yale University Press, 1982), 74.

34 Tyler Cowen, *The Great Stagnation: How America Ate All the Low-Hanging Fruit of Modern History, Got Sick, and Will (Eventually) Feel Better* (New York: Dutton, 2011).

35 Bari Weiss, "We Got Here Because of Cowardice. We Get Out with Courage," *Commentary*, November 2021.

36 "Civilian Labor Force Participation Rate," U.S. Bureau of Labor Statistics, accessed June 2021, https://www.bls.gov/charts/employment-situation/civilian-labor-force-participation-rate.htm; and Nicholas Eberstadt, "Education and Men without Work," *National Affairs* no. 51 (Spring 2022), https://www.nationalaffairs.com/publications/detail/education-and-men-without-work.

37 Social Capital Project, "The Demise of the Happy Two-Parent Home," SCP Report No. 3–20, Washington: Joint Economic Committee—Republicans, July 2020.

38 Timothy P. Carney, *Alienated America: Why Some Places Thrive While Others Collapse* (New York: HarperCollins, 2019).

39 Rachel Louise Ensign and Shane Shifflett, "College Was Supposed to Close the Wealth Gap for Black Americans. The Opposite Happened," *Wall Street Journal*, August 7, 2021.

40 Bruce Stokes, "Global Publics More Upbeat About the Economy" (Washington: Pew Research Center, 2017), 15.

41 "National: More Americans Struggling: Inflation, Gas Prices Top Family Concerns" (Press Release, Monmouth University, July 5, 2022).

42 Emily Badger, "Americans Are Afraid. Not for Themselves, but for the Country," *New York Times*, November 1, 2020.

Chapter 2

1 David G. Tarr, "The Steel Crisis in the United States and the European Community: Causes and Adjustments," in *Issues in US-EC Trade Relations*, Robert E. Baldwin, Carl B. Hamilton, and Andre Sapir, eds. (Chicago: University of Chicago Press, 1988), 175.

2 Bill Toland, "In Desperate 1983, There Was Nowhere for Pittsburgh's Economy to Go but Up," *Pittsburgh Post-Gazette*, December 23, 2012.

3 See, for example, Alan Blinder and William J. Newton, "The 1971–1974 Controls Program and the Price Level: An Econometric Post-Mortem" (October 1981), NBER Working Paper No. 0279.

4 See, for example, Jack Knott and Aaron Wildavsky, "Jimmy Carter's Theory of Governing," *Wilson Quarterly* 1, no. 2 (Winter 1977): 49–67.

5 Pew Research Center, "Public Trust in Government: 1958–2021," accessed June 2021, https://www.pewresearch.org/politics/2021/05/17/public-trust-in-government.

6 Gallup, "Confidence in Institutions," accessed June 2022, https://news.gallup.com/poll/1597/confidence-institutions.aspx.

7 See Ron Nessen, "The Brookings Institution's Arthur Okun—Father of the 'Misery Index,'" Brookings Institution, December 17, 2008, https://www.brookings.edu/opinions/the-brookings-institutions-arthur-okun-father-of-the-misery-index/.

8 Alan Greenspan and Adrian Wooldridge, *Capitalism in America: An Economic History of the United States* (New York: Penguin Press 2018), chapter 9.

9 "Labor Force Employment and Unemployment (LAUS)," Pennsylvania Department of Labor & Industry, accessed July 2021, https://www.workstats.dli.pa.gov/Research/Pages/default.aspx.

10 Bernard Gwertzman, "The Gloomy Side of the Historian Henry A. Kissinger," *New York Times*, April 5, 1976.

11 Michel J. Crozier, Samuel P. Huntington, Joji Watanuki, "The Crisis of Democracy," Report on the Governability of Democracies to the Trilateral Commission (New York: New York University Press, 1975).

12 Aidan Connaughton, "Prevailing view among Americans is that U.S. influence in the world is weakening—and China's is growing," *Pew Research Center*, June 23, 2022, https://www.pewresearch.org/fact-tank/2022/06/23/prevailing-view-among-americans-is-that-u-s-influence-in-the-world-is-weakening-and-chinas-is-growing/.

13 Aaron L. Friedberg, *The Weary Titan: Britain and the Experience of Relative Decline, 1895*–1905 (Princeton: Princeton University Press, 1988), 290.

14 Henry Olsen, The Working-Class Republican: Ronald Reagan and the Return of Blue-Collar Conservatism (New York: Broadside Books, 2017).

15 Ronald Reagan, "Inaugural Address" (Speech, Presidential Inauguration, Washington, DC, January 20, 1981).

16 Ronald Reagan, "Commencement Address to the Graduating Class of Eureka College" (Speech, Eureka College, Eureka, IL, May 10, 1982).

17 Hal Brands, *Making the Unipolar Moment* (Ithaca: Cornell University Press, 2016), 11.

18 Robert Ajemian, "Where Is the Real George Bush?" *Time*, January 26, 1987.

19 James Wilson, *The Triumph of Improvisation: Gorbachev's Adaptability, Reagan's Engagement, and the End of the Cold War* (Ithaca: Cornell University Press, 2014), 10.

20 Ronald Reagan, "Remarks to Members of the Commonwealth Club of California" (Speech, Commonwealth Club, San Francisco, CA, March 4, 1983).

21 American Academy of Arts and Sciences, "Historical Trends in Federal R&D," accessed July 2021, https://www.aaas.org/programs/r-d-budget-and-policy/historical-trends-federal-rd: Gerald M. Boyd, "Reagan Hails U.S. Technology's Role," *New York Times*, April 10, 1987.

22 Harold Brown with Joyce Winslow, *Star Spangled Security: Applying Lessons Learned over Six Decades Safeguarding America* (Washington: Brookings Institution Press, 2012).

23 Hal Brands, "The Vision Thing," *First Year 2017* no. 2 (January 2016).

24 John B. Taylor, "Paul Volcker Was Inflation's Worst Enemy," *Wall Street Journal*, December 9, 2019.

25 Peter Baker and Susan Glasser, *The Man Who Ran Washington: The Life and Times of James A. Baker III* (New York: Doubleday, 2020), 223.

26 George P. Shultz, *Turmoil and Triumph: My Years as Secretary of State* (New York: Charles Scribner's Sons, 1993), 263.

27 Quoted in E.J. Dionne Jr., "Kennedy Says Democrats Can Learn From Reagan," *New York Times*, March 7, 1989.

28 Ronald Reagan, "Address Accepting the Presidential Nomination," Speech, Republican National Convention, Detroit, July 17, 1980.

29 Peter Baker and Susan Glasser, *The Man Who Ran Washington: The Life and Times of James A. Baker III* (New York: Doubleday, 2020), 223.

30 "Address on Behalf of Senator Barry Goldwater: 'A Time for Choosing.'" October 27, 1964. https://www.presidency.ucsb.edu/documents/address-behalf-senator-barry-goldwater-time-for-choosing.

31 Ibid.

32 Ronald Reagan, "Inaugural Address," Speech, Presidential Inauguration, Washington, DC, January 20, 1981.

33 Ibid.

34 Ronald Reagan, "Address to the Members of the British Parliament," Speech, Palace of Westminster, London, June 8, 1982.

35 See, for example, George Packer, *Last Best Hope: America in Crisis and Renewal* (New York: Farrar, Straus and Giroux, 2021), 78–82.

36 Ronald Reagan, "Farewell Address to the Nation," Speech, White House, Washington, DC, January 11, 1989.

37 "Labor Force Employment and Unemployment Statistics (LAUS)."

38 Rachel Louise Ensign and Shane Shifflett, "College Was Supposed to Close the Wealth Gap for Black Americans. The Opposite Happened," *Wall Street Journal*, August 7, 2021.

Chapter 3

1 William S. Dietrich II, "A Very Short History of Pittsburgh," *Pittsburgh Quarterly*, August 25, 2008.
2 Stefan Lorent, *Pittsburgh: The Portrait of an American City* (New York: Derrydale Press, 2000).
3 Guhan Venkatu, "Rust and Renewal: A Pittsburgh Retrospective," *Industrial Heartland Series* (Cleveland: The Cleveland Federal Reserve, 2018).
4 Scott Andes et al., "Capturing the Next Economy: Pittsburgh's Rise as a Global Innovation City," Brookings Institution, September 13, 2017, https://www.brookings.edu/wp-content/uploads/2017/09/pittsburgh_full.pdf.
5 Jeffery Fraser, "A Slow but Continuing Decline," *Pittsburgh Quarterly*, Fall 2019.
6 "Labor Force Employment and Unemployment (LAUS)," Pennsylvania Department of Labor & Industry, accessed July 2021, https://www.workstats.dli.pa.gov/Research/Pages/default.aspx.
7 James Risen, "The Struggle to Rebuild After Big Steel Moved Out: A Whole Region Was Almost Ruined When the Mills Closed," *Los Angeles Times*, September 27, 1989.
8 Scott Andes, et al., "Capturing the Next Economy: Pittsburgh's Rise as a Global Innovation City," Brookings Institution, September 13, 2017, https://www.brookings.edu/wp-content/uploads/2017/09/pittsburgh_full.pdf.
9 "SAP to Expand Cloud Presence With Acquisition of Ariba," Press Release, SAP News Center, May 22, 2012, https://news.sap.com/2012/05/sap-to-expand-cloud-presence-with-acquisition-of-ariba/.
10 Taylor Soper, "Pittsburgh Forges a New Future, Remaking Iconic Steel Town into a Modern Innovation Factory," *GeekWire*, January 25, 2018.
11 Scott Andes et al., "Capturing the Next Economy: Pittsburgh's Rise as a Global Innovation City," Brookings Institution, September 13, 2017, https://www.brookings.edu/wp-content/uploads/2017/09/pittsburgh_full.pdf.
12 Michael Machosky, "Vacant 1915 Ford Plant Coming Back to Life as $330 Million Pitt Biomedical Research Hub," *Next Pittsburgh*, May 25, 2021.
13 W. W. Abbot, ed., *The Papers of George Washington*, Confederation Series 3, 19 May 1785 – 31 March 1786 (Charlottesville: University Press of Virginia, 1994), 148–15.
14 Charles I. Jones, "Sources of U.S. Economic Growth in a World of Ideas," *American Economic Review* 92, no. 1 (March 2002): 220–239.

15 James Manyika and Michael Spence, "A Better Boom: How to Capture the Pandemic's Productivity Potential," *Foreign Affairs*, July/August 2021, https://www.foreignaffairs.com/articles/united-states/2021-06-22/better-boom.

16 Harry S. Truman, "Statement by the President Announcing the Use of the A-Bomb at Hiroshima" (Prepared statement, Washington, August 6, 1945).

17 See, for example, Robert M. Solow, "Technical Change and the Aggregate Production Function," in *The Review of Economics and Statistics* 39, no. 3 (August 1957): 312–320.

18 Oren Cass, "Putting Dynamism in Its Place," *National Affairs* no. 51 (Spring 2022), https://www.nationalaffairs.com/publications/detail/putting-dynamism-in-its-place.

19 Edward Glaeser, "How to Fix American Capitalism," *City Journal*, Autumn 2020, https://www.city-journal.org/end-insider-privileges-of-socialism-to-fix-american-capitalism.

20 Roger Hilsman memorialized his service in World War II in his memoirs, *American Guerrilla: My War Behind Enemy Lines* (Washington: Brassey's, 1990).

21 "Remarks by the President in Meeting with High-Tech Leaders" (Speech, White House, Washington, DC, March 28, 2001), https://georgewbush-whitehouse.archives.gov/news/releases/2001/03/20010328-2.html.

22 David H. McCormick, "High Technology Trade with China" (Speech, Commonwealth Club, San Jose, CA, July 27, 2006).

23 Ufuk Akcigit and Sina T. Ates, "New Insights for Innovation Policy," *Aspen Economic Strategy Group*, July 2022; and Charles I. Jones, "Sources of U.S. Economic Growth in a World of Ideas," *American Economic Review* 92, no. 1 (March 2002): 220–239.

24 United States President and Council of Economic Advisers, *Economic Report of the President Together with the Annual Report of the Council of Economic Advisers* (Washington: Government Printing Office, 2020), https://trumpwhitehouse.archives.gov/wp-content/uploads/2020/02/2020-Economic-Report-of-the-President-WHCEA.pdf.

25 United States President and Council of Economic Advisers, *Economic Report of the President Together with the Annual Report of the Council of Economic Advisers* (Washington: Government Printing Office, 2021). https://trumpwhitehouse.archives.gov/wp-content/uploads/2021/01/Economic-Report-of-the-President-Jan2021.pdf.

26 Megan Cassella, "The Pandemic Drove Women out of the Workforce. Will They Come Back?" *Politico*, July 22, 2021, https://www.politico.com/news/2021/07/22/coronavirus-pandemic-women-workforce-500329.

27 Abraham Lincoln, *Abraham Lincoln Papers: Series 1. General Correspondence. 1833–1916: Abraham Lincoln, May–June 1861 Message to Congress, July 4, 1861,*

Second Printed Draft, with Changes in Lincoln's Hand, May 1861, Abraham Lincoln Papers at the Library of Congress, Manuscripts Division, Library of Congress, https://www.loc.gov/item/mal1057200/.

28 Clayton M. Christensen, *The Innovator's Dilemma: The Revolutionary Book That Will Change the Way You Do Business* (Cambridge: Harvard Business School Press, 1997).

29 "'Made in China 2025' Plan Issued," State Council of the People's Republic of China, May 19, 2015, http://english.www.gov.cn/policies/latest_releases/2015/05/19/content_281475110703534.htm.

30 Eric Schmidt, "I Used to Run Google. Silicon Valley Could Lose to China," *New York Times*, February 27, 2020.

31 Vannevar Bush, "As We May Think," *The Atlantic*, July 1945.

32 Jeff Desjardins, "How Much Data Is Generated Each Day?" *Visual Capitalist*, April 15, 2019.

33 According to research provided by McKinsey Global Institute.

34 Sharon LaFraniere et al., "Politics, Science and the Remarkable Race for a Coronavirus Vaccine," *New York Times*, November 21, 2020.

35 Task Force on Manufacturing Competitiveness. *A Manufacturing Renaissance: Bolstering U.S. Production for National Security and Economic Prosperity*. Washington: Ronald Reagan Presidential Foundation and Institute, 2021.

36 *Review of Findings of the President's Commission on Industrial Competitiveness, Before the Senate Finance Comm.*, 99th Cong. 5 (1985). Attached memo from Finance Committee Staff.

37 Gary P. Pisano and Willy C. Shih. "Restoring American Competitiveness." *Harvard Business Review* 87, no. 7–8 (July–August 2009); and James Manyika et al, "Building a More Competitive US Manufacturing Sector." Working paper, McKinsey Global Institute, April 15, 2021.

38 Arjun Kharpal, "How Asia Came to Dominate Chipmaking and What the U.S. Wants to Do about It," *CNBC*, April 11, 2021.

39 Interviews conducted by the Ronald Reagan Institute Task Force, May–October 2021.

40 John VerWey, "No Permits, No Fabs: The Importance of Regulatory Reform for Semiconductor Manufacturing" (Center for Security and Emerging Technology, October 2021). https://doi.org/10.51593/20210053.

41 Dylan Patel, "Why America Will Lose Semiconductors," *SemiAnalysis*, newsletter, June 13, 2022, https://semianalysis.substack.com/p/why-america-will-lose-semiconductors.

42 Stephanie Yang, "Chip Makers Contend for Talent as Industry Faces Labor Shortage," *Wall Street Journal*, January 2, 2022.

43 Interviews with semiconductor industry representatives, July–October 2021.
44 Nadia Schadlow, Arthur Herman, and Brady Helwig, "Powering Innovation: A Strategic Approach to America's Advanced Battery Technology," A Report of the Hamilton Commission on Securing America's National Security Industrial Base. Washington: Hudson Institute, 2021.
45 Stephen Ezell, "Going, Going, Gone? To Stay Competitive in Biopharmaceuticals, America Must Learn From Its Semiconductor Mistakes," Information Technology & Innovation Foundation, November 22, 2021.
46 Interagency Task Force in Fulfillment of Executive Order 13806, *Assessing and Strengthening the Manufacturing and Defense Industrial Base and Supply Chain Resiliency of the United States*. Washington: Office of the Undersecretary of Defense for Acquisition and Sustainment and Office of the Deputy Assistant Secretary of Defense for Industrial Policy, 2018.
47 The CHIPS and Science Act of 2022, H.R. 4346, 177th Cong. (2021).
48 John F. Cogan and Kevin Warsh, "Reinvigorating Economic Governance," (Stanford: Hoover Institution, 2022).
49 Mike Allen, "Republicans and Democrats Agree—the Country Is Falling Apart," *Axios*, January 14, 2021.
50 Victoria Balara, "Fox News Poll: Pride in US down significantly." FoxNews.com, June 30, 2022, https://www.foxnews.com/official-polls/fox-news-poll-pride-us-down-significantly.
51 Ronald Reagan, "Explosion of the Space Shuttle *Challenger*," Address to the Nation, White House, Washington, DC, January 28, 1986.

Chapter 4

1 McCormick Family History, 2018.
2 Lauren Camera, "High School Seniors Aren't College-Ready," *U.S. News & World Report*, April 27, 2016, https://www.usnews.com/news/articles/2016-04-27/high-school-seniors-arent-college-ready-naep-data-show.
3 Eric A. Hanushek et al., "The Achievement Gap Fails to Close," *Education Next* 19, no. 3 (Summer 2019), 8–17.
4 National Security Commission on Artificial Intelligence, *Final Report*, by Eric Schmidt, et al. (Washington: Government Printing Office, 2021), 173, https://www.nscai.gov/wp-content/uploads/2021/03/Full-Report-Digital-1.pdf.
5 National Science Board, National Science Foundation. *Elementary and Secondary STEM Education: Science and Engineering Indicators 2022*, NSB-2021-1 (Alexandria: National Science Board), https://ncses.nsf.gov/pubs/nsb20211.
6 See, for example, Sarah Mervosh, "The Pandemic Erased Two Decades of Progress in Math and Reading," *New York Times*, September 1, 2022.

7 Max Eden, "The K-12 Cartel Is Holding Children Hostage," *Washington Examiner*, January 13, 2022, https://www.washingtonexaminer.com/restoring-america/community-family/the-k-12-cartel-is-holding-children-hostage.

8 Corey A. DeAngelis and Matthew Nielsen, "No, We Haven't 'Defunded Education for Years,'" *Washington Examiner*, June 11, 2020, https://www.washingtonexaminer.com/opinion/no-we-havent-defunded-education-for-years.

9 Ira Stoll, "Growth in Administrative Staff, Assistant Principals Far Outpaces Teacher Hiring," *Education Next*, October 1, 2020, https://www.educationnext.org/growth-administrative-staff-assistant-principals-far-outpaces-teacher-hiring/.

10 For a dissection of critical race theory, see Jeffrey J. Pyle, "Race, Equality and the Rule of Law: Critical Race Theory's Attack on the Promises of Liberalism," *Boston College Law Review* 40, no. 3 (1999), https://lawdigitalcommons.bc.edu/bclr/vol40/iss3/6.

11 "The 2021 College Free Speech Rankings," Foundation for Individual Rights in Education, September 21, 2021, https://www.thefire.org/the-2021-college-free-speech-rankings.

12 Komi German and Sean Stevens, "The Targeting of Scholars for Ideological Reasons from 2015 to Present," The Foundation for Individual Rights in Education (2021), https://www.thefire.org/research/publications/miscellaneous-publications/scholars-under-fire/scholars-under-fire-full-text/; and Gabriel Scheinmann, "The Intellectual Conformity of International-Relations Faculty," *National Review*, September 5, 2021, https://www.nationalreview.com/2021/09/the-intellectual-conformity-of-international-relations-faculty.

13 Yuval Levin, *A Time to Build: From Family and Community to Congress and the Campus, How Recommitting to Our Institutions Can Revive the American Dream* (New York: Basic Books, 2020), 105.

14 Ibid, 103.

15 Pete Hegseth with David Goodwin, *Battle for the American Mind: Uprooting a Century of Miseducation* (New York: Broadside Books, 2022).

16 Frederick M. Hess, "The Next Conservative Education Agenda," *National Affairs*, no. 51 (Spring 2020), https://www.nationalaffairs.com/publications/detail/the-next-conservative-education-agenda.

17 Katherine B. Stevens and Elizabeth English Smith, "Does Pre-K Work? The Research on Ten Early Childhood Programs—and What It Tells Us," Washington: American Enterprise Institute, April 2016.

18 Albert Cheng and Paul E. Peterson, "How Satisfied Are Parents with Their Children's Schools," *Education Next* 17, no. 2 (Spring 2017), https://www.educationnext.org/how-satisfied-are-parents-with-childrens-schools-us-dept-ed-survey.

19 Macke Raymond, "Improving Educational Outcomes Through Innovation with Macke Raymond: Policy Perspectives," April 22, 2019, produced by PolicyEd, video, 4:07, https://www.policyed.org/perspectivesonpolicy/improving-educational-outcomes-through-innovation-macke-raymond/video.

20 Patrick J. Wolf et al., "Education Freedom and Student Achievement: Is More School Choice Associated with Higher State-Level Performance on the NAEP?" March 2021, University of Arkansas, School Choice Demonstration Project, https://scdp.uark.edu/education-freedom-and-naep-scores.pdf.

21 Jeb Bush, "Unlocking the Power of Technology for Better Governance," *Governance in an Emerging World*, no. 819 (October 2019), https://www.hoover.org/research/unlocking-power-technology-better-governance.

22 Matthew Chingos, Tomás Monarrez, and Daniel Kuehn, "The Effects of the Florida Tax Credit Scholarship Program on College Enrollment and Graduation," Urban Institute, February 4, 2019, https://www.urban.org/research/publication/effects-florida-tax-credit-scholarship-program-college-enrollment-and-graduation.

23 David Osborne, "A Tale of Two Systems: Education Reform in Washington, D.C." (Washington: Progressive Policy Institute, 2015).

24 Research provided by American Federation for Children.

25 Paul E. Peterson, "Lockdowns Give School Choice a Boost," *Wall Street Journal*, April 28, 2021.

26 AEI/Brookings Working Group on Poverty and Opportunity, *Opportunity, Responsibility and Security: A Consensus Plan for Reducing Poverty and Restoring the American Dream* (Washington: American Enterprise Institute, 2015), 61.

27 Mike Gallagher, "Wisconsin 2030: The Education Path to Prosperity within the Decade," Washington: American Enterprise Institute, 2021, 1.

28 Edmund DeMarche, "Hundreds of College Professors Blast 'Woke' Math Movement," *New York Post*, December 7, 2021.

29 Ian Rowe, "Here's Why All Students Need Agency Rather than 'Equity,'" *New York Post*, June 4, 2022.

30 Henry Kissinger, *Leadership: Six Studies in World Strategy* (New York: Penguin Press, 2022), 415.

31 See, for example, Gabriel Scheinmann, "The Intellectual Conformity of International-Relations Faculty," *National Review*, September 5, 2021, https://www.nationalreview.com/2021/09/the-intellectual-conformity-of-international-relations-faculty/.

32 Robert J. Zimmer, "Free Speech Is the Basis of a True Education," *Wall Street Journal*, August 26, 2016.

33 Geoffrey R. Stone et al, *Report of the Committee on Freedom of Expression*. Chicago: University of Chicago, 2015.

34 Joy Addison, "Skilled Labor Workforce Sees Severe Nationwide Shortage," *Fox Business*, February 4, 2022, https://www.foxbusiness.com/features/skilled-labor-workforce-severe-nationwide-shortage.

35 Irene Petrick and Faith McCreary, "Creating Lasting Value in the Age of AI + IoT—Futureproofing Your Business," *Intel*, December 2019, https://newsroom.intel.com/wp-content/uploads/sites/11/2019/12/futureproofing-your-business.pdf.

36 Bureau of Labor Statistics, "Job Openings and Labor Turnover Survey," News release USDL-21-1616 (September 8, 2021); and "Beyond Hiring: How Companies Are Reskilling to Address Talent Gaps," *McKinsey*, February 12, 2020, https://www.mckinsey.com/business-functions/people-and-organizational-performance/our-insights/beyond-hiring-how-companies-are-reskilling-to-address-talent-gaps.

37 Paul Wellener et al., "Creating Pathways for Tomorrow's Workforce Today," *Deloitte*, May 4, 2021, https://www2.deloitte.com/us/en/insights/industry/manufacturing/manufacturing-industry-diversity.html.

38 *The America Works Report: Quantifying the Nation's Workforce Crisis* (Washington: Chamber of Commerce, June 2021).

39 Bill Strickland, "Environments Change Behavior," 10:24. TED Video, filmed March 2014, https://www.youtube.com/watch?v=bnhSLAmDRh0.

40 Jim Jacobs and Maria Cormier, "Workforce Development and an Opportunity for Change," *Inside Higher Ed*, May 28, 2020, https://www.insidehighered.com/views/2020/05/28/three-factors-will-impact-community-college-efforts-make-workforce-training.

41 David McCormick, "Reshaping America's Views of Veterans," *Wall Street Journal*, December 6, 2015.

42 Kathy Matsui, Hiromi Suzuki, and Yoko Ushio, "Womenomics: Buy the Female Economy," Goldman Sachs, August 1999, https://www.goldmansachs.com/our-firm/history/moments/1999-womenomics.html.

43 Kathy Matsui, Hiromi Suzuki, and Kazunori Tatebe, "Womenomics 5.0." Goldman Sachs, April 18, 2019, https://www.goldmansachs.com/insights/pages/womenomics-5.0/.

44 George W. Bush, *Out of Many, One: Portraits of America's Immigrants* (New York: Crown Publishers, 2021), 148.

45 National Foundation for American Policy, "Immigrants and Nobel Prizes: 1901–2020," October 2020, https://nfap.com/wp-content/uploads/2020/10/Immigrants-and-Nobel-Prizes-1901-to-2020.NFAP-Policy-Brief.October-2020.pdf; and Remco Zwetsloot et al, *Keeping Top AI Talent in the United States: Findings and Policy Options for International Graduate Student Retention*, Georgetown University School of Foreign Service, Center for Security and

Emerging Technology, December 2019, https://cset.georgetown.edu/research/keeping-top-ai-talent-in-the-united-states/.

46 Stuart Anderson, "Immigrants and Billion-Dollar Companies," National Foundation for American Policy, October 2018, https://nfap.com/wp-content/uploads/2019/01/2018-BILLION-DOLLAR-STARTUPS.NFAP-Policy-Brief.2018-1.pdf; and New American Economy, "New American Fortune 500 in 2019: Top American Companies and Their Immigrant Roots," July 22, 2019, https://data.newamericaneconomy.org/en/fortune500-2019/.

47 Shai Bernstein et al., "The Contribution of High-Skilled Immigrants to Innovation in the United States," Working paper, Stanford Graduate School of Business, Stanford, CA, November 6, 2018, https://www.gsb.stanford.edu/faculty-research/working-papers/contribution-high-skilled-immigrants-innovation-united-states.

48 United Nations, Department of Economic and Social Affairs, Population Division, *International Migration 2019*, 2019, https://www.un.org/en/development/desa/population/migration/publications/migrationreport/docs/InternationalMigration2019_Report.pdf; and Rohen d'Aiglepierre et al., "A Global Profile of Emigrants to OECD Countries: Younger and More Skilled Migrants from More Diverse Countries" (working paper, Organisation for Economic Co-operation and Development, Paris, France, February 2020), https://doi.org/10.1787/0cb305d3-en.

49 Matthew Boyle, "PA's David McCormick Outlines America First Immigration Vision after Border Trip," *Breitbart*, February 14, 2022, https://www.breitbart.com/politics/2022/02/14/exclusive-pas-david-mccormick-outlines-america-first-immigration-vision-after-border-trip/.

50 Jon Kamp, José de Córdoba, and Julie Wernau, "How Two Mexican Drug Cartels Came to Dominate America's Fentanyl Supply," *Wall Street Journal*, August 30, 2022.

51 Michelle Hackman, "Border Patrol Makes About 1.66 Million Arrests at Southern Border in 2021 Fiscal Year," *Wall Street Journal*, October 22, 2021.

52 Christopher Wray, "The Threat Posed by the Chinese Government and the Chinese Communist Party to the Economic and National Security of the United States," Federal Bureau of Investigation, July 7, 2020, https://www.fbi.gov/news/speeches/the-threat-posed-by-the-chinese-government-and-the-chinese-communist-party-to-the-economic-and-national-security-of-the-united-states; Larry Diamond and Orville Schell, *China's Influence & America's Interests: Promoting Constructive Vigilance*, Hoover Institution, 2019, https://www.hoover.org/sites/default/files/research/docs/00_diamond-schell-chinas-influence-and-american-interests.pdf.

53 Remco Zwetsloot and Zachary Arnold, "Chinese Students Are Not a Fifth Column," *Foreign Affairs* (April 23, 2021), https://www.foreignaffairs.com/articles/united-states/2021-04-23/chinese-students-are-not-fifth-column.

54 Matthew Sussis, "Untold Stories: The American Workers Replaced by the H-1B Visa Program," Center for Immigration Studies, May 4, 2019, https://cis.org/Report/Untold-Stories-American-Workers-Replaced-H1B-Visa-Program.

55 US Department of Homeland Security, "Lawful Permanent Residents (LPR)," https://www.dhs.gov/immigration-statistics/lawful-permanent-residents.

56 Oren Cass, *The Once and Future Worker* (Encounter Books; New York, 2018).

57 Donald J. Trump, "Modernizing Our Immigration System for a Stronger America," Remarks, White House, Washington, DC, May 16, 2019.

58 Ronald Reagan, "Ronald Reagan: Immigrants Recognize the Intoxicating Power of America," *Kansas City Star*, July 23, 2019, https://www.kansascity.com/opinion/opn-columns-blogs/syndicated-columnists/article232864812.html.

Chapter 5

1 Lingling Wei, "Beijing Drops Contentious 'Made in China 2025' Slogan, but Policy Remains," *Wall Street Journal*, March 5, 2019; and Arjun Kharpal, "China Has a 15-Year Plan to Shape the Future of Tech. But Some Call It Hype," *CNBC*, June 22, 2020.

2 See, for example, Marco Rubio, "American Industrial Policy and the Rise of China" (Remarks, National Defense University, Washington, DC, December 10, 2019). See also, Task Force on 21st-Century National Security Technology and Workforce. *The Contest for Innovation: Strengthening America's National Security Innovation Base in an Era of Strategic Competition*. Washington: Ronald Reagan Institute, December 3, 2019.

3 For a good story of CRISPR and its potential, see Carl Zimmer, "CRISPR, 10 Years On: Learning to Rewrite the Code of Life," *New York Times*, June 27, 2022.

4 Huawei has received, by some measures, as much as $75 billion in subsidies, tax breaks, and other forms of state support. Chuin-Wei Yap, "State Support Helped Fuel Huawei's Global Rise," *Wall Street Journal*, December 25, 2019.

5 "The Global AI Talent Tracker," Marco Polo, accessed August 2021, https://macropolo.org/digital-projects/the-global-ai-talent-tracker/.

6 National Security Commission on Artificial Intelligence, *Final Report*, by Eric Schmidt, et al. (Washington: Government Printing Office, 2021), 57.

7 Paul Mango, *Warp Speed: Inside the Operation that Beat Covid, the Critics, and the Odds* (New York: Republic, 2022), 15.

8 Vannevar Bush, *Science—the Endless Frontier* (Washington: United States Government Printing Office, 1945).

9 "Perils of Complacency: America at a Tipping Point in Science and Engineering," American Academy of Arts & Sciences and Baker Institute for Public Policy, September 2020, https://www.amacad.org/publication/perils-of-complacency.

10 Ashish Aroroa and Sharon Belenzon, "American Innovation Under Threat: Restrictive Legislation and Global Competition," Report of the Innovation Frontier Project, Progressive Policy Institute, Washington, DC, November 18, 2021.

11 John P. A. Ioannidis, "Fund People Not Projects," *Nature* 477, September 28, 2011, 529–531.

12 Daniel E. Ho et al., "Building a National AI Research Resource," White paper, Human-Centered Artificial Intelligence Initiative, Stanford University, Stanford, CA, October 2021.

13 Eric and Wendy Schmitt, "How to Spur Scientific Breakthroughs," *Boston Globe*, June 16, 2022.

14 As Chris Brose, the former staff director of the Senate Armed Services Committee, once said, would-be defense contractors "need one thing more than any other from the U.S. government: revenue." *Supercharging the Innovation Base: Hearing before the Future of Defense Task Force of the House Armed Services Comm.*, 116th Cong. (2020). Statement of Christian Brose.

15 See, for example, Dani Rodrik, "Industrial Policy for the Twenty-First Century," November 2004, https://drodrik.scholar.harvard.edu/publications/industrial-policy-twenty-first-century.

16 "U.S. Government Support of the Entrepreneurial Space Age," Report by Space Angels for the National Aeronautics and Space Administration, June 17, 2019, 2.

17 These funds facilitate defense and intelligence community procurement of new technologies, particularly from nontraditional contractors, and they encourage new entrants into the contractor market.

18 *Supercharging the Innovation Base: Hearing before the Future of Defense Task Force of the House Armed Services Comm.*, 116th Cong. (2020) (Comment made by Raj Shah, former managing partner of the Defense Innovation Unit).

19 The federal government currently supports innovative small businesses through the Small Business Innovation Research (SBIR) program, created during the Reagan administration, and the Small Business Technology Transfer (STTR) program. Federal agencies administer the programs. Agencies identify something they need, and firms submit proposals to develop that needed capability. All told, agencies award roughly $3 billion per year through the two programs. They're a vital piece of the innovation puzzle, but a few billion dollars is not enough.

20 The CHIPS and Science Act of 2022, H.R. 4346, 177th Cong. (2021).

21 Mission Statement of America's Frontier Fund, provided by founders.

22 For comparison, the Chinese Communist Party established "guiding funds" to incentivize private investment and establish venture funding for technology development. See the discussion of these funds in, Kai-Fu Lee, *AI Superpowers: China, Silicon Valley, and the New World Order* (Boston: Houghton Mifflin Harcourt, 2018), 64–65.

23 See Matt Ridley, *How Innovation Works: And Why It Flourishes in Freedom.* (New York: HarperCollins, 2020); and Christian Brose, *The Kill Chain: Defending America in the Future of High-Tech Warfare* (New York: Hachette Books, 2020).

24 Prospectus provided by founder.

25 Mark Perry, "Monday Afternoon Links," *Carpe Diem* (blog), August 31, 2015.

26 Energy Policy Act of 2005, 42 U.S.C. § 15801–16359 (2005).

27 Salena Zito, "Pennsylvania Town Saved by Fracking Fears Biden Will Kill Its Prosperity," *New York Post*, April 10, 2021.

28 PricewaterhouseCoopers, "Impacts of the Oil and Natural Gas Industry on the US Economy in 2019," Report prepared for American Petroleum Institute, July 20, 2021.

29 "Global CO2 emissions in 2019," International Energy Agency, February 11, 2020.

30 United States President and Council of Economic Advisers, *Economic Report of the President Together with The Annual Report of the Council of Economic Advisers* (Washington: Government Printing Office, 2020), 95.

31 See *Economic Report of the President Together with The Annual Report of the Council of Economic Advisers*, 2020; and United States Department of the Treasury Office of Economic Policy, the Council of Economic Advisers, and the Department of Labor, *Occupational Licensing: A Framework for Policymakers* (Washington: Government Printing Office, 2015).

32 Adam Thierer, *Permissionless Innovation: The Continuing Case for Comprehensive Technological Freedom* (Arlington: Mercatus Center at George Mason University, 2014).

33 The Council of Economic Advisers, *The Economic Effects of Federal Deregulation since January 2017: An Interim Report* (Washington: Government Printing Office, 2019).

34 The Federal Aviation Administration, for example, is working with drone developers to modernize regulations. Patrick McGee, "US Considers How to Open Skies to Drones and Flying Cars," *Financial Times*, February 27, 2020.

35 James Manyika and William H. McRaven, "Innovation and National Security: Keeping Our Edge," Task Force Report No. 77 (Council on Foreign Relations, Washington, DC, September 2019), 27.

36 Mitch Daniels, "Purdue President Daniels: 'Biggest risk of all is that we stop taking risks at all.'" News Release, Purdue University, West Lafayette, Indiana, May 15, 2021.

Chapter 6

1 Ray Dalio, *Principles* (New York: Simon & Schuster, 2017).
2 According to research provided by McKinsey Global Institute.
3 Alan Greenspan and Adrian Wooldridge, *Capitalism in America: An Economic History of the United States* (New York: Penguin Press, 2018), 16.
4 Ibid.
5 "Not Everything Can Be Digitized. But Everything That Can Be Digitized Will Be" (Press release, IESE, Munich, Germany, November 30, 2017), https://www.iese.edu/stories/not-everything-can-be-digitized-but-everything-that-can-be-digitized-will-be/.
6 According to analysis from Bridgewater Associates.
7 See, for example, Anna Lembke, *Dopamine Nation: Finding Balance in the Age of Indulgence* (New York: Dutton 2021); and Brian A. Primack et al., "Social Media Use and Perceived Social Isolation Among Young Adults in the U.S.," *American Journal of Preventive Medicine* 53, issue 1 (July 1, 2017), 1–8.
8 "The World's Most Valuable Resource Is No Longer Oil, but Data," *Economist*, May 6, 2017, https://www.economist.com/leaders/2017/05/06/the-worlds-most-valuable-resource-is-no-longer-oil-but-data.
9 Matthew J. Slaughter and David H. McCormick, "Data Is Power," *Foreign Affairs*, 100, no. 3 (May/June 2001): 54.
10 "Economic Impact of the Human Genome Project," Batelle Technology Partnership Practice, May 2011, https://web.ornl.gov/sci/techresources/Human_Genome/publicat/BattelleReport2021.pdf.
11 Ezra Klein, "TikTok May Be More Dangerous Than It Looks," *New York Times*, May 8, 2022.
12 Liz Sly, "U.S. Soldiers Are Revealing Sensitive and Dangerous Information by Jogging," *Washington Post*, January 29, 2018.
13 Emily Baker-White, "Leaked Audio From 80 Internal TikTok Meetings Shows That US User Data Has Been Repeatedly Accessed From China," *Buzzfeed*, June 17, 2022, https://www.buzzfeednews.com/article/emilybakerwhite/tiktok-tapes-us-user-data-china-bytedance-access.
14 Senators Mark Warner and Marco Rubio to the Honorable Lina Khan, Chairwoman of the Federal Trade Commission, July 5, 2022, https://www.warner

.senate.gov/public/_cache/files/3/e/3eeb87b3-e9b5-4aa4-8ea1-361a8472ff46/A42795C63518B32671F9ACCF82B1E26A.khan-ssci-tiktok-letter.pdf.

15 Georgia Wells, Jeff Horwitz, and Deepa Seetharaman, "Facebook Knows Instagram Is Toxic for Teen Girls, Company Documents Show," *Wall Street Journal*, September 14, 2021.

16 Nihal Krishan, "Big Tech Faces Renewed Scrutiny for Hunter Biden Laptop Censorship," *Washington Examiner*, March 31, 2022.

17 Lima Cristiano, "Facebook No Longer Treating 'Man-Made' Covid as a Crackpot Idea," *Politico*, May 26, 2021. The Editorial Board. "Facebook's Lab-Leak About-Face," *Wall Street Journal*, May 27, 2021.

18 Brad Parscale, "Trump Is Right: More Than Facebook & Twitter, Google Threatens Democracy, Online Freedom," *USA Today*, September 10, 2018.

19 For example, in 2021, it removed a book on the transgender movement by respected scholar Ryan T. Anderson. See Rod Dreher, "Amazon Cancels Ryan T. Anderson Book," *American Conservative*, February 21, 2021.

20 Daisuke Wakabayashi and Scott Shane, "Google Will Not Renew Pentagon Contract That Upset Employees," *New York Times*, June 1, 2018.

21 See, for example, Nick Bilton, "Silicon Valley Won't Own Up to Its China Problem," *Vanity Fair*, January 21, 2022.

22 Jack Nicas, Raymond Zhong, and Daisuke Wakabayashi, "Censorship, Surveillance and Profits: A Hard Bargain for Apple in China," *New York Times*, June 17, 2012; and Wayne Ma, "Inside Tim Cook's Secret $275 Billion Deal with Chinese Authorities," *The Information*, December 7, 2021.

23 As I write this, Congress is debating bipartisan legislation to protect user privacy. What comes of those discussions may obviate the need for some of what I propose here. John D. McKinnon, "Online Privacy Protection Bill Gets Bipartisan Push," *Wall Street Journal*, June 3, 2022.

24 Similar to proposals from the National Security Commission on Artificial Intelligence. National Security Commission on Artificial Intelligence, *Final Report*, 192.

25 For a catalog of social media's effects, see Jonathan Haidt, "Why the Past 10 Years of American Life Have Been Uniquely Stupid," *Atlantic*, May 2022.

26 John F. Cogan and Kevin Warsh, "Reinvigorating Economic Governance." Stanford: Hoover Institution, 2022.

27 "Differences in How Democrats and Republicans Behave on Twitter." Pew Research Center, October 15, 2020, https://www.pewresearch.org/politics/2020/10/15/differences-in-how-democrats-and-republicans-behave-on-twitter/.

28 For a detailed summary of the law and its effects, see Valerie C. Brannon, and Eric N. Holmes, "Section 230: An Overview." Congressional Research Service no. R46751, April 7, 2021.

29 Tom Cotton, "Big Tech Reboot—Time to Stop Further Consolidations, Revive Competition, and Promote Free Speech," *Fox News*, November 16, 2021, https://www.foxnews.com/opinion/big-tech-revive-competition-promote-free-speech-sen-tom-cotton.

30 Mark Lapedus, "The Great Quantum Computing Race," *Semiconductor Engineering*, July 26, 2021, https://semiengineering.com/the-great-quantum-computing-race/.

31 Robert C. O'Brien, "Breaking Up Tech Is a Gift to China," *Wall Street Journal*, December 26, 2021.

32 Xi Jinping, "Speech to the Politburo Collective Study Session on China's Digital Economy," Rogier Creemers, et al., trans. Remarks, Beijing, CN, October 18, 2021.

33 Paul Mozur, Raymond Zhong, and Aaron Krolik, "In Coronavirus Fight, China Gives Citizens a Color Code, with Red Flags," *New York Times*, March 1, 2020.

34 Matt Pottinger and David Feith, "The Most Powerful Data Broker in the World Is Winning the War Against the U.S.," *New York Times*, November 30, 2021.

35 Jonathan E. Hillman and Maesea McCalpin, "Huawei's Global Cloud Strategy," *Reconnecting Asia*, May 17, 2021, https://reconasia.csis.org/huawei-global-cloud-strategy/.

36 Cate Cadell, "China Harvests Masses of Data on Western Targets, Documents Show," *Washington Post*, December 31, 2021; and Muyi Xiao and Paul Mozur, "A Digital Manhunt: How Chinese Police Track Critics on Twitter and Facebook," *New York Times*, January 1, 2022.

37 Michael Mink, "How the Clean Network Alliance of Democracies Turned the Tide on Huawei in 5G," *Life & News*, December 2, 2020, https://www.lifeandnews.com/articles/how-the-clean-network-alliance-of-democracies-turned-the-tide-on-huawei-in-5g/.

38 Andrew Imbrie et al., "Privacy Is Power," *Foreign Affairs*, January 19, 2022, https://www.foreignaffairs.com/articles/world/2022-01-19/privacy-power.

39. "The Trust Machine," *Economist*, October 31, 2015.

Chapter 7

1 "Trade Official Outlines Approach for Economic Growth," Pittsburgh *Business Times*, May 8, 2006.

2 See, for example, "U.S. Improving Controls on 'Dual Use' Exports to China; Commerce Department Sees Increasing High-Tech Trade, Enhanced Security," Press Release, State Department, Washington, DC, June 13, 2006.

3 David McCormick, "Don't Use Exports to China to Develop Military," *Financial Times*, June 8, 2006.

4 Policy Planning Staff, "The Elements of the China Challenge" (Washington: Office of the Secretary of State, 2020).

5 " 'Made in China 2025' Plan Issued," State Council of the People's Republic of China, May 19, 2015, http://english.www.gov.cn/policies/latest_releases/2015/05/19/content_281475110703534.htm.

6 Office of the United States Trade Representative. *Findings of the Investigation into China's Acts, Policies, and Practices Related to Technology Transfer, Intellectual Property, and Innovation Under Section 301 of the Trade Act of 1974.* Washington: Government Printing Office, March 2018.

7 Aaron L. Friedberg, *Getting China Wrong* (Cambridge: Polity, 2022), 1.

8 Export Control Reform Act of 2018, 50 U.S.C. § 4801 (2018); and Foreign Investment Risk Review Modernization Act of 2018, 50 U.S.C. § 4501 (2018).

9 David McCormick, "Time for America's leaders to confront China's Communist Party head on," *Fox Business*, January 13, 2022, https://www.foxbusiness.com/politics/americas-leaders-chinas-communist-party-dave-mccormick.

10 David H. McCormick, "Remarks at Wharton's Eleventh Annual Investment Management Conference," Speech, Wharton School of the University of Pennsylvania, Philadelphia, PA, October 3, 2008.

11 *Findings of the Investigation into China's Acts, Policies, and Practices Related to Technology Transfer, Intellectual Property, and Innovation Under Section 301 of the Trade Act of 1974.*

12 Robert E. Lighthizer, "How to Make Trade Work for Workers," *Foreign Affairs* 99, no. 4 (July/August 2020): 87.

13 Review of Findings of the President's Commission on Industrial Competitiveness, Before the Senate Finance Comm., 99th Cong. 5 (1985) (Attached memo from Finance Committee Staff).

14 "U.S.-China Trade Facts," Office of the United States Trade Representative, accessed January 2022, https://ustr.gov/countries-regions/china-mongolia-taiwan/peoples-republic-china.

15 President Trump laid the groundwork for energy exports by securing China's commitment to buying $50 billion worth of U.S. energy. Ariel Cohen, "Phase One Trade Deal: China Pledges to Buy Ambitious $50 Billion in US Energy Exports," *Forbes*, January 15, 2020.

16 Austen Hufford, "Harley-Davidson Finds Partner to Make Small Motorcycles in China," *Wall Street Journal*, June 19, 2019.

17 Kate O'Keeffe, Heather Somerville, and Yang Jie, "U.S. Companies Aid China's Bid for Chip Dominance Despite Security Concerns," *Wall Street Journal*, November 12, 2021.

18 Ryan Fedasiuk, Jennifer Melot, and Ben Murphy, "Harnessed Lightning: How

the Chinese Military Is Adopting Artificial Intelligence" (Washington: Georgetown University Center for Security and Emerging Technology, October 2021).

19 Kate O'Keeffe, Natalie Andrews, and Heather Somerville, "Lawmakers Make Bipartisan Push for New Government Powers to Block U.S. Investments in China," *Wall Street Journal*, June 14, 2022.

20 Thanks to H.R. McMaster for his recommendations on how to structure this committee.

21 Derek Scissors, "The Most Important Number for China Policy," *AEIdeas* (blog), January 3, 2022, https://www.aei.org/foreign-and-defense-policy/the-most-important-number-for-china-policy/.

22 My disagreements with Ray Dalio were reported in Bloomberg: Sridhar Natarajan and Katherine Burton, "Bridgewater CEO Clashes With Dalio Over China Before Senate Race," *Bloomberg*, December 4, 2021.

23 For data on exports and exporting companies, see U.S. Census Bureau, "A Profile of U.S. Importing and Exporting Companies," release no. CB21-52, April 7, 2021, https://www.census.gov/foreign-trade/Press-Release/edb/2019/edbrel.pdf.

24 Benjamin Bain and Robert Schmidt, "US Regulators Move Step Closer to Delisting Chinese Firms," *Bloomberg*, December 2, 2021.

25 Office of the United States Trade Representative, *Findings of the Investigation into China's Acts, Policies, and Practices Related to Technology Transfer, Intellectual Property, and Innovation Under Section 301 of the Trade Act of 1974* (Washington: Government Printing Office, March 2018).

26 Christopher Wray, "The Threat Posed by the Chinese Government and the Chinese Communist Party to the Economic and National Security of the United States." Remarks, Hudson Institute, Washington, DC, July 7, 2020.

27 Export Control Reform Act of 2018, 50 U.S.C. § 4801 (2018); and Foreign Investment Risk Review Modernization Act of 2018, 50 U.S.C. § 4501 (2018).

28 Phelim Kine, "The War on Drugs Puts a Target on China," *Politico*, February 7, 2022; and Edward Wong and Chris Buckley, "U.S. Says China's Repression of Uighurs Is 'Genocide,'" *New York Times*, January 19, 2021.

29 For example, the drone manufacturer DJI hid Beijing's support and its ties to the Chinese Communist Party, even as it sold drones to U.S. law enforcement. See Cade Cadell, "Drone Company DJI Obscured Ties to Chinese State Funding, Documents Show," *Washington Post*, February 1, 2022.

30 President of the United States, *National Security Strategy of the United States* (Washington: Government Printing Office, 2017), 2.

31 Task Force on Manufacturing Competitiveness. *A Manufacturing Renaissance: Bolstering U.S. Production for National Security and Economic Prosperity*. Washington: Ronald Reagan Presidential Foundation and Institute, 2021.

32 See, Arjun Kharpal, "Power Is 'Up for Grabs': Behind China's Plan to Shape the Future of Next-Generation Tech," *CNBC*, April 26, 2020.

33 Xi Jinping, "Certain Major Issues for Our National Medium- to Long-Term Economic and Social Development Strategy," trans. Etcetera Language Group, Inc., ed. Ben Murphy (speech, Central Financial and Economic Affairs Commission, Beijing, CN, April 10, 2020).

34 Rufus E. Miles, "The Origin and Meaning of Miles Law," *Public Administration Review* 38, no. 5 (1978), 399.

35 Robert M. Kimmitt, "Give Treasury Its Proper Role on the National Security Council," *New York Times*, July 23, 2012.

36 *History of the National Security Council, 1947–1997* (Washington: National Archives, 1999).

37 Christopher DeMuth, "Can the Administrative State Be Tamed?" *Journal of Legal Analysis* 8, no. 1, Spring 2016.

38 Ibid, 121.

39 Alexis de Tocqueville, *Democracy in America*, volume II, trans. Henry Reeve (London: Saunders and Otley, 1835), chapter 5.

Chapter 8

1 Wayne Stewart, *America's Football Factory: Western Pennsylvania's Cradle of Quarterbacks from Johnny Unitas to Joe Montana* (Kent: Kent State University, 2018).

2 Yuval Levin, *A Time to Build: From Family and Community to Congress and the Campus, How Recommitting to Our Institutions Can Revive the American Dream* (New York: Basic Books, 2020), 163.

3 Milton and Rose Friedman, *The Tyranny of the Status Quo* (New York: Houghton Mifflin Harcourt, 1984), 115.

4 Eric Gibson, "Woke Ideologues Are Taking Over American Art Museums," *Wall Street Journal*, September 2, 2022; Stanley Goldfarb, *Take Two Aspirin and Call Me By My Pronouns: Why Turning Doctors into Social Justice Warriors is Destroying American Medicine* (New York: Bombardier Books, 2022); and Thomas Spoehr, "The Rise of Wokeness in the Military," *Imprimis* 51, issue 6/7 (June/July 2022).

5 Meimei Xu, "More than 80 Percent of Surveyed Harvard Faculty Identify as Liberal," *Harvard Crimson*, July 13, 2022.

6 "2022 Edelman Trust Barometer," *Edelman*, 2022, https://www.edelman.com/sites/g/files/aatuss191/files/2022-01/2022%20Edelman%20Trust%20Barometer%20FINAL_Jan25.pdf.

7 Milton Friedman, "The Social Responsibility Of Business Is to Increase Its Profits," *New York Times*, September 13, 1970.

8 "ESG Should Be Boiled Down to One Simple Measure: Emissions," *The Economist*, July 21, 2022.

9 Marin Wolf and Kim Bhasin, "Wells Fargo, Delta Join Nascent Push into Racial Hiring Quotas," *Bloomberg*, September 1, 2020.

10 Sanjai Bhagat, "An Inconvenient Truth About ESG Investing," *Harvard Business Review*, March 31, 2022; Vivek Ramaswamy and Riley Moore, "The Market Can Curtail Woke Fund Managers," *Wall Street Journal*, June 9, 2022; and Vivek Ramaswamy and Alex Acosta, "Biden's ESG Tax on Your Retirement Fund," *Wall Street Journal*, July 19, 2022.

11 Paul Kiernan, "SEC Proposes More Disclosure Requirements for ESG Funds," *Wall Street Journal*, May 25, 2022.

12 See, for example, Aaron Ross Sorkin et al., "The Pushback on E.S.G. Investing," *New York Times*, May 11, 2022.

13 As others have shown, the best teams are composed of people with diverse perspectives and backgrounds. See Scott E. Page, *The Diversity Bonus: How Great Teams Pay Off in the Knowledge Economy* (Princeton: Princeton University Press, 2017).

14 Lydia Moynihan and Theo Wayt, "Nancy Pelosi Makes Millions Off Tech Stocks—And Scoffs at Push to Ban Congressional Trades," *New York Post*, January 7, 2022.

15 Niall Ferguson, *The Great Degeneration: How Institutions Decay and Economies Die* (New York: Penguin Books, 2014), 10.

16 Bari Weiss, "The New Founders America Needs," Common Sense, July 10, 2022, https://www.commonsense.news/p/the-new-founders-america-needs.

17 See Greg Lukianoff and Jonathan Haidt, *The Coddling of the American Mind: How Good Intentions and Bad Ideas Are Setting Up a Generation for Failure* (New York: Penguin Press, 2018).

18 Sally C. Curtin and Paul D. Sutton, "Marriage Rates in the United States, 1900–2018," Center for Disease Control and Prevention, accessed March 2022, https://www.cdc.gov/nchs/data/hestat/marriage_rate_2018/marriage_rate_2018.htm; Joyce A. Martin et al., "Births: Final Data for 2019." National Vital Statistics Reports 70, no. 2 (March 23, 2021), https://www.cdc.gov/nchs/data/nvsr/nvsr70/nvsr70-02-508.pdf; "Federal Policies in Response to Declining Entrepreneur ship," Congressional Budget Office, December 2020, https://www.cbo.gov/system/files/2020-12/56906-entrepreneurship.pdf; and Kevin Rector, "Study Finds Majority of Teens Delay Pursuit of Driver's Licenses," *Baltimore Sun*, August 1, 2013.

19 "Our Precarious Democracy: Extreme Polarization and Alienation in Our Politics," Chicago: University of Chicago's Institute of Politics, 2022.

20 John Hillen, "Restoring Trust and Leadership in a Vacuous Age," *Law & Liberty*, April 27, 2021, https://lawliberty.org/restoring-trust-and-leadership-in-a-vacuous-age/.

21 Megan Brenan, "Americans' Confidence in Major U.S. Institutions Dips," Gallup, July 12, 2021, https://news.gallup.com/poll/352316/americans-confidence-major-institutions-dips.aspx.

22 Pew Research Center, "Public Trust in Government: 1958-2021," accessed March 2022, https://www.pewresearch.org/politics/2021/05/17/public-trust-in-government.

23 Gallup, "Confidence in Institutions," accessed June 2022, https://news.gallup.com/poll/1597/confidence-institutions.aspx.

24 Justin McCarthy, "In U.S., Trust in Politicians, Voters Continues to Ebb," Gallup, October 7, 2021, https://news.gallup.com/poll/355430/trust-politicians-voters-continues-ebb.aspx.

25 Emily Badger, "Americans Are Afraid. Not for Themselves, but for the Country," *New York Times*, November 1, 2020.

26 Adam Smith, *The Wealth of Nations* (London: Strahan, 1776), book 1, chapter 8.

27 Ibid, 176.

28 Edgar H. Schein, *Organizational Culture and Leadership* (San Francisco: Jossey-Bass, 2010), 1.

29 United States Marine Corps, "Force Design 2030," Washington: Department of the Navy, 2020.

30 Gary Anderson, "The Marine Corps' Intellectual Civil War," Military.com, April 28, 2022, https://www.military.com/daily-news/opinions/2022/04/28/marine-corps-intellectual-civil-war.html.

31 James M. Cunningham and Thomas Donnelly, "Army Readiness Assessment, Vol.1," Washington: American Enterprise Institute, 2017.

32 Michael Bayer and Gary Roughead, *Strategic Readiness Review* (Washington: Department of the Navy, 2017).

33 Christopher Dougherty, "Gradually and then Suddenly: Explaining the Navy's Strategic Bankruptcy," War on the Rocks, June 30, 2021.

34 Kimberly Jackson et al., *Raising the Flag: Implication of U.S. Military Approaches to General and Flag Officer Development* (Santa Monica: Rand Corporation, 2020).

35 Robert E. Schmidle and Mark Montgomery, A Report on the Fighting Culture of the United States Navy Surface Fleet, 9. Conducted at the direction of Senator Tom Cotton et al. (Washington: Government Printing Office, 2021).

36 Stanley McChrystal, "Leading to Chaos: A Conversation with General Stanley McChrystal," interview by Joe Mariani, *Deloitte Review* 9 (July 25, 2016).

37 Steve Blank, "The Red Queen Problem: Innovation in the Defense Department and Intelligence Community," War on the Rocks, October 17, 2017.

38 United States Army, "Climate Strategy" (Washington: Department of the Army, 2022).

39 Nadia Schadlow, "The Distracted Defense Department," *Wall Street Journal*, October 21, 2021.

40 Courtney Kube and Molly Boigon, "Every Branch of the Military Is Struggling to Make its 2022 Recruiting Goals, Officials Say," NBC News, June 27, 2022, https://www.nbcnews.com/news/military/every-branch-us-military-struggling-meet-2022-recruiting-goals-officia-rcna35078; and Davis Winkie, "Citing Recruiting Woes, Army Will Shed Up to 28,000 Troops in Next Year," *Army Times*, July 19, 2022.

41 *Providing for the Common Defense*. Report of the National Defense Strategy Commission, November 2018.

42 Seth Moulton and Mike Gallagher, "Send In the Marines for a Modernization," *Wall Street Journal*, May 30, 2022.

43 The legendary military scholar Stephen Rosen wrote about this three decades ago, calling for "a new promotion pathway for junior officers practicing a new way of war." Stephen P. Rosen, *Winning the Next War: Innovation and the Modern Military* (Ithaca: Cornell University Press, 1991), 251. See also, Long, "Shoot, Move, Communicate, and Innovation: Harnessing Innovative Capacity in the Ranks," Modern War Institute, March, 16, 2020, https://mwi.usma.edu/shoot-move-communicate-innovate-harnessing-innovative-capacity-ranks/.

44 As I argued in my first book. David McCormick, *The Downsized Warrior: America's Army in Transition* (New York: New York University Press, 1998).

45 Nina Kollars and Emma Moore, "Every Marine a Blue-Haired Quasi-Rifleperson?" War on the Rocks, August 21, 2019, https://warontherocks.com/2019/08/every-marine-a-blue-haired-quasi-rifleperson/.

46 John Kroger, "Office Life at the Pentagon Is Disconcertingly Retrograde," *Wired*, August 20, 2020, https://www.wired.com/story/opinion-office-life-at-the-pentagon-is-disconcertingly-retrograde/.

47 See, for example, Vivian Hunt, Dennis Layton, and Sara Prince, "Why Diversity Matters," McKinsey, January 1, 2015, https://www.mckinsey.com/business-functions/people-and-organizational-performance/our-insights/why-diversity-matters; and David Rock and Heidi Grant, "Why Diverse Teams Are Smarter," *Harvard Business Review*, November 4, 2016, https://hbr.org/2016/11/why-diverse-teams-are-smarter.

48 *The Downsized Warrior: America's Army in Transition*.

49 Bradley Saacks and Shana Lebowitz, "Bridgewater is mandating its employees take off at least 15 days a year. Its deputy CEO explains how the new policy will combat burnout," *Insider*, June 17, 2021.

50 David McCormick and James Cunningham, "America's Military Needs an Innovation Overhaul," *Fast Company*, December 8, 2020.

51 Richard Nixon, *Leaders: Profiles and Reminiscences of Men Who Have Shaped the Modern World* (New York: Warner Books, 1982), 319.

Chapter 9

1 Selim Algar, "Hundreds of College Professors Blast 'Woke' Math Movement," *New York Post*, December 7, 2021; and Naomi Schaefer Riley, "'The 1619 Project' Enters American Classrooms," *EducationNext* 20, no. 4 (May 2020).

2 Henry Kissinger, *Leadership: Six Studies in World Strategy* (New York: Penguin Press, 2022), xv.

3 Noah Wasserman, "The Founder's Dilemma," *Harvard Business Review* (February 2008).

4 Kip McDaniel and Alicia McElhaney, "Bridgewater Is Having a Bad Year. David McCormick Has a Plan," *Institutional Investor* (August 26, 2020).

5 For the full story of the Bridgewater transition, see "A Perpetual Motion Machine: An Oral History of Bridgewater Associates' Leadership Transition," *Leaders* (October, November, December 2021). See also Juliet Chung, "Bridgewater Names New Co-CEOs as McCormick Steps Down for Possible Senate Run," *Wall Street Journal*, January 3, 2022; and Katherine Burton, "Bridgewater's Flagship Hedge Fund Gains 32% for First Half of Year," *Bloomberg*, July 5, 2022.

6 Joe Dawson, "Introduction of President Bill Clinton," Remarks, 50th Anniversary of D-Day, Normandy, France, 1994.

7 Lindsey Fortado and Robin Wigglesworth, "Former US Ranger ready to take command at Bridgewater," *Financial Times*, December 6, 2019.

8 Dr. Rice has made similar comments elsewhere. See, for example, Peter Robinson, "Interview with Condoleezza Rice," Uncommon Knowledge, September 11, 2020, https://www.hoover.org/research/condoleezza-rice-director-hoover-institution-1.

9 William F. Buckley, *Gratitude: Reflections on What We Owe to Our Country* (New York: Random House, 1990).

10 Katherine Schaeffer, "The Changing Face of America's Veteran Population," Pew Research Center, April 5, 2021, https://www.pewresearch.org/fact-tank/2021/04/05/the-changing-face-of-americas-veteran-population/.

11 "War and Sacrifice in the Post-9/11 Era," Paul Taylor ed., Washington: Pew Research Center, 2011.

12 As reported in *Warriors and Citizens*. James Mattis and Kori Schake eds. (Stanford: Hoover Institution Press, 2016).

13 David Ignatius, "Congress's Bipartisan National-Service Bill Would Be a Powerful Tonic for What's Ailing America," *Washington Post*, July 8, 2022.

14 John Feinstein, *A Civil War: Army vs. Navy Tag—A Year Inside College Football's Purest Rivalry* (New York: Little, Brown and Company, 1996), 12–14.

15 Wilfred M. McClay, "Remarks at the 18th Annual Bradley Prize Ceremony," Washington, DC, May 17, 2022.

INDEX

ABOUT THE AUTHOR

David H. McCormick is a prominent business executive, combat veteran, and public servant. David served as the chief executive officer of Bridgewater Associates, one of the world's largest investment management firms, before pursuing a U.S. Senate seat in his home state of Pennsylvania in 2022. Prior to Bridgewater, he was the U.S. Treasury undersecretary for international affairs and held senior posts on the National Security Council and at the Department of Commerce. From 1999-2005, David was the CEO and then president of two publicly traded software companies. He is a graduate of the United States Military Academy, a former army officer, and a veteran of the first Gulf War. David holds a PhD from Princeton's School of Public and International Affairs and previously served on the Defense Policy Board.

James M. Cunningham was an associate at Bridgewater Associates when he and David McCormick began writing this book, later joining David's campaign for the U.S. Senate as a senior policy adviser. Previously, James worked as a policy analyst at the Hoover Institution under former secretary of state George Shultz and at the American Enterprise Institute. He holds a bachelor of science and engineering from Princeton University.